# Diaspora and Identity

This book investigates the identity issues of South Asians in the diaspora. It engages the theoretical and methodological debates concerning processes of culture and identity in the contemporary context of globalisation and transnationalism. It analyses the South Asian diaspora – a perfect route to a deeper understanding of contemporary socio-cultural transformations and the way in which information and communication technology functions as both a catalyst and indicator of such transformations. The book will be of interest to scholars of diaspora studies, cultural studies, international migration studies, and ethnic and racial studies.

This book is a collection of papers from the journal *South Asian Diaspora*.

**Ajaya Kumar Sahoo** is currently an Assistant Professor and Director of the Centre for Study of Indian Diaspora, University of Hyderabad. His areas of research interests comprise international migration, South Asian diaspora, transnationalism, religion, and ageing. He is the Editor of *South Asian Diaspora* and Reviews Editor of *Journal of Intercultural Studies*.

**Gabriel Sheffer** is Professor of Political Science at the Hebrew University of Jerusalem, Israel. His research interests are in the field of diaspora and transnationalism, diaspora-homeland relations, and ethnic politics. He has authored numerous publications on topics related to his research interests. He is the editor of *Modern Diasporas in International Politics* (Croom Helm/St. Martin's Press, a pioneering text in the political study of diasporas).

# Diaspora and Identity
Perspectives on South Asian Diaspora

*Edited by*
**Ajaya Kumar Sahoo and Gabriel Sheffer**

Routledge
Taylor & Francis Group

LONDON AND NEW YORK

First published 2014
by Routledge
2 Park Square, Milton Park, Abingdon, Oxfordshire OX14 4RN

Simultaneously published in the USA and Canada
by Routledge
711 Third Avenue, New York, NY 10017

First issued in paperback 2014

*Routledge is an imprint of the Taylor & Francis Group, an informa business*

© 2014 Taylor & Francis

This book is a reproduction of papers from several issues of *South Asian Diaspora*. The Publisher requests to those authors who may be citing this book to state, also, the bibliographical details of the special issue on which the book was based.

*British Library Cataloguing in Publication Data*
A catalogue record for this book is available from the British Library

ISBN 13: 978-0-415-82544-3 (hbk)
ISBN 13: 978-1-138-85071-2 (pbk)

Typeset in Times New Roman
by Taylor & Francis Books

**Publisher's Note**
The publisher would like to make readers aware that the chapters in this book may be referred to as articles as they are identical to the articles published in the special issue. The publisher accepts responsibility for any inconsistencies that may have arisen in the course of preparing this volume for print.

# Contents

# CONTENTS

# Citation Information

The following chapters were originally published in various issues of *South Asian Diaspora*. When citing this material, please use the original page numbering for each article, as follows:

**Chapter 2**
*Diasporic subjectivity as an ethical position*
Dibyesh Anand
*South Asian Diaspora*, volume 1, issue 2 (September 2009) pp. 103-111

**Chapter 3**
*Another world of experience? Transnational contexts and the experiences of South Asian Americans*
Bandana Purkayastha
*South Asian Diaspora*, volume 1, issue 1 (March 2009) pp. 85-99

**Chapter 4**
*Revisiting the UK Muslim diasporic public sphere at a time of terror: from local (benign) invisible spaces to seditious conspiratorial spaces and the 'failure of multiculturalism' discourse*
Pnina Werbner
*South Asian Diaspora*, volume 1, issue 1 (March 2009) pp. 19-45

**Chapter 5**
*'My language, my people': language and ethnic identity among British-born South Asians*
Rusi Jaspala and Adrian Coyle
*South Asian Diaspora*, volume 2, issue 2 (September 2010) pp. 201-218

**Chapter 6**
*The Sikh gurdwara in Finland: negotiating, maintaining and transmitting immigrants' identities*
Laura Hirvi
*South Asian Diaspora*, volume 2, issue 2 (September 2010) pp. 219-232

**Chapter 7**
*Communal networks and gender: placing identities among South Asians in Kenya*

# Introduction

## Issues of identity in the South Asian diaspora

Ajaya Kumar Sahoo and Gabriel Sheffer

This volume investigates the issues of identity of South Asians in the diaspora. Using various theoretical, methodological and political standpoints, the chapters in this volume present a nuanced understanding of the processes of culture and identity in the contemporary context of globalisation and transnationalism. It argues that South Asians in the diaspora have not only maintained the homeland culture and identities but also created, recreated and negotiated such identities under different circumstances in the multiracial and multicultural societies. The first part of this introduction details the theoretical and methodological debates surrounding diaspora and identity while the second part provides a brief outline of the chapters[1] included in this volume.

## Theoretical approaches to diasporas

It is quite widely known and recognised that at the beginning of the twenty-first century both the general diasporic phenomenon and specific diasporas are far from vanishing. Quite the contrary and, furthermore, as it is pretty well known, the numbers and varieties of diasporas and diasporans (that is, members of diasporas entities) are growing.

By the same token, as a result of current more favourable cultural, social, political and economic processes occurring in various democratic and democratising states, diasporas' and diasporans' influence and impact on their homelands (countries of origin), hostlands (countries in which they permanently reside), regional organisations (such as the European Union) and the general international system are also expanding all over the world. Hence, some negative reactions notwithstanding, mainly generated by hostlands' governments and various social groups, including in some 'liberal' democracies and societies, diasporas' and diasporans' various capabilities and influences will only continue to increase.

It does not mean, however, that diasporic individuals and entities are totally free to develop and behave in their hostlands strictly according to their own or according to their homelands' inclinations and interests. Like other non-diasporic minorities existing in diasporas' hostlands, the diasporas and diasporans are under a range of pressures originating in various relevant environments and institutions. As a result of such processes that eventually affect the 'quadrangular relationships' between diasporas and diasporans,[2] on the one hand, and homelands, hostlands and other actors, on the other hand, there is a continuous need to reevaluate the past, present and future situation of the entire phenomenon in tandem with the theoretical approaches to this vastly significant phenomenon.

Politicians and academics alike have realised that as a result of past and current developments diasporas constitute a highly intricate phenomenon, that this phenomenon is becoming even more complicated, that therefore the challenges facing the various existing and emerging diasporas and their homelands and hostlands are mounting too, and consequently the need for their explanation is growing too.

The general views and positions *vis-à-vis* diasporas revealed by the general public, by most politicians and by most students of the diaspora phenomenon is to treat all dispersed migrants, cross-states human networks and actual diasporas as one uniform phenomenon and lump all of them together. This pattern makes it somewhat difficult to understand the different basic natures and behaviours of these entities and no less difficult to assess the challenges facing them. This is particularly evident in the academic literature that has been written based on what is known as the 'transnational' theoretical approach,[3] an approach that will be discussed later in this introduction in comparison with the approach that I call the 'trans-state' ethno-national-religious diasporic phenomenon.[4]

Following is a critical reexamination of the two main theoretical and analytical approaches to the study of 'transnational communities' and 'trans-state diasporas'. More specifically, the purpose here is to reexamine these approaches' comparative relevance and contribution to a better understanding of the general and specific people's dispersal phenomena.

In this vein, and as part of these introductory comments, the following are relatively brief distinctive characterisations of these two categories: essentially, the first category – the transnational one – argues that these entities consist of large groups, some of which, but certainly not all members of these entities, regard themselves as forming coherent diasporas. Actually, however, not all persons who regard themselves, or are regarded by others, as forming such diasporas, are of the same ethno-national origin, or are migrants or descendants of migrants. Rather, many of them have in common some other characteristics that in their own perception and in the eyes of outsiders – such as the general public in their hostlands, politicians and analysts – determine their belonging to such entities, which are usually ill defined. Thus, they may have in common religious beliefs and affiliations with certain churches or sects, or the same regional geographical background, or the same language, or even shared ideological beliefs, but not the same ethno-national background. Hence, respectively, groups such as the 'Moslem', 'Buddhist', 'Catholic', 'African', 'Latino', 'Arab', 'Francophone', 'Chinese' and also the 'Greens' and in the past the 'Communists' worldwide, can be included in this category. Here it should be noted that these entities are included in this category mainly on the basis of the basically subjective views of their members and outside observers. The significant argument here is that it is most significant that other dispersed groups should not be included in this category.

Furthermore, a broadly accepted, but a quite problematic, and by now also a contested view, which has been held by writers in the field of the study of dispersed 'others' and migrants of various types, has been that most of the lumped together dispersed Moslems, Arabs, Latinos, Chinese, Indians, Irish, Jews and many others are members of transnational, or multicultural, or hybrid or borderless globalised entities. However, and among other things, by lumping together all such individual persons, their families and their wider social groups, and by stressing the multiplicity and hybridity of their identities and sense of belonging, this view has to a large degree opposed and challenged the significance of these individuals and groups' specific ethno-national identities, their modes of identification and their connections to their old or new countries and societies of origin. According to 'postmodernist', 'postcolonial', 'globalist', 'transnationalist' and 'hybridist' writers and practitioners, such factors characterise and should be applied to many Diasporas.

Based on close observations of actual developments and academic studies of various aspects of the identities, organisation, patterns of behaviour and activities of specific ethno-national diasporas, including their 'positive' roles in the economic development of their hostlands and homelands and the political support they render to their brethrens, on the one hand, and their 'negative' involvement in terrorism and criminal activities on behalf of their homelands and brethrens, on the other hand, one of the main arguments here is that in view of the perseverance and even strengthening of nationalism and ethno-nationalism, the significant role and various impacts of ethno-nationalism in most states and among most of 'their' dispersed persons, and the continuation of the ethnic revival worldwide, much greater significance should be attributed to the ethno-national identity, the background and the connections between various dispersed persons and groups, and their actual or perceived ethno-national homelands. The argument here is that rather than the transnationalist theoretical approach this second basic approach should be applied to most diasporas.

In this context, here there is an essential need to realise and state that the vastly and rapidly growing numbers as well as the growing variety of dispersed persons and entities further contribute to the vast complexity of both the diasporic and the transnational entities phenomena. Consequently, ancient and historical diasporas, such as the Greek, Armenian and Jewish historical diasporas, as well as modern and incipient diasporas, such as the Italian and Polish modern diasporas and the Mexican and Palestinian incipient diasporas, have both certain similar and different characteristics to what are now regarded as transnational communities or 'transnational diasporas', referring, for example, to the above mentioned Moslem, African, Asian, Latino, Green and Catholic entities.[5] Again, and basically speaking, despite certain similarities between the perceived and widely stated meanings of the terms 'diaspora' and 'transnational communities', as well as between such concrete entities, there are also certain inherent actual differences between them, between the terms that are used to characterise each of these groups, and the various usages of these terms by politicians, media persons and academic researchers.

In view of the variety of dispersed groups, and the complexity of each of these entities, very clear distinctions should be made between the veteran/historical, modern and incipient entities. For example, such distinctions should be made between the worldwide general historical Moslem religious dispersal and the various newer Moslem or more accurately Arab ethno-national-religious entities, whose cores mostly maintain their original ethno-national identity and close relations with their actual or imagined homelands. A very similar distinction should be made, for example, between what is called the 'Latino diaspora' and the various South American entities that maintain their ethno-national identities and intensive connections with their perceived and actual homelands.

One of the main differences between the two types of entity mentioned already is related to the fact that while not all members of the various transnational entities have migrated from one country of origin (this observation applies, for example, to the

Moslems, the Marxists in the past and to the Greens these days), all members of diasporas are migrants themselves or descendants of migrants who permanently reside in hostlands.

As mentioned earlier, it is important to note again that despite the tremendous increase in their numbers in hostlands, which is created either by various types of migration or by demographic growth, and their greater inclination to separately organise and maintain various ties with their countries of origin, the common tendency of the general public, politicians, media persons and researchers is still to lump together and to treat all transnational entities and actual diasporas as belonging to the same homogeneous category and specific entities. For example, many observers have not paid adequate attention to the fact that not all 'others' in hostlands actually constitute organised diasporas. In fact, those others fall into seven subcategories: tourists; refugees and asylum seekers; legal and illegal non-organised newly arrived migrants; irredentist groups; members of various transnational entities; and ethno-national diasporans.

Furthermore, clear distinctions should be made between the various types of transnational entity. At the least there are cultural, religious, ideological and professional such entities. By the same token, again as mentioned earlier, distinctions should be made between various types of ethno-national diaspora: historical (some of these were formed already in the ancient period), modern (started to be formed in the seventeenth century) and incipient (those who started to be shaped after World War II and are still organising).

A further distinction is between state linked (that is, diasporas' linked with 'their' nation-states in their countries of imagined or actual origin) and stateless (that is, entities that are linked with an ethno-national entity in the country of origin that is not controlled by the same ethno-national group) diasporas. Thus, for example, in accordance with these categorisations while the Jewish diaspora should be typified as a historical state-linked diaspora, the dispersed Palestinians should be typified as a modern stateless diaspora.

Furthermore, it should be strongly emphasised that specific diasporas and transnational entities are very far from being homogeneous communities. Thus, a critical distinction should be made between core and peripheral members of such entities. Core members are all those who emotionally, cognitively and actually cling to the common identity characterising their entire group, who regard themselves and are regarded as members of such entities, and who, whenever it is needed, publicly identify with the entire ethno-national entity and the country of origin. Peripheral members are those persons who have been fully or partly integrated (but not fully assimilated) into their host countries' culture, society, politics etc., but still maintain their original ethno-national identity, even if this identity has become hybridised. These persons also maintain some contacts with their organised groups of brethrens in the hostland and with some individuals, organisations and groups in their country of origin. Totally and finally assimilated persons in their hostland societies should not be considered as members of such diasporic entities.

As can be fairly easily seen and understood, all these distinctions are stemming from and connected to the very fundamental differences among the members of these entities' assorted identities. This issue will be further dealt with later.

In short, when discussing the nature and main issues facing ethno-national-religious diasporas and transnational entities at the beginning of the twenty-first century, one should avoid generalisations and make very careful and clear distinctions between the origins, nature and patterns of behaviour of the various types of such entity. In fact, all human dispersals exhibit characteristics of their identities that partly fit both theoretical approaches and hence there is a need for a 'theoretical synthetic approach' to this major question concerning the composition of these entities.

The following is a further elaboration of the different meanings of each of the basic two approaches to current diasporism. Briefly and generally speaking, for many observers and analysts transnationalism means streams of people, ideas, goods and capital that extend across the borders of national territories and nation-states in ways that are opposed to nationality and nationalism as major, or even as the only, sources of identity, identification, economic structures and political arrangements (see Braziel & Mannur 2003; Glick-Schiller 2003). Most adherents to this approach view all such groups as entirely constructed and imagined entities,[6] which are espousing imagined deterritorialised identities that are strongly influenced by postmodern, globalised, glocalised and hybridising environments and processes. The main argument of this school/ approach is that dispersed persons who fit that characterisation do not maintain actual and perceptual ties with their countries of origins and they exist as totally independent or highly autonomous entities that constitute parts of the new global, globalising and glocalising environments. Membership in such entities is conceptually imagined, entirely self-selected and self-determined by each member or by small groups of these entities.

The second approach – the 'trans-state' approach – contends that because of their inherent ethno-national identities, their voluntary or forced migration, but nevertheless deeply rooted connections to a real or imagined country of origin, most ethno-national-religious diasporas, including some entities that are incorrectly regarded as, for example, the Moslem, African, Asian, Latino diasporas, cannot be viewed as 'pure' transnational entities.

Further to the rather brief but vital clarifications of the two different theoretical approaches to transnational entities and ethno-national-religious diasporas that have been suggested earlier, the following are more detailed characterisations of the two phenomena.

First, let us deal with transnationalism. Actually, most adherents to the transnational approach, which has been the more popular approach when dealing with these entities, regard and portray all present-day dispersed persons permanently residing out of their countries of origin as transnational entities (see for example, Brubaker 2005; Butler 2001; Safran 1991; Schnapper 2005; Tölölyan 1991, 1996; Vertovec 1997). They strongly argue that, like other existing nations and ethnic groups such diasporas are, to use Ben Anderson's famous term, 'imagined communities' (Anderson 1991, 1994). They also argue that essentially transnational diasporism is an utterly modern phenomenon. This approach is strongly influenced by postmodern epistemological trends, as well as by various actual aspects of globalisation, such as current ease of movement from one country to another, migration, modern communication, individualisation and spreading hybrid cultures.

The main specific arguments of the transnational approach are pretty well known and therefore the following is not an exhaustive list of their characterisations, but only the very significant elements.

Essentially, the adherents to this approach argue that membership in these entities is based on utterly subjective feelings and decisions of individuals, who, especially when they do not have noticeable physical markers, can relatively easily change their affiliations and loyalties up to the stage of full assimilation into their hostlands' societies; that the main glue binding together these persons, and hence also their entities, is cultural elements; that these entities are constantly changing and therefore both the entities' borders and their history are not so significant; that their social boundaries are very far from being clearly drowned, fixed and stable; that most of these entities and their members who permanently reside in certain hostlands experience continuous processes of cultural hybridisation (Werbner 2002), that cause substantive heterogeneity in the entity at large, and also in smaller subgroups residing in the same country, region or city; that consequently they tend to either assimilate or fully integrate into their host societies; that memories of their historical and more recent ancestors, or of their 'original homelands', are not very significant for their existence; and that the possibility of their return to their homelands is almost inconceivable.

Adherents to this transnationalist approach also argue that the current processes of globalisation and glocalisation constantly influence and cause major changes in the identity and identification of such persons. As perceived from the specific viewpoints of the entities' various leaders and members, these changes are either 'positive' or 'negative'. Thus, on the one hand, globalisation processes diminish the numbers of such cohesive entities and make their cultural and social boundaries even less defined and more porous. But on the other hand, due to current sophisticated means of communication such processes increase the number of members in such entities and enhance their solidarity and connections to their 'communities', or rather to their entities. As mentioned earlier, one of the main entities that are supposed to fit this characterisation is the 'Moslem diaspora'. But there are serious doubts concerning the inclusion in this category of, for example, the 'Arab' and 'Latino' diasporas.

Generally, it seems that in fact there is a certain decline in the acceptance and application of the transnational approach and that more scholars are moving again to the other approach – the trans-state diasporic theoretical approach (see, for example, Braziel and Mannur 2003). Without any attempt to generalise or to claim that these are utterly homogeneous entities, adherents to this approach argue that a clear distinction should be made concern in the fact that as far as their age, the collective and personal identity of their members, their borders, their organisation and their patterns of behaviour are concerned, ethno-national diasporas constitute a perennial phenomenon (Sheffer 1986; Smith 1986). This means that although over the centuries certain historical diasporas, which still exist today, such as the Chinese, Indian, Jewish and Armenian, have changed somewhat, in fact these are ancient entities that have overcome many actual as well as more abstract acute threats to their identity and thus to their organised existence. They have survived planned and actual attempts to totally annihilate or assimilate their members – this has been certainly the case of the Jewish and Armenian diasporas. From a different but connected perspective it also means that their members are capable of surviving as distinct groups in today's globalised postmodern world in which there have emerged some expectations that ethnic minorities and diasporas will totally disappear either through total assimilation or 'return' to their homelands. This portrayal also applies to modern and incipient stateless and state-linked diasporas, such as Basque, Palestinian, Polish and even some Scandinavian reawakening diasporas in the USA.

Furthermore, according to this second approach, the cores of such diasporas are more united and demonstrate higher degrees of cohesion and solidarity than what are regarded as transnational diasporas. This is the case because of a number of factors: first and foremost is that the identity of many of their members is more built in and inherent because it is an integrative combination of primordial, psychological and instrumental factors (Kelass 1991; Sheffer 2006); there is no tremendous gap between their identity and identification, namely, these days at the beginning of the twenty-first century such diasporans are not so shy or reluctant to publicly identify as belonging to these entities. Actually, it is becoming even fashionable to do so and behave accordingly. In comparison to the purported transnational entities, diasporans are more widely and better organised; their connections with their real or perceived original homelands are more inherent, constant and intensive; their involvement in their homelands' cultural, social, political and economic affairs, and in the affairs of various hostlands in which their brethrens reside, is significant; on various occasions they are involved in conflicts in or pertaining to their homelands and to other states that host their brethrens; and some members of such diasporas consider a return, or they actually return, to their homelands. All these factors apply, for example, to the Irish, Turks, and even Japanese and, of course, the Jews (Sheffer 2006).

The most significant feature that determines the similarity between the trans-state entities is that their core members as well as some peripheral members of each of these diasporas are of the same ethno-national origin and they maintain their ethno-national religious identity. According to their ethno-national background, according to their own awareness and self-definition, according to the perception of relevant external observers, and according the fact that their identification with their entity is either not questionable or not objectionable by the societies and politicians in their host countries, these are persons that very clearly belong, to a certain clear diasporic entity that maintains it boundaries and organisations. Here it should be re-emphasised that this applies not only to first generation of diaspora members, but also to later generations of historical, modern and incipient diasporas, whether these are state linked or stateless.

In sum, as a result of the growing realisation that perceptually and also actually such two types of diaspora exist and therefore distinctions should be made between them, and because of the current extreme complexity of the trans state diasporic phenomenon it is vital to expand existing short and comprehensive definitions by providing longer profiles of these entities.[7]

## The South Asian diaspora

The South Asian diaspora, comprising well over 30 million settled either temporarily or permanently in almost all the countries in the world, today constitute one of the largest ethnically diverse diasporas. India, Pakistan, Bangladesh, Nepal, Sri Lanka, Bhutan and the Maldives all anchor a sense of home for people who have moved outside the region through the centuries. These territories evoke emotional, social, political, economic, cultural and literary affiliations as well, which find expression in multiple ways. The diaspora is also marked by struggles over meanings and tensions both among the diasporics and with people in the countries that the diasporics now inhabit. It has developed institutions, orientations and patterns of living specific to the institutional structures and socio-political contexts of different host lands. These patterns have been marked not only by the influences of the host land culture but by relations with the homeland.

While in some countries South Asians constitute the largest ethnic minority, in other countries they represent a numerical majority of the population. With collective mobilisation and extensive use of information and communication technology, South Asians today have created transnational communities. Perhaps no other diaspora in the world is characterise by such diversity in its population as the South Asian diaspora in terms of culture, including languages, regions, religions and other forms of social stratification such as caste, gender and class. Compared to other ethnic groups of immigrant origin, South Asians in the diaspora have the distinction of being one of the most successful economic and political groups who have contributed significantly to the society and culture of the host society (see, for example, Das Gupta 2006; Leonard 1997; Rai and Reeves 2009; Visram 2002) and simultaneously maintained strong relations with the homeland (see for example, Clarke et al. 1990; Koshy and Radhakrishnan 2008; Shukla 2001; Vertovec 1997). As Judith Brown (2007: 3) rightly pointed out, South Asians have made significant contribution 'to the economies, societies and cultures of the places to which they have gone, whether as semi-free labourers on contracts of indenture on plantations in Natal, the Caribbean and Malaya; a traders and entrepreneurs in East Africa; as semi-skilled industrial in Europe ... Moreover, they have increasingly influenced the politics, economies and cultures of the places which they and their ancestors left.'

The first chapter in this volume by Dibyesh Anand highlights some of the ways in which diasporas challenge the dominant narratives of belonging that give primacy to the bounded community of nation-states. He argues that diaspora is not only a social formation, but also a subject position, since it 'allows one to witness and understand the ways in which culture is sought to be manufactured through different voices and silences, through inclusions and exclusion'.

Bandana Purkayastha examines how globalisation and technological transformations in the present context shapes the lives of South Asians in the United States. Using the data on immigrant and post-immigrant generation South Asian Americans, she examines mainly three dimensions of the transnational context: the role of global security blocs, companies that market cultures as products and the world wide web as a social space. She shows how ideologies, institutions and interactions in coalescing real and virtual transnational spaces add another layer of experience that, in turn, intersects with the multi-layered diasporic experiences extant within nations.

Pnina Werbner's chapter highlights the recent developments of public dialogue between British politicians and leaders of Muslim community in the British media. Addressing the 'failure of multiculturalism' discourse, she questions, first, whether talk of multiculturalism in the UK is really about 'culture' at all? Second, she explores why Muslim integration into Britain – the so-called success or failure of multiculturalism – has come to be 'tested' by Muslim national leaders' willingness to attend Holocaust Memorial Day commemorations. The public dialogue reflecting on these issues in media, ethnic and mainstream press, the chapter proposes, highlights a signal development in the history of the UK Muslim diasporic public sphere: from being hidden and local to being highly visible and national, responsive to British politicians, investigative journalists and the wider British public.

Rusi Jaspal and Adrian Coyle in their chapter explore how second-generation British South Asians understood and defined heritage language that played an important role in ethnic identity construction. Based on the data collected through in-depth interviews, they present four superordinate themes: mother tongue and self, a sense of ownership and affiliation, negotiating linguistic identities in social space and the quest for a positive linguistic identity. They argue that an imperfect knowledge of the heritage language was said to have a negative impact on psychological well-being. Hence they offer recommendations for interventions that might aid the management of bilingualism among second-generation Asians.

For immigrants in the diaspora, religion came to be identified with ethnicity and identity. Gurdwara (Sikh temple) – as a place of worship – played an important role in the history of Sikh diaspora. Based on primary data collected in Helsinki, Finland, among 26 Sikh immigrants from northern India and through participant observation, Laura Hirvi's chapter investigates how gurdwara, its foodways and its role in transmitting religious as well as cultural traditions to Sikh youth, helps in the process of negotiating, maintaining and transmitting immigrants' identities in the diaspora.

Pascale Herzig's chapter examines the intra-ethnic relations of South Asians in Kenya. South Asians in Kenya are divided, as they are in South Asia, on the lines of caste, language, region and religion, which are discernible through their construction of separate community centres or places of worship. The 'established' Asians have developed a specific East African identity and they tend to dissociate themselves from recent South Asian immigrants. The creation of communities has assisted the migrants in feeling more at home – or in place – in their new environment. Based on the data collected through participant observation and in-depth interviews among respondents in Nairobi, Herzig shows two important findings. First, the appropriation of communal places is gendered and divided by age and migratory generation and, second, the mutually interlinked relation of place and identity is important for the comfort and the sense of belonging of the migrants.

Rupam Saran's chapter examines the intergenerational and intragenerational social mobility of post-1965 Indian immigrants' children in the metropolis of New York. Based on ethnographic study on social mobility and second-generation Asian Indian immigrants, the chapter explores two important issues: first, to what extent the current challenges in the US economy hinder upward social mobility of the children of Indian immigrants. Second, how parental messages of taking advantages of both worlds contributes to second-generation Asian Indians' success or failure in American society. The author argues that while globalisation facilitated mobilisation across national borders, the recent economic crisis in the USA poses tough challenges for Indian immigrants and their children. However, the study found that the younger generations have adaptive strategy to challenge the mainstream society by way of their social mobility and cultural capital.

In their chapter, Arshia Zaidi, Amanda Couture and Eleanor Maticka-Tyndale examine how young South Asians use digital technologies to maintain cross-gender intimate relationships. Using 42 qualitative interviews conducted with second-generation South Asian Canadians living in the Greater Toronto Area and Durham region, the authors argue that South Asian youth use computer-mediated communication (CMC) to initiate and build relationships, remain connected with partners, engage in discreet communication, to ease uncomfortable and intimate discussions, and to communicate when face-to-face interaction is not available. Negative consequences of CMC use volunteered by participants include parent–child conflict over restriction and questioning CMC use and its use leading to parents' discovery of a 'secret' relationship.

They point out that CMC provides a means for second-generation South Asian youth in Canada to overtly adhere to norms of gender separation while covertly engaging in cross-gender relationships.

The last chapter in this volume by Pratap Kumar examines how caste identity, unlike in South Asia, has made significant transformations in the diaspora. He focuses on the case study of the Indian diaspora in South Africa, the West Indies and UK by showing evidence of the dissolution of subcaste (*jati*) identities, which has given rise to various other formations of groups replacing the endogamous relationships with other arbitrary group formations. Further, he analyses how caste has been transformed in these places and what it means for a discourse on caste that is historically rooted in subcaste identity.

It is hoped that this volume will help the readers to understand some of the complex issues confronted by South Asians in the diaspora.

## Notes

1 The chapters included in this volume were published earlier in the journal *South Asian Diaspora* (visit the journal homepage: http://www.tandfonline.com/toc/rsad20/current).
2 On this issue which is part of a definition of diasporas, see Sheffer (1986).
3 On the concept of transnationalism in general and on its applications to diasporas in particular see, for example, Anthias (1998); Brubaker (2005); Clifford (1994); Glick-Schiller et al. (1992, 1995); Lie (1995); Morawska (2001); Smith (1986); Tambiah (2000); Vertovec (2004); Vertovec and Cohen (1999); Waldinger and Fitzgerald (2004).
4 For this distinction, see Miles and Sheffer (1998). On the 'trans-state' approach see, for example, Braziel and Mannur (2003); Sheffer (2006).
5 The term 'entities' is used here since in the case of these dispersals the term 'communities' is quite problematic. This is the case unless we are ready to think that these are spiritual or abstract communities. Among other things, this is connected to the question of the almost non-existent borders of these specific entities. On the complexity of borders problems, see, for example, Brubaker (1995).
6 This is in line with Benedict Anderson approach (Anderson 1991, 1994).
7 For a profile of these diasporas see Sheffer (2006, Chapter 2).

## References

Anderson, B., 1991. *Imagined communities: reflections on the origins and spread of nationalism.* London: Verso.

Anderson, B., 1994. Exodus. *Critical Inquiry*, 20 (2), 314–327.

Anthias, F., 1998. Evaluating 'diaspora' beyond ethnicity. *Sociology*, 32 (3), 557–580.

Braziel, A. and Mannur, J.E., 2003. *Theorizing diaspora: a reader.* Oxford: Blackwell.

Brown, J., 2007. *Global South Asians: introducing the modern diaspora.* Cambridge: Cambridge University Press.

Brubaker, R., 1995. National minorities, nationalizing states, and external national homelands in the new Europe. *Daedalus*, 124 (2), 107–132.

Brubaker, R., 2005. The 'diaspora' diaspora. *Ethnic and Racial Studies*, 28 (1), 1–19.

Butler, K., 2001. Defining diaspora, refining a discourse. *Diaspora*, 10 (2), 189–219.

Clarke, C., Peach, C. and Vertovec, S., eds., 1990. *South Asians overseas: migration and ethnicity.* Cambridge: Cambridge University Press.

Clifford, J., 1994. Diasporas. *Cultural Anthropology*, 9 (3), 302–338.

Das Gupta, M., 2006. *Unruly immigrants: rights, activism, and transnational South Asian politics in the United States.* Durham, NC: Duke University Press.

Glick-Schiller, N., 2003. The centrality of ethnography in the study of transnational migration. *In*: N. Foner, ed., *American arrivals: anthropology engages the new immigration.* Sante Fe, NM: School of American research Press, 99–128.

Glick-Schiller, N., Basch, L. and Blanc-Szanton, C., 1992. *Toward a transnational perspective on migration: race, class, ethnicity and nationalism reconsidered.* New York: New York Academy of Science.

Glick-Schiller, N., Basch, L. and Blanc-Szanton, C., 1995. From immigrant to transmigrant: theorizing transnational migration. *Anthropological Quarterly,* 68 (1), 48–63.

Kelass, J., 1991. *The politics of nationalism and ethnicity.* London: Macmillan.

Koshy, S. and Radhakrishnan, R., eds., 2008. *Transnational South Asians: the making of a neo-diaspora.* New Delhi: Oxford University Press.

Leonard, K.I., 1997. *The South Asian Americans.* Westport, CT: Greenwood.

Lie, J., 1995. From international migration to transnational diaspora. *Contemporary Sociology,* 24 (4), 303–306.

Miles, W. and Sheffer, G., 1998. Francophone and Zionism: a comparative study of transnationalism and transstatism. *Diaspora,* 7 (2), 119–148.

Morawska, E., 2001. Immigrants, transnationalism, and ethnicization: a comparison of this great wave and the last. *In:* G. Gerstle and J. Mollenkopf, eds., *E pluribus unum? Contemporary and historical perspectives on immigrant political incorporation.* New York: Rusell Sage, 157–212.

Rai, R. and Reeves, P., 2009. *The South Asian diaspora: transnational networks and changing identities.* London: Routledge.

Safran, W., 1991. Diasporas in modern societies: myths of homeland and return. *Diaspora,* 1 (1), 83–93.

Schnapper, D., 2005. De l'état-nation au mond transnational: du sens et de l'utilité du concept de diaspora. *In:* L. Anteby-Yemini, W. Berthomière and G. Sheffer, eds., *Les diasporas: 2000 ans d'histoire.* Rennes: Press Universitaires de Rennes, 21–50.

Sheffer, G., 1986. A new field of study: modern diasporas in international politics. *In:* G. Sheffer, ed., *Modern diasporas in international politics.* New York: St. Martin's Press, 1–15.

Sheffer, G., 2006. *Diaspora politics: at home abroad.* Cambridge: Cambridge University Press.

Shukla, S., 2001. Locations for South Asian diasporas. *Annual Review of Anthropology,* 30, 551–572.

Smith, A., 1986. *The ethnic origins of nations.* Oxford: Basil Blackwell.

Tambiah, S., 2000. Transitional movements, diaspora, and multiple modernities. *Daedalus,* 129 (1), 163–194.

Tölölyan, K., 1991. The nation-state and its others: in lieu of a preface. *Diaspora,* 1 (1), 3–7.

Tölölyan, K., 1996. Rethinking diaspora(s): stateless power in the transnational moment. *Diaspora,* 5 (1), 3–36.

Vertovec, S., 1997. Three meanings of diasporas exemplified among South Asian religions. *Diaspora,* 6 (3), 277–297.

Vertovec, S., 2004. Migrant transnationalism and modes of transformation. *International Migration Review,* 38 (3), 970–1001.

Vertovec, S., 2005. The political importance of diasporas. *Migration Policy Institute,* http://www.migrationinformation.org [accessed on 25 October 2012].

Vertovec, S. and Cohen, R., eds., 1999. *Migrations, diasporas and transnationalism.* Cheltenham: Edward Elgar.

Visram, R., 2002. *Asians in Britain: 400 years of history.* London: Pluto Press.

Waldinger, R. and Fitzgerald, D., 2004. Trans-nationalism in question. *American Journal of Sociology,* 109 (5), 1177–1195.

Werbner, P., 2002. *Imagined diaspora among Manchester Muslims: the public performing of Pakistani transnational identity politics.* Oxford: James Currey.

# Diasporic subjectivity as an ethical position

Dibyesh Anand

*Centre for the Study of Democracy, Westminster University, London, UK*

The paper highlights some of the ways in which diasporas challenge the dominant narratives of belonging that give primacy to the bounded community of nation-states. It argues for a critical appropriation of diasporic subjectivity as an ethical position that reveals the contested and constructed nature of culture. This position requires analytical frameworks that recognise power relations behind cultural claims and allow us to appreciate the silenced and marginalised voices subsumed under the categories of diaspora and culture.

The emergence of diaspora as a subject of academic study followed the emergence of identity politics that challenged the simplistic equation of political community with the bounded community of nation-states in the West. As Tölölyan says, diaspora, 'once saturated with the meanings of exile, loss, dislocation, powerlessness and pain has become a useful, even desirable way to describe a range of dispersions' (1996, p. 9). The launch of a new journal *South Asian Diaspora* is timely since it will provide a forum for discussing issues, themes and concerns affecting diasporic formations around the world that imagine one or the other country in South Asia as its homeland. Rather than focus on a South Asian diaspora elsewhere or a diaspora residing within the region, this paper reminds us that diaspora is not only a social formation, but also a subject position. Agreeing with works that highlight hybridity and identity politics within diasporas (see Brah 1996; Hall 1990; Radhakrishnan 1996), I argue for conceptualising diasporic subjectivity as an ethical political position that rejects cultural conformity and celebrates culture as a site of contestation.

This position breaks the monopoly of social formation of diasporas over diasporic subjectivity. One need not be socially diasporic to possess diasporic subjectivity. And many members of a diaspora may not possess diasporic subjectivity of the kind I am highlighting here – an approach to culture that refuses to privilege what is shared within a community over erasures and debates that get papered over in dominant narratives. Diasporic ethical subjectivity should serve as a constant reminder to the observers of South Asian diasporas of four things. First, that their investigation is as much about conceptualisation as it is about empirical realities on the ground. Second, an understanding of diaspora entails excavating marginalised, silenced and dissenting voices as well as the dominant ones. Third, what role do the host states and civil societies play in shaping and disciplining the narratives of diaspora? Fourth, belonging and alienation within diaspora is better studied in terms of a mix of politics of identification (that sees identity as always already a political process) and identity politics (that sees identity as a category that can be mobilised for politics; for an extended discussion, see Kaul 2007). To provoke an intellectual debate, I focus on this reimagined diasporic subjectivity as a normative endeavour and make no claim that it is always ethnographically mappable onto actually existing diasporic populations.

## Diaspora and problematic belongingness

In the second half of the twentieth century, diaspora as a designation moved away from its original association with Jewish (and to some extent Armenian) experience to encompass the imaginaries and lived realities of many different groups of people. In its commonly used sense, it refers to a collective of people with shared ethnic markers of identity who live away from their homeland and in significantly large numbers in their new hostland. Let us be clear, diaspora is a collective entity – a single person cannot constitute a diaspora. She would be a rebel or an exile but never a diaspora. For instance, had only the Dalai Lama and few of his followers exiled themselves in 1959, there would be no Tibetan diaspora. The latter exists because a sizeable population moved out of Tibet and formed a community-in-exile in South Asia and elsewhere (see Anand 2003, 2007). For diasporas to exist, there needs to be a collective of people with a reasonable level of self-consciousness of their own existence as a collective. Diaspora thus is a group of people sharing a cultural and ethnic background that separates them from where they live and links them to where they come from. This definition privileges affiliation and emotional affectivity with a distant place over material reality and geography of the immediate environment.

Diasporas by their very existence problematise the notion of political allegiance because their loyalty can never be unambiguously to one or the other. They are privileged, or condemned, depending on one's point of view, to forever straddle across boundaries. While their existence is tied to one place, their affective connections are with more than one place, including with where they 'come from', their original homeland. This coming from could have taken place a few years, or a few centuries or forever ago. If the people who have moved no longer have emotional connections with their homeland, they are not diasporic. If they live in one place (their hostland) but have complete loyalty to their homeland, they are not diasporic but temporary migrants. Rejecting a comprehensive notion of diaspora that includes all types of migrants, I propose confining the term to those collectivities within which individual subjectivity is marked by an ambiguity, a confusion, a productive anxiety, an affective pull from different directions, all of which creates a hyper-awareness and not a predominant sense of regret. The advantage of this narrow conception of diaspora is that it shifts away the emphasis from ethnicity and identity to a politics of identification and thus foregrounds agency. 'The diaspora experience … is defined, not by essence or purity, but by the recognition of a necessary heterogeneity and diversity; by a conception of "identity" which lives with and through, not despite, difference; by hybridity' (Hall 1990, p. 235).

Migrants who have lost all sense of belonging to their homeland and have no connections with it whatsoever except ethnic ties are not diasporic. They might be socially diasporic but their subjectivity is too resolved and settled to be diasporic. For instance, branding all overseas Chinese, including those who have no ties with China at all, as Chinese diaspora privileges an essentialist and primordial conception of ethnicity. In contrast, Chinese diaspora should refer only to those ethnic Chinese people living overseas who retain emotional connections with China and see it as their homeland. Even the most hyper-nationalistic activists within the diaspora who try their level best to ground their identity cannot exorcise the uncertainty that stems from their existence within a different polity. Rather than treating such displacement as only an occasion of loss and regret (for instance, as represented in many Hindi movies and songs), one should accept the diasporic subjectivity as an opportunity. An opportunity to re-read and re-imagine one's own culture is also problematic. This may allow a more nuanced politics of identity and culture that focuses more on routes than roots for a rooted notion of culture (see Clifford 1997) may foster a sense of irreconcilability with difference. Diasporic condition serves as a reminder to all of 'anxious identities we inhabit' (Kaul 2003). Diaspora thus has a psychogeography of displacement and desire of belonging built into itself.

## De(stabilising) the (inter)national

Empirical examples of different diasporas constantly remind us of their influence on domestic as well as international politics. Yet, international relations moored in a statist paradigm has largely ignored diasporas. Instead of dwelling on the role of diaspora in international politics (see Cohen 1997; Esman 1986; Sheffer 1986) and examples of how specific diasporas impact upon foreign policies of states (most research here has focused on the influences of Jewish, Armenian and other diasporas on American foreign policy; for example, see Shaffer 2006), let me explain how the diasporas by their very logic call for a questioning of narrow realpolitik way of looking at the international.

A focus on diasporas as conspicuous phenomena destabilises the familiarity of identity politics underpinning international relations. International relations adopts a jigsaw puzzle view of the world with discrete and distinct bounded national communities interacting with each other. The ideal subjectivity is that of a nation-state, one where the population = territory = government = sovereignty, but this putative equation is put into question with the presence of diasporas. Diasporas make a neat division of the world into fully formed, clearly demarcated units with secure sense of national identity impossible. And rightly so. For they could also act as a check against narrow exclusivist notions of national identity. If the state wants stability and security, it cannot afford to be exclusionary. Instead of acting merely as pressure groups working in tandem (as in the case of Jewish diaspora or Indian diaspora in the USA) or in opposition (like the Cuban diaspora in the USA) with their homeland government, diasporas could potentially occupy a role that makes a progressive difference and ensures an inclusionary nationalism within and accommodative foreign relations without. The existence of such diasporas could make the world more peaceful by complicating international relations, by criss-crossing boundaries and making mobilisation of violence around a specific narrow identity difficult. Diasporas, instead of jostling for political power and influence, could transform themselves into interlocutors and negotiators. We recognise that this normative exhortation for diasporas to challenge the key characteristics of international relations – war and peace, statism, national interest, pursuit of power – instead of subscribing to them is far from reality. Diasporas have often acted as extensions of nationalist discourse of the homeland or even encouraged a more exclusionary nationalism than that existing back in the homeland. Diasporas often contribute toward hypernationalism in their homeland. The oft reported financial support by the Hindu Non-Resident Indians to various Hindu nationalist organisations back in India is a case in point (see articles in *Ethnic and Racial Studies* 2000), but this need not be the case as a thought experiment at the very least.

Diasporas have a multifarous relationship with the notion of national identity. The diasporic condition forces one to confront difference. You cannot be comfortable and ignorant about your identity if you are diasporic. Your identity plays an important role in how you negotiate your daily life. You cannot but be aware of how you are similar and different from the majority around you. Some in the diaspora find it hard to reconcile their 'original' beliefs and values in a different context. I put 'original' under scare quotes because what may be perceived as original is often a product of nostalgic imagination and myth-making. Diasporas even when they have striven to be part of the host country's national identity have often found it is easier said than done. Racialised discourses and discomfort with difference often makes diasporic subjects targets of resentment on the part of sections of the 'native' population.

And then there are members of some diasporas who may claim to move beyond national identity to a global one. Rejection of narrow national identity does not automatically indicate a progressive broadening of horizon. The conspicuous examples of some radicalised British Muslims of Asian descent show how loyalty is neither to the host country nor to the original home country, but to the universal *umma*. In practice, their attempt to adopt a universal placeless identity cannot but be mediated through negotiations with concrete places, but these radical Islamists in the West pose an altogether different kind of challenge. Unlike diasporas who negotiate their identity between two particularities (one place *vis-à-vis* another), radical Islamists living outside their place of origin deny the very existence of specificity and locatedness. They fight battles in the name of a place-free notion of Islam and *umma* and are not concerned with homeland–hostland interactions. Even when they wage territorial wars, say in Palestine or Kashmir, they do so in the name of deterritorialised Islam. It is because of this reason, I propose expunging extremism, in the name of globalist ideology, out of the concept of diaspora. Diaspora involves negotiations across boundaries and between particular spatialities (even though imagined) and should not be applicable to universal spatial formations (global jihadi Islamism is one obvious example). Diasporas are always already cultural formations that involve perpetual negotiations between the universal and the particular and not a negation of one or the other. The end of the negotiation is the end of diasporic subjectivity.

## Diaspora and culture

Most studies on diaspora focus on the specificity of cultural identity that marks them out from the rest of the population in specific geographical locations. No analysis of diaspora can avoid engaging with the issue of culture and cultural identity. Questions of politics or social practices or economic relations in the diaspora emerge out of their cultural identity. An investigation into diaspora is thus an investigation of culture.

> Culture is one of the two or three most complicated words in the English language. This is so partly because of its intricate historical development, in several European languages, but mainly because it has now come to be used for important concepts in several distinct intellectual disciplines and in several distinct and incompatible systems of thought. (Raymond Williams in Duncombe 2002, p. 36)

One cannot but agree with Williams about the difficulty of providing a clear definition of culture. The dominant understanding of culture is that it is something that a social group shares, that defines the we and us, and allows for recognising the boundaries between us and them, Self and the Other. Culture is not about I but about Us. It is a collective phenomenon. It has various aspects to it but the main one is the common thread (or threads) that bind us together. Culture involves 'objective' commonalities such as language, way of thinking, songs, dances, literature, music, poetry, perceptual lens, morality, ethics, food and dress, sense of history, collective myths and legends, etc. For instance, American culture could be understood in terms of mass consumerism, Coke, KFC, Hollywood, Marilyn Monroe, Andy Warhol, big gas guzzlers, *The Great Gatsby*, Broadway and so on, but culture also involves a *recognition* of commonality, a subjective consciousness of who we are, an awareness of us. Culture cannot just exist, it has to be felt. Without a consciousness of commonality among the collective, culture has little significance. This does not mean that everyone has to be equally conscious for it to exist, but a general consensual consciousness has to be there.

Can there be a universal culture then? In the post-Cold War era especially, there is a discussion about global culture. Some may see it in terms of cultural imperialism (American culture dominating the world and destroying the local cultures). The problem with this sense of global culture is that it is too wide and too thin-layered to be effective. Such global uniformity or universalism remain mostly gestures. This is not to say that claims in the name of umma by the Islamists or global sisterhood by the feminists are empty rhetoric. Not at all; they might be heartfelt, but if you scratch under the surface, you would see that specific understandings of actors making the claims are context and culture specific. To remind you, universalist ideas of Reason, Rationality and Progress provided by European Enlightenment were always parochial (see Chakrabarty 2000). The fact that one speaks on behalf of a universal spirit does not mean it is universal. For the world is too complicated and diverse to be anything but pluriversal. Thus, culture is always about boundaries, about us and them, about we and you (plural). Culture is something that distinguishes us from them, that defines we. It is what makes us different and unique! In that sense it is always particularistic.

A definition of culture in terms of shared sense of belonging has an important impact. It can be mobilised differently by different actors. It allows for a sense of pride in owns own cultural identity. It encourages appreciation of cultural difference and avoidance of cultural arrogance. It can contribute to cross-cultural understanding. Alternatively, it might lead to cultural antagonism and an assumption of cultural supremacy. Defining culture in terms of shared identity can therefore be mobilised for different political purposes. For instance, right-wing nationalists may insist that any dissent from their version of national culture is unpatriotic and a treason, while critical dissidents may argue that their national culture is accommodative and allows for plurality of views.

How is this relevant in a discussion on diaspora? Diaspora is an entity whose very existence is a product of interactions across cultures. The presence of diaspora is a constant reminder that there is always more than one culture. At the very least, there are two cultures – one in the host country and another in the home country. For instance, the presence of Iranian diaspora in Canada implies that there is an Iranian culture and there is also a Canadian culture. The Canadians as well as the Iranian diasporic population will be aware of this, but many Iranians when they go back to Iran for a visit are likely to realise that there are at least three cultures – one Canadian, one Iranian and the third that is Canadian–Iranian. Even this ignores wide differences *within* Canadian, Iranian and Canadian–Iranian cultures. Thus, diasporic subjectivity can inculcate an awareness of multiplicity and difference and serve as a caution against narrow self-focused understandings of culture. This is not often the case, for the actually existing diasporic subjects may deny this emancipating diasporic subjectivity promoting humility and go for a different, more commonplace, understanding of culture. How diasporic subjects act toward those not belonging to their culture depends on their notion of culture. Hence this lengthy discussion on culture.

While cultural studies, anthropology and few other disciplines adopt a sophisticated notion of culture, often in other social sciences, culturalist frameworks are commonplace. These frameworks argue that culture is an important explanatory phenomenon. Let me illustrate how such explanations work and what assumptions about culture they make. Huntington is explicit about how culture matters – culture conceived as 'the values, attitudes, beliefs, orientations and underlying assumptions prevalent among people in a society ... affects the extent to which and the ways in which societies achieve or fail to achieve progress in economic development and political democratization' (2000, p. xv). The main danger with this is that culturalist frameworks while calling for recognition of cultural difference, often end up promoting one culture as better than the others. To illustrate using Huntington again, he gives an example – while in the 1960s, South Korea and Ghana's economic data were alike, by the early 1990s, Ghana's per capita GNP was about one-fifteenth of South Korea's and while many factors may have played their role, 'culture had to be a large part of the explanation. South Koreans valued thrift, investment, hard work, education, organization and discipline. Ghanaians had different values. In short cultures count' (2000, p. xiii). While saying that 'cultures count', it is clear from the statement that in this framework it is mainly, if not only, culture that counts. The role of neo-colonialism, American presence in East Asia in its war of containment, American (and Japanese) security and economic priorities in East Asia which then contributed to the rise of the 'Asian tigers', the more pernicious legacy of longer-term European colonialism in Africa, etc. – all these are seen as unimportant by Huntington in his example. All that matters is the superiority of South Korean culture. Another good example of this can be found in Fisher who sees culture as a 'pretested design, a store of knowledge and an entire system of coping skills ... learned behavior ... shared behavior, which is important because it systematizes the way people do things, thus avoiding confusion and allowing cooperation ...' (1997, p. 44). It then allows him to study the role of culture and perception in international relations in terms of mindsets. For instance, he argues how because of the legacy of Iberian forms of society and Catholic notions, 'Latin America is more static. Emphasis is placed less on managing things than on managing affiliations with other people' (1997, p. 52). A similar homogenising conception of culture can be found in various contexts.

Diasporas when they adopt such a notion of culture – as almost a fixed shared sense of belonging – are prone to vacillate between exclusion and inter-cultural dialogue, but they underplay inter-mixing, and any inter-mixing that is inevitable is seen as an impurity and an attack on culture. In contrast, I put forward culture as a site of debate and contestation. Culture is about contestations and conversations within it. The view of an Iranian feminist or a Revolutionary Guard about what is the core of Iranian-Islamic culture would be very different. Some may argue that tea and being reserved is essential characteristic of British culture, others might argue that it is tolerance and liberty. In this sense, cultures are always in process. They are not the end product which can be easily identified. After all, cultures are about 'circuits of mean-ing' and different actors always debate these meanings and in the process construct cultures. Such a social constructionist approach studies culture as a constitutive process, as processual (see Hall 1997). It understands identity of culture as well as cultural identity as always in flux and as a product of representations. While in academia there are plenty of writings which illustrate the constructed and contested nature of culture and diaspora, cultural entrepreneurs and self-appointed guardians of diaspora often retain a more conventional understanding of culture as about common-ality within and difference from without.

Culture, following Michel Foucault, should be seen in terms of relations of power and resistance. Identification of the knowledge–power (*pouvoir/savoir*) nexus reveals the linkage of truth claims with systems of power:

> (T)ruth isn't outside power, or lacking of power: contrary to a myth whose history and functions would repay further study, truth isn't the reward of free spirits, the child of protracted solitude, nor the privilege of those who have succeeded in liberating themselves. (Foucault 1980, p. 291)

This Foucauldian identification and exploration of link between power, knowledge and truth is radical in its implication. It shifts the terrain of inquiry from the question 'what is truth?' to the question 'how do discursive practices constitute truth claims?' In terms of culture, we no longer ask what are the authentic features of a culture but rather how do some features get represented as authentic and what power and interests lie behind those representations. This is similar to what Bhabha has to say about culture as transnational and translational:

> Culture as a strategy of survival is both transnational and translational. It is transnational because contemporary political discourses are rooted in specific histories of cultural displacement … . Culture is translational because such spatial histories of displacement … make the question of how culture signifies, or what is signified by culture, a rather complex issue. (Bhabha 1994, p. 172)

## Reconceptualising diaspora

Thus conceptualising culture as a site of contestation encourages us to read diaspora as a problematic and fragile imagined category and pay more attention to silences, marginalisations and erasures in the dominant narratives coming out of the diaspora. This is ethnographically rigorous as well as ethnically sound. For anything else will make analysts complicit with the dominant narratives in diaspora which often paper over differences within and accentuate differences without. For instance, in the UK context, the dominant narratives are the ones that are often used by the so-called community leaders. These communities – say 'Asian' or 'Black' or 'Bangladeshi' or 'Indian' – are ethnic minorities within Britain while also being diasporic. This is different from the status of minorities in China for instance. Minorities in China are not a product of modern diasporic movements, but because most visible minorities in the West have come to be through recent migrations, they are also diasporic. The interaction between this minority status and diasporic status is pregnant with multiple meanings. We can only point out to some here. The state, the media, the civil society – all use the language of 'community' for ethnic minorities and often talk of 'commu-nity elders' and 'community leaders'. This vocabulary needs an unpacking for there are unanswered questions about agency – who defines the community, who selects the community spokesmen (yes, they are almost always men), what are the assumptions behind the institutions and personnels of the host state and host civil society who perceive diasporic-ethnic minorities, how does the language of community reflect and reshape identity politics within the diaspora? How about those members of the diaspora who refuse to conform, who refuse to adhere to the cultural norms, who contest a certain given sense of what it means to belong to their culture? Does the 'community' have a space for them or are they outcasted? We argue for seeing the diaspora, its culture and its identity through the eye of these outsiders. The limits are always fluid and an arena for struggles.

Those who push the boundaries of culture, the limits of diasporic culture, are in a better position to have a critical understanding of 'their culture' (we use this for want of a better phrase) and appreciate commonalities across cultural formations. This does not imply that they are better 'cultural ambassadors' because no one, including they themselves, would see it as such. They are non-ambassadors and dissenters. Note that diplomacy (of which ambassadors are crucial part) is never questioning of one's own country or identity but always promoting it. An ambassador represents her country, she will only project an uncritical view of her country. A diasporic subject as an ambassador of his native culture or as a representative of her homeland culture – this native culture or homeland could be another country or another sub-national group or even a non-national entity – is similarly involved in shoving under the carpet differences and power relations within his or her own cultural community. In contrast, the figure of the dissenter lends a critical distance. Even if the dissenter is marginalised or outcast, she knows how it feels to bear the burden of culture (non)confirmity, he has felt the culture operate through his body and being in not so pleasant ways. The disciplining, mostly through social and moral sanctions, of dissidents of diaspora reveals the arbitrariness and artificiality of the cultural claims made in the name of diaspora. An understanding of this can also put the other cultures – especially of the hostland – under erasure and questioning. In this, we call for reconceptualising diasporic subjectivity as an ethical political positioning that can be occupied by anyone with a consciousness of the contested and constructed nature of the culture to which they are seen as belonging. This normative take on diaspora allows one to witness and understand the ways in which culture is sought to be manufactured through different voices and silences, through inclusions and exclusion.

## Notes on contributor

Dr Dibyesh Anand is a Reader (Associate Professor) in International Relations at the Centre for the Study of Democracy, Westminster University, UK. His publications are in the areas of Global Politics, Tibet, China, Hindu nationalism and Security. He is the author of *Geopolitical Exotica: Tibet in Western Imagination* (2007), *Tibet: A Victim of Geopolitics* (2009) and *Hindu Nationalism in India and the Politics of Fear* (2010). He is currently working on his book 'China's Tibet', Indian diaspora in Tanzania, a research project on Sino-Indian border regions and majority–minority relations in India and China.

## References

Anand, D., 2003. A contemporary story of diaspora: the Tibetan version. *Diaspora: a journal of transnational studies,* 12 (3), 211–229.

Anand, D., 2007. *Geopolitical exotica: Tibet in Western imagination*. Minneapolis: University of Minnesota Press.

Bhabha, H.K., 1994. *The location of culture*. London: Routledge.

Brah, A., 1996. *Cartographies of diaspora: contesting identities*. London: Routledge.

Chakrabarty, D., 2000. *Provincializing Europe: postcolonial thought and historical difference*. Princeton: Princeton University Press.

Clifford, J., 1997. *Routes: travel and translation in the late twentieth century*. Cambridge, MA: Harvard University Press.

Cohen, R., 1997. *Global diasporas: an introduction*. London: University College London Press.

Duncombe, S., 2002. *Cultural resistance reader*. London: Verso Books.

Esman, M.J., 1986. Diasporas and international relations. *In:* G. Sheffer, ed. *Modern diasporas in international politics*. London: Croom Helm, 333–349.

*Ethnic and Racial Studies,* 2000. Special issue on Hindutva in the West. 23 (3), 401–623.

Fisher, G., 1997. *Mindsets: the role of culture and perception in international relations*. Yarmouth, ME: Intercultural Press.

Foucault, M., 1980. *Power/knowledge: selected interviews and other writings 1972–1977,* (C. Gordon, ed.). London: Harvester Wheatsheaf.

Hall, S., 1990. Cultural identity and diaspora. *In:* J. Rutherford, ed. *Identity: community, culture, difference*. London: Lawrence & Wishart, 222–237.

Hall, S., 1997. The spectacle of the 'other'. *In:* S. Hall, ed. *Representation: cultural representations and signifying practices*. London: Sage/Open University, 223–290.

Huntington, S.P., 2000. Foreword: cultures count. *In:* L.E. Harrison and S.P. Huntington, eds. *Culture matters: how values shape human progress*. New York: Basic Books, xiii–xvi.

Kaul, N. 2003. The anxious identities we inhabit … post'isms and economic understandings. *In:* D. Barker and E. Kuiper, eds. *Toward a feminist philosophy of economics*. London: Routledge, 194–210.

Kaul, N., 2007. *Imagining economics otherwise: encounters with identity/difference*. London: Routledge.

Radhakrishnan, R., 1996. *Diasporic mediations: between home and location*. Minneapolis, MN: University of Minnesota Press.

Shaffer, B., 2007. 'Shiite Crescent' might not be what it seems. *The Baltimore sun,* April 25. Available from: http://belfercenter.ksg.harvard.edu/publication/1681/shiite_crescent_might_not_be_what_it_seems.html?breadcrumb=%2Fexperts%2F283%2Fbrenda_shaffer [Accessed on 15 February 2009].

Sheffer, G., 1986. A new field of study: modern diasporas in international politics. *In:* G. Sheffer, ed. *Modern diasporas in international politics*. London: Croom Helm, 1–15.

Tölölyan, K., 1996. Rethinking diaspora(s): stateless power in the transnational moment. *Diaspora: a journal of transnational studies,* 5 (1), 3–36.

# Another world of experience? Transnational contexts and the experiences of South Asian Americans

Bandana Purkayastha

*Department of Sociology & Asian American Studies, University of Connecticut, Storrs, CT, USA*

Despite discussions about freely circulating people, ideas, media images, money, technology in a flat world in the popular media, new political, economic, and technological formations continue to construct restrictive social hierarchies that disproportionately affect socially marked groups. This paper focuses on South Asian Americans to systematically examine how these forces have created a transnational context that works through and across multiple nations to shape the lives of diasporic groups today. Drawing on a meta analysis of three previous studies, the paper examines three dimensions of this transnational context: the role of global security blocs, companies that market cultures as products, and the World Wide Web as a social space. It shows how ideologies, institutions, and interactions in coalescing real and virtual transnational spaces adds another layer of experience that, in turn, intersects with the multi-layered diasporic experiences extant within nations.

## Introduction

Contemporary globalisation has been marked by rapid circulation of people, ideas, media images, money, technology (Appadurai 1996) in ways that distinguish it from earlier historical eras such as colonialism. Indeed, the some influential opinion-makers have assumed that these current types of global-level circulation have led to the creation of a flat world (Freidman 2005). Yet discussions of flat worlds, with their suggestion of easy passage and interactions across national boundaries, elide the realities of existing ideologies, interactions, and institutions that continue to construct social hierarchies that restrict the lives of racialised groups (Kibria 2002; Purkayastha 2005; Tuan 2001). This paper focuses on South Asian Americans to suggest that we need to study the transnational context that is adding a new realm of experience for diasporic groups. The transnational context is an outcome of contemporary globalisation, it exists across and through multiple nation-states. The factors that shape the transnational context intersect with processes within nation-states to deepen, dilute, and/or change experiences of marginalisation. The paper examines dimensions of this transnational context – focusing on the role of global security blocs, companies that market cultures as products, and the Word Wide Web as a social space – to discuss some ways in which new global forces affect diasporic groups.

## Transnationalism and transnational contexts

Most scholars in Europe and America recognise that contemporary migrant groups construct lives across countries facilitated by improved communication technology, ease of travel, and political moves by countries to claim 'their' overseas citizens (e.g. Anthias 1998; Kistivo 2001; Levitt and De La Rahesa 2002; Portes 1997; Vertovec 2002). But, following the route charted by assimilation studies, these Western scholars (and researchers in other parts of the world who use Western models) have mostly focused on the networks and links that diasporic groups – immigrants and their children – maintain between their home and host countries.[1] For instance, Glick-Schiller, Basch, and Blanc-Szanton (1992), introduced the term transnationalism to describe 'the processes by which immigrants forge and sustain multi-stranded social relations that link together their *societies of origin and settlement*' (p. 7, my italics). A series of studies on first generation migrants – e.g. Peggy Levitt's *Transnational Villagers* (2001) – documented how migrants build and maintain lives in the home country and the country where they settled. The work on the post-immigrant generation continued the same trajectory, examining the ways in which the children of migrants maintain ties with their parent's homelands (e.g. Portes 1995; Waters and Levitt 2002).

However, this home-host framework is inadequate to understand the lives of contemporary diasporic groups. The concepts of 'home' and 'host' become complicated when we consider post-immigrant generations or groups that have, over generations, migrated multiple times. The home-host framework does not explicitly examine how groups that identify with a country, the country of origin or the ancestors' country of origin, may, nonetheless, be outsiders to these places; and a range of laws and policies in these 'home countries' offer opportunities and/or impede their lives. More importantly, this framework does not provide a way to examine the series of political, economic and technological transformations that have worked *through and across multiple nations* to create a *transnational* context that shapes the lives of diasporic groups today. Among the key factors that shape this context are the growth of global security blocs, economic processes that sell cultures and lifestyles to 'ethnic consumers', and the rapid development of the Web as a social space through which ideas – including ideas about identities – are developed and shared among members of geographically dispersed communities. Ideologies, institutions, and interactions that emanate from multiple countries are structuring a transnational context that is marked by power inequalities and gendered racialised hierarchies.

The transnational context that works through and across nations is inflected with political, economic, social and cultural power hierarchies extant at the global level, and these intersect with hierarchies existing within nation-states. This idea can be illustrated with reference to political hierarchies. Depending on their citizenship, and the relative power of their country of citizenship to influence the global political agenda, some diasporic groups might experience the transnational context as an arena of relative freedom, an arena that allows them the opportunity to experience life beyond nation-state boundaries with very few social costs. For instance, white diasporic groups in Western countries – such as white South African diasporic groups in the US – might experience relative freedom to travel anywhere in the world if their countries of residence wield sufficient power and the social will to create benign political status for them in the transnational context. However, diasporic groups that are classified as 'other' within powerful nation-states that shape the transnational political agenda might find their marginalised experiences deepening. Afghani diasporic groups who hold American or British citizenship might find themselves in such ambiguous positions; their marginalisation is further accentuated since their country of origin is not able to mitigate the marginalised status of Afghans within the transnational context. Diasporic groups that are marginalised in states that wield less power in shaping the transnational context might experience a dilution of their marginalised status in this context. Indian diasporic groups from Kenya might experience a dilution of their local marginalised status compared to their fellow-country people. Or diasporic groups might simultaneously benefit from some of the power of their countries of citizenship in this context, along with a degree of marginalisation. Indian diasporic groups from the UK might experience both the power of their citizenship status along with the negative effects of their 'other' designation by Britain.

In addition to the practices of nation-states, a variety of groups use diverse political mobilisations and tactics to attempt to influence the political positioning of diverse diasporic groups. For instance, terrorist groups have attempted to interrupt the relative ability of citizens from selected countries to travel freely and feel secure. In recent times, terrorists have targeted 'foreigners' on the basis of their 'other' religion and nationality. At the same time, diasporic groups work to improve their relative position within the transnational context by mobilising to challenge their marginalisation and/or protecting their political status. There is, for example, a long history of diasporic Sikhs who work through and across countries to challenge their marginalisation (Rex 1995; Tatla 1999). These political processes do not work in isolation: a range of economic, social, and cultural factors work in conjunction with these political processes through and across countries to structure diasporic group experiences in the transnational context.

Overall, the transnational context is the site of an additional layer of experience for diasporic groups. But the transnational experiences are not entirely separable from nation-based experiences. These transnational encounters *interact and intersect* with experiences within countries of residence to deepen, dilute, and/or change the experiences of diasporic groups. Thus, in order to understand the effects of contemporary globalisation on diasporic groups, it is important to understand some of the contours of the transnational context. South Asian Americans, who benefit from some of the power of their American citizenship while experiencing continued marginalisation, provide an adequate case for understanding this other 'world of experience'.

**A note on the data**

This discussion is based on three studies on South Asian Americans. The first study focuses on a post immigrant generation group of young adults, the children of relatively affluent, highly educated-immigrant parents (Purkayastha 2005). Most were born in the US, all are US citizens; they grew up in middle-class-to-affluent, mostly-white suburbs, and were either in college or were in professional careers. They are Hindus, Muslims, Sikhs and Christians who trace their origins to India, Pakistan, Bangladesh and Nepal. They had family members all over the world. The purpose of this study was to analyse the factors that shaped post-immigrant generation South Asian American identities, with a particular focus on why they chose hyphenated identities in spite of being objectively assimilated according to locally accepted indicators – their linguistic abilities, education, residence current or prospective occupation – in the US. The study examined how these hyphenated identities – Asian Indian, Indian American, South Asian American, desi, etc. – are shaped by the processes of racialisation of these young people in the US, their experience in multiple countries as they maintain meaningful ties with geographically dispersed family members, the racial/gendered dynamics within nuclear families and ethnic communities, their ability to consume ethnic cultural items – music, art, literature, films, fashions – and through the efforts of organised ethnic groups.

This article uses two strands of this study – *Negotiating Ethnicity* by Purkayastha – to describe the transnational context. It draws upon the barriers these young people experienced as they travelled, to discuss the effects of global security blocs. The ways in which the boundaries within the transnational context coalesce with some of their experiences within the US is discussed with reference to the original study. This article also focuses on the cultural items these young people consumed and the entities that sell 'cultural' items to discuss some economic factors that shape the transnational context. While the original study examines many ways in which ethnic identity is shaped, the focus here is on transnational politics and economic processes. Some of the examples are drawn from this study, but these are used to develop a different theoretical argument.

The second study is on Hindu and Muslim women's experiences in living their religions in the US, Bangladesh, India, Nepal, and Pakistan (Narayan and Purkayastha 2008). In this study, immigrant and post immigrant generation women discussed the opportunities and barriers they encounter as they live their religions. The study sought to identify the institutional structures and ideologies within the women's ethno-cultural groups, the mainstream in the US and one or more South Asian countries that supported or impeded their efforts to live their religions. The objective of the book was to showcase how religions dynamically respond to diverse local and national socio-political contexts, as well as women's views of their status and agency as practitioners and interpreters of these religions. The current article draws upon the discussions about the ideological constructions of religions for political purpose. Unlike the original study, the discussion about the political use of religions is linked to the ideologies underpinning the development of global security blocs.

The third study focuses on the construction of ethno-religious identities on the Web (Narayan 2005; Purkayastha and Narayan 2009). The main focus was to identify the recurring themes that student groups use in the US and UK to publicly profess their identities. Narayan's seminal study critically analysed the shifts and changes that are being constructed as 'traditional Hinduism' and 'traditional Indian-ness' through these websites. An additional focus of her study was to track the networks of websites through which these college students interpret and challenge their racialisation. In this article, the data is used to illustrate the contours of a virtual transnational context, rather than the exact content of the messages.

I draw upon some insights of these empirical studies to discuss factors that shape the contemporary transnational context within which diasporic groups live their lives. Given the hegemonic power of the US in world political and economic systems, South Asian Americans are a particularly interesting group to consider for such a discussion.[2] Since the US continues to play a major role in shaping many of the political and economic initiatives in the transnational context, the experiences of South Asian Americans illustrate dimensions of power and marginalisation – gendered racialisation – that are experienced by diasporic groups.[3] By focusing on South Asian Americans, I showcase people who are able to move relatively easily around the world

– i.e., they are less constrained by visa requirements – and they constitute a particular type of American ethnic markets targeted by multinational companies because of their perceived buying power. They enjoy the advantages of America's access to technology (compared to other diasporic South Asian groups). But, as the next sections show, they experience gendered racialisation processes that unlink them from the full benefits of being American citizens. Their experiences form the basis of the discussion of three important factors shape facets of the transnational context.

## Transnational political boundaries: the role of ideologies and institutions

The development of a transnational context is related to a number of global-level initiatives and changes that have been underway for decades. Soysal (1998) and others have pointed to the transformation of the international state system towards an increasing interconnectedness and interdependence since the middle of the twentieth century. International instruments such as the Universal Declaration of Human Rights (UDHR) have offered the promise of a universally applicable set of rights. UDHR and its conventions continue to create political spaces for notions of universal personhood. As these instruments gather more political force, nation-states are expected *not* to discriminate on the basis of citizenship as they grant civil and political and social rights to traditionally excluded groups. Soysal (1998), therefore, argues that in addition to national citizenship – which provides political rights – there now exists post-national citizenship, which, albeit fragmentary, provides a series of conduits for claiming human rights across states. Diasporic groups have used these instruments to claim their political and cultural rights, for instance, the recent case of Sikhs protesting the banning of 'religious apparel' in French schools. In the US, Indian origin Dalit groups have organised to claim human rights; their efforts have been opposed by Hindu fundamentalist groups that have claimed the Dalit-USA efforts violate *their* human rights (Majumdar 2008).

However, the growth of this transnational political sphere, where diasporic groups can claim human rights and contest structural restrictions, is challenged by an opposing political trend: the rapidly developing supra-national security blocs that are creating a global-level hierarchy of who can claim these human rights and who cannot (Vertovec 2001). As countries join these security blocs – at least eighty have done so – they share detailed information about racially profiled individuals, their communications and their movements. These new supra-national racial profiles classify which groups are to be subject to extra scrutiny and which ones are considered benign, irrespective of citizenship. As a result, 'benign', unmarked groups are able to travel more easily through the supra national zones marked by fewer political boundaries, while marked groups – such as Muslims and Muslim-looking people – have become more politically vulnerable in larger swaths of the globe as many countries adopt similar racial classifications to 'secure' their nations (see Luban 2005; Robinson 2005, for critiques).

Racial profiling in this transnational political context is based on ideologies about appropriate and inappropriate people. While such ideologies have been key to creating unequal citizenships within countries (see Glenn 2002), they now act as restraints on transnational claims to political personhood. For instance, a-historical, over-generalised ideology of clashing civilisations, the idea that 'Islamic culture explains, in large part, the failure of democracy to emerge in much of the Muslim world' (Huntington 1998, p. 4), has resulted in a renewed marking of geographic zones into civilised and non-civilised areas of the world, reminiscent of earlier colonial classification of the world

(Purkayastha and Narayan 2009). People who are assumed to have roots in the not-civilised regions, are supposed to be essentially different from modern, secular, freedom-loving people; hence the justification for widespread profiling. Embedded within this ideology are ideas of female subordination, extreme patriarchy, and lack of progressive ideas or practices characteristic of just societies. Religion, as the précis of civilisation, has become *the* race-marker in the ideologies that shape the transnational political context; Muslims are particularly affected negatively, though other religions have not fared well (Narayan and Purkayastha 2008).

The data on immigrant and post-immigrant generation South Asian Americans suggest that both ideologies and social structures shape their experiences in national and transnational contexts. Studies focusing on the US show that South Asian Americans have long been relegated to the status of 'other' in the ideological tropes about incommensurable cultures within the US (Purkayastha 2005; Narayan and Purkayastha 2008; Purkayastha and Narayan 2009). They face overt racism – racial epithets, hate crimes, institutional barriers to work, education access – as well as ideological racism which describes them as practitioners of less modern or traditional cultures (Purkayastha 2005). The ideological distinctions between modernity and tradition are constructed broadly in terms of female subordination and corresponding inappropriate masculinities – for instance, 'they practice arranged marriages' – religious beliefs that are antithetical to Western secularism – they practice religions of darkness – and suspected loyalties to other nation-states that are at odds with US foreign policy objectives.

The widespread discourse about the United States as a country built on Christian values places them in outsider positions: Muslims are at the bottom of this religious hierarchy, though Hindus and Buddhists are also marginalised (Grillo 2001). Along with the Sikhs – especially males who have been targets of hate crimes because of their turbans – Hindus, Buddhists, Christians, Muslims, and Zoroastrian South Asian Americans are rarely seen as people who actively construct the secular character of the US through *their* lives and achievements. They remain as the other, with secularism being defined mostly in terms of Christianity (and, sometimes, Jewishness). The persistent belief that religion is only practiced in the ways Christianity is practiced – in religious institutions, on designated days, membership in congregations, with centralised priestly hierarchies, according to a key text – deprives Hindus, Muslims, Sikhs and others of their right to practice their religions in ways that are consistent with their cultural moorings. Such barriers to religious freedom impede the ability of South Asian Americans to claim full citizenship within the US, even if they are US citizens.[4]

Given hegemonic role of the US in the formation of security blocs, similar political boundaries are evident in the transnational context. Since the transnational political context is constructed on the basis of acceptable and unacceptable individuals and groups – based on a combination of phenotype, nationality, and religion – South Asian Americans experience a decoupling of their status as American citizens from their racialised master-status as Muslim or Muslim-looking people (irrespective of their religious affiliation). People with roots in Pakistan and Bangladesh have been subjected to periods of being on 'country-watch' lists. South Asian Americans who are permanent residents or hold other legal visa status are even more vulnerable. Since South Asian Americas tend to have geographically dispersed families,[5] they travel to multiple countries for weddings, funerals, family gatherings, and for religious purposes. The ideologies about them and their actual movement subject them to surveillance at a far greater level than that of their peers. Young South Asian Americans described how officials and residents of other countries would repeatedly ask them where they were 'really from' after they announced they were American. These questions were mostly followed by questions about the location of their families. Equally important, depending on where their geographically dispersed families live, repeated communications with 'people in suspect countries', can trigger racial profiling and extra surveillance across the security blocs (instead of single nation-states). Since countries share data, 'suspect profiles' can be, and now are, invoked by many countries. Accounts by Muslim South Asian Americans show, for instance, that they are as likely to be negatively profiled by India – questioned about their extended family lineage – just as they are 'racially profiled' in the UK (see Chowdhury 2008). The chances of being indicted because of their links to cousins and family in different countries if those family members are detained on suspicion of being 'security risks' has become a concern among diasporic South Asian American groups.[6]

Gendered racialised hierarchies remain very salient in this transnational context. Who is likely to be under surveillance – e.g. turban-wearing males, hijab-wearing females, males with Muslim sounding names, sari-clad Hindu females – is an outcome of the political imperative that is important within the transnational context. South Asian American women reported being questioned about their 'original country' and the country of origin of their husbands and fathers by immigration officials in multiple countries. Just as these questions emphasised their lack of political personhood – except through their relationship with male family members – they are, in effect, deprived of the political status to directly seek protection of a state – as refugees, or as victims of racism in these global security regimes – on their own right, unless they are willing to repudiate, disown and vilify 'their civilization', like the Somali-Dutch politician Ayan Hirsi Ali, who has emerged as a leading crusader against Islam (Zakaria 2008).

## Transnational markets and the sale of cultures

Economic transformations of the global economy also shape the experiences of diasporic groups in a transnational context. The shift towards a post-industrial economy in the Euro-American countries has led to the increasing emphasis on the production of knowledge and services (e.g. Davilla 2001; Lury 1996; Zukin 1995). A specific aspect of this shift is the development of industries that sell cultures. Companies with global reach target groups of consumers by appealing to their 'fundamental' identities and sell cultural products – include clothing, art, music, films, books, make-up – that are supposed to help these consumers express their ethnic lifestyles. These companies may be located anywhere in the world, just as their marketing targets could be located in any corner of the world. In order to create market demands and develop loyal consumer bases, companies spend a great deal of money in *creating* segmented ethnic markets across nations to which they sell cultures (Halter 2000).

Scholars have pointed out that the availability of these consumption items has led to new ways of participating in societies. Traditional sources of identity, which have been related to nationality, family, long-term employment, and relationships to people in geographic proximity, are now being replaced by more fluid identities based on the construction of lifestyles (Hebdige 1988). The hallmark of being a citizen of post-industrial societies – in the sense of what makes a person culturally American or British – is the ability to exercise individual choice, in other words, free of the fetters of family or other loyalties to exercise their option to consume items and construct lifestyles (Canclini 2001). Issues of citizenship, political affiliation, and other differences are wiped out in these appeals to 'fundamental' identities and desires as companies try to create and sell to new markets.

While groups that are marked politically as 'other' do not enjoy the privilege of having fluid identities, nonetheless, they can and do use ethnic items as material symbols to express who they are (Davilla 2001). The degree of affiliation with ethnic institutions and organisations – that act as nodes of many ethnically identified networks – vary for post immigrant generations, but, irrespective of their affiliations, they can independently exercise their choice of buying ethnic items to showcase their 'roots'. The growth of the economy of selling cultures provides a variety of material cultural items to achieve such consumption-driven ways of doing ethnicity. What these items mean to ethnic individuals fluctuates depending on how they construct their ethnic-ness – some might construct their lives primarily on the basis of ethnic consumption, others might add ethnic 'touches' to episodic events such as an 'Indian-themed' party, yet others might consume ethnic items along with maintaining strong ethnic networks and relationships – but the consumption items are available for all, including people who are not otherwise invested in their ethnic identities.[7]

The growth of the transnational economy of selling cultures has opened up new ways of doing ethnicity. Shared consumption allows diasporic groups to develop pan-ethnic bonds within nations: South Asian Americans, like other South Asian diasporic groups, use cultural consumption as a neutral way to bridge linguistic, religious, regional cultural divides among themselves. Gujarati Indians might bond with Punjabi Indians over dance sequences; Bengali Indians might bond with Assamese Indians over shared admiration for some singers. The post immigrant generations also adopt the marketing ideologies to equate their consumption choices with exercising individualism, which they describe as expressing their modern Westernised selves (Bhachu 1995). According to this logic women can overcome gender inequality through their equal opportunity with men to consume ethnic fashions, much like the process described by Canclini (2001) or Hebdige (1988). This 'safe' way of practicing ethnicity becomes particularly important to them as practicing religion, belonging to ethnic community groups, charitable giving to organisations that might later be labelled security problems, are increasingly scrutinised and are likely to cause problems within global security regimes.

The economy of selling cultures promotes homogeneity. Since diasporic cultures are always dynamic, responding to structural and cultural contexts within which the group is situated, these processes of selling cultures also create a level of homogenisation *across* countries in powerful ways. Shared patterns of consumption develop across countries – affluent groups in the US and the UK might buy ethnic designer clothing from the same designer outlets across the world or enjoy the same types of music and movies marketed globally – and these shared patterns lead to the development of common lifestyles across nations. As artists and musicians are 'promoted' to travel on a global circuit each year, diasporic groups in multiple countries can claim to have heard the same artists 'live', a level of commonality of experience that emphasises homogeneity across countries. Irrespective of the South Asian country (and specific South Asian cultural region) to which they trace their roots, South Asian diasporic groups participate in common consumption of Bollywood movies (Gillespie 1995). A rapidly growing range of 'South Asian' designers in India, United Kingdom, the US and other countries are setting the similar standards of fashions across countries (Purkayastha 2005). The selling of religious artifacts also exhibits this tendency towards picking and marketing common symbols even though the two major South Asian American religions, Hinduism and Islam, are very diverse culturally (Narayan and Purkayastha 2008). Since this homogenisation occurs across several nation-states, South Asian 'culture' tends to assume an aura of essentialism and changelessness making local and national specificities less salient.

It is important to note that such homogenisation at the transnational level is not an outcome of a 'flat world', where ideas and people circulate seamlessly. It is an outcome of economic power and works at several levels. First, as South Asian Americans construct their ethnic lifestyles, they often draw most heavily on materials that are easily accessible (that is, widely marketed) and suitable for leisure time activities, the only time-space when they can be ethnic without incurring social costs. Thus they turn to products marketed by companies that have the greatest economic power to generate brand-name identification. Second, the cultures of Hindi and Urdu speaking people – who are the demographic majority in South Asian diasporas – are marketed most often; thus these cultures subsequently assume the status of 'the culture' and 'the tradition', pushing regional cultures – for instance of Bangladeshis or the Kannadigas from India – to the margins in this transnational 'Indian' cultural formation process. Third, since the aim of marketing is to create desire and identification with cultural products of particular companies, ethnic consumers across countries have, over time, begun to cede the 'authority' and 'expertise' to decide what represents 'a culture' in public fora to these large-scale commercial producers. Many local, regional, and national cultural producers – artists, authors, performers, designers, intellectuals – who are well known and valued in South Asian countries are pushed to the margins within this transnational context. In addition, diasporic cultural producers are marketed as the voices of the cultures of *South Asian* countries.[8] Fourth, the need to find new ways to conduct identity marketing each season leads companies to invent traditions. For instance, fashions that hark back to a Muslim identity or extol the virtues of a Hindu musician emphasise distinctions based on religious identities that may not have been as salient in the same way in the era that is evoked through such marketing initiatives.

The boundaries constructed through the economy of selling cultures overlap with the political boundaries described in the previous section. The ideology of clashing cultures that provides the contemporary impetus for racial profiling based on religions, is mirrored in the marketing of cultures. As the staple of such marketing, appeals to tradition and to 'home' cultures continue to reinforce the idea of essential cultures that are distinctively different from the mainstream in countries where diasporic groups reside. Marketing motifs that are widely deployed emphasise specific tropes of gender and ethno-religious imageries that are borrowed from widely circulating racial ideologies. Equally important, the emphasis on consumption as a way of being modern and exercising choice deflects attention from the racist premise of profiling based on religion – the idea of essential cultures incommensurable with secular states. As politically conscious South Asian Americans have pointed out, the freedom to consume also deflects this group's energies from organising to claim the human right to practice other aspects of their cultures.

## Transnational virtual social spaces

While the intersecting political and economic processes described above have shaped a transnational context that is replete with gendered racialised boundaries, the development of the technologically derived transnational social space, contributes further to shaping this context. Political and economic actors use the Web for a variety of activities (see e.g. Chadwick 2006; Howard 2006). For diasporic groups the Web has emerged as a site for ideologically challenging the racially denigrating 'controlling images' by offering alternative ways of thinking about ethno-racial identities. The process through which such alternatives are offered involves building networks in cyberspace. These activities further underscore the ways in which nation-states do not act as containers of people's lives.

Emily Ignacio's (2005) study on Filipino diasporas demonstrates how Internet technologies facilitate the creation of 'communities of sentiment' and computer-mediated 'diasporic public spheres'. The Web provides a context within which individuals and groups can reach geographically dispersed others – for keeping in touch, socialising, facilitates meeting-and-dating, and for group-organising – since it allows a new arena for self-expression and self-representation and a venue for constructing ethnic (ethno-religious, ethno-national) identities. Marked groups challenge ascribed identities, often using cultural tools – e.g. versions of histories, ideologies of superiority, re/invented beliefs and practices – strategically to promote a sense of ethno-nationalism.

While earlier studies of the Web raised questions about the real impact of interactions on this arena compared to interactions in tangible geographic domains, the activities of younger groups – those who use the Internet for everyday socialising and communications – have begun to challenge this assumed hierarchy of real and virtual spaces. The Web can, at the least, be considered to complement tangible social spaces for the technologically 'wired' generation. As young people become more and more woven into virtual world networks and socialising patterns, the Web becomes an increasingly crucial component of the transnational context. Studies that document who links to whom, where, and how frequently, are beginning to reveal the contours of this social space.

Anjana Narayan's (2005) study of Hindu student websites reveals some of the dimensions of the virtual transnational context. This large scale, empirical study, of the discourse of student groups in the US and UK, shows that there is now a similarity of discourse – a similarity that is statistically significant – about Hinduism across the US and UK. Despite the fact that Hinduism is extremely diverse and that it is dependent on family-and-regional cultural context in India and Nepal, the Web versions emphasise a few key components: that Hinduism is a superior, world religion, it has a unified set of beliefs, India is the homeland for Hindus and that Hindus believe in the superiority of females.

Along with the striking similarity of recurrent themes across two countries, it is also important to note the reconstruction of this public presentation of Hinduism on terms salient to the Western diasporic context. While Hinduism's lack of 'a book', congregations, and multiple-coexisting belief-practice systems have made it difficult to fit it into the preset descriptions of religion, these transnational constructions fit quite well into Western definitions of religion. Reconstructed, homogenised Hinduism assumes significance through the activities within this transnational virtual social space.

The gendered racialised imageries about subordinated women (and inappropriate men who ill-treat women) that are the staple of ideologies about clashing civilisations also appear consistently among the top themes in both countries according to Narayan's content analysis. The student websites, irrespective of the country in which they are hosted, repeatedly challenge the stereotypes about the 'ill-treatment' of women by practitioners of 'other' religions to create alternative ways of considering the status of women. The websites portray strong women – mostly goddesses and historical characters – as proof of the problems with racist ideologies.[9]

These websites contribute to the construction of the transnational context in two ways. A key impact of these websites that push a unified transnational message about Hinduism is evident through a simple search of the Web. The top ranked sites that are revealed through Web searches are sites with these homogenised fundamentalist messages. Hence these versions begin to represent the universe of Hinduism on the Web and groups within countries can simply borrow and use or adopt these homogenised messages. In addition, an assessment of the hyperlinks of the websites shows that these frequently link to 'nodal' websites in other countries, offering visitors seamless ways of reading the messages of groups in different nations simultaneously, facilitating the participation in a transnational context.

## Concluding remarks

The literature on diasporas is large and interdisciplinary, ranging from empirical documentation of groups around the world (Clark *et al.* 1990; Cohen 1997; Peach 1994; Singh 2007; Tatla 1999) to postcolonial studies and discussions of imperial power and its effects on marginalised groups (Gilroy 1993; Hall 1990). This paper focused on the social science approaches to diasporic groups, especially the recent American studies on transnationalism, arguing that home-and-host-country frameworks are inadequate to capture political and economic forces emanating from multiple countries. It pointed to global-level changes that are, together, crafting a transnational context focusing on the effects of institutions and entities engaged in securing the boundaries of supranational blocs, of corporations engaged in constructing and selling cultures to segmented consumer markets, and of organised groups constructing and mobilising a constituency to challenge their gendered racialisation, on the lives of South Asian Americans.

For diasporic groups, this transnational context, spanning real and virtual worlds, offer unparalleled opportunities to network across countries and participate in shared experiences. The promise of universal human rights, global-level economic recognition of multiple cultures, or the freedom, via the Web, to construct new transnational identities that are loosened from specific localities, are associated with this layer of experience. At the same time, an array of political, economic and social boundaries continue to restrict and constrain opportunities for diasporic groups. This view contradicts some of the assumptions of the home-and-host-country models of understanding transnationalism.

This account of a transnational context does not override the relevance of national and local contexts. National contexts are still the repositories of formal laws and policies that construct different strata of citizenship. Access to a transnational context does not allow groups to avoid gendered, racialised interactions, though transnational ideologies and interactions can help minimise and parochialise the outcomes. In other words, the existence of a transnational context adds another layer of experience that deepens, changes, and/or challenges gendered, racist marginalisation. As this article shows, the transnational layer can come together and/or clash with the national layer of diasporic experience.

While a focus on the South Asian American experience might appear to indicate a seamlessness between national and transnational experiences, this is simply a function of US hegemony in the politics and economic trends in the world. South Asian diasporic groups from other nations would experience transnationalism in different ways, depending on how their political status – and its intersection with religion, phenotype, gender, age, etc. – is constructed in the supra-national geographic areas where several nation-states co-operate to share information and impose one set of surveillance rules to track people who are negatively profiled as security risks. Other diasporic groups, especially those that are not seen as security concerns currently, are likely to encounter even different experiences. In other words, this context is not a neutral realm of experience; rather, the experiences are likely to vary depending on the node – the social identity created through an association with a nation-state. Thus these transnational experiences add another layer that intersects with multilayered diasporic group identities emerging within nations (Joshi 2006; Kibria 2002).

This discussion indicates another emerging reality that needs to be taken into account in the future study of diasporic groups. The growing importance of the Web as a social space suggests that any consideration of the transnational – transnational context, transnational identities – needs to consider both real and virtual social spaces. These two spaces are not only likely to coalesce and coexist; conflicts and disjunctures between these spaces are equally likely. Together they shape the emerging arenas within which social identities of diasporic groups are being formed.

## Notes

1. In his book on global diasporas, Robin Cohen (1997) developed several criteria for defining diasporic groups. The criteria include forced dispersal from a homeland to two or more societies, a continued sense of ties with that homeland, a strong ethnic-group consciousness constructed and sustained over a long period of time, a sense of solidarity with co-ethnic members in other countries. Scholars such as Tatla (1999) have claimed diasporic status for Sikhs. The concept has been used more expansively by others (e.g. Clark *et al.* 1990; Peach 1994) to describe groups that do not meet these stringent criteria. In this paper the term diaspora is used in the latter sense, to describe a migrant group which maintains strong ties with people in other countries, based on a shared sense of culture and/ or family ties.

2. As the world shifts towards a more multi-polar distribution of power, there are many emerging questions about the dominant position of the US. However, US hegemony remains distinctive in several areas that are pertinent to this discussion. US citizens do not need visas to travel in many parts of the world, where visas are a requirement for nationals of other countries. This provides US citizens with unparalleled power to move across countries without encountering too many political barriers. US-issued credit cards and US shipping addresses are recognised in most parts of the world thus promoting ease of buying from different parts of the world. US publication markets hold a pre-eminent position because of their global reach, i.e. they are able to market their publications across the globe, and the US way of constructing and presenting knowledge – the content, form and style – dominates in publishing. Thus, in the rest of this section, my discussion of US hegemony refers specifically to the hegemonies outlined above.

3. There are many other dimensions of marginalisation within this context. I am focusing on gender and race primarily because the studies I draw upon were originally stratified by class; these data do not answer questions about other forms of social hierarchies.

4. I am referring to social and cultural citizenship following the schema proposed by T.H. Marshall (1964) and Will Kymlicka (1995). This idea of deprivation can also be described as deprivation of cultural human rights according to the Universal Declaration of Human Rights (Purkayastha 2008).

5. Immigration restrictions in Europe, America and other parts of the world have long limited South Asian migrants' ability to relocate entire families to single countries. Thus most South Asian diasporic groups have geographically dispersed families.

6.  The case of the Indian doctor, Muhammed Haneef, who lived and worked in Australia, and was arrested because the activities of his British cousins is a well publicised example of this phenomenon (http://www.independent.co.uk/news/world/australasia/australian-police-charge-indian-doctor-over-british-terror-plot-457234.html, accessed 15 October 2008).
7.  The content of ethnicity is shaped by many institutions. This discussion on the effects of consumption is not intended to suggest that consumption erases other types of ethnic prac-tice. Nonetheless, this discussion is intended to emphasise the growing importance of ethnic and non-ethnic purveyors of ethnic cultural items in shaping the lives of diasporic groups.
8.  For instance, Indian-American author Chitra Banerjee Divakaruni's 'retelling' of the Mahabharata through Draupadi's eyes, in 'Palace of Illusions', is being marketed as a feminist interpretation of a classic story, without reference to the fact that it is similar to Saoli Mitra's rendering of Nathabati-Anathabat, in the early 1980s in Kolkata (www.chitradivakaruni.com/books/palace_of_illusions). The marketing tropes are consis-tent with the ideologies about modernities and empowerment that reside mainly in 'the West', as explained in Somdatta Mandal's discussion of several diasporic authors and their representations of India (Mandal 2007).
9.  While they challenge their racialisation, the websites offer several ethnocentric and gendered messages as well since Muslims and Christians are vilified, and women, despite the symbolic representation of strong women, are advised to exercise their traditions through their selfless support of fathers, brothers and husbands. We have been extremely critical of the overall message of these sites elsewhere (see Narayan and Purkayastha 2008; Purkayastha and Narayan 2009).

## Notes on contributor

Bandana Purkayastha is Associate Professor of Sociology & Asian American Studies at the University of Connecticut. She was educated in India (Presidency College) and the US. She has published more than twenty-five peer reviewed journal articles and chapters and four books on gender/race/class, ethnicity, peace and human rights. She currently serves on the executive board of the research committees on Armed Forces & Conflict Resolution, and Women in Society of the International Sociological Association. She is the Deputy Editor of *Gender & Society*.

## References

Appadurai, A., 1996. *Modernity at large: cultural dimensions of globalization.* Minneapolis, MN: University of Minnesota Press.
Bhachu, P., 1995. New cultural forms and transnational South Asian women: culture, class and consumption among British South Asian women in the diaspora. *In:* P. van der Veer, ed. *Nation and migration: the politics of space in the South Asian diaspora.* Philadelphia, PA: University of Pennsylvania Press, 222–244.
Anthias, F., 1998. Evaluating diaspora: beyond ethnicity? *Sociology,* 32, 557–580.
Canclini, N., 2001. *Consumers and citizens: globalization and multicultural conflicts.* Minneapolis, MN: University of Minnesota Press.
Chadwick, A., 2006. *States, citizens, and new communication technologies.* New York: Oxford University Press.
Chowdhury, E.H., 2008. Bengali, Bangladeshi yet Muslim. *In:* A. Narayan and B. Purkayastha, *Living our religions: Hindu and Muslim South Asian American women narrate their experiences.* Stirling, MD: Kumarian Press, 211–230.
Clark, C., Peach, C., and Vertovec, S., eds., 1990. *South Asians overseas: migration and ethnicity.* Cambridge: Cambridge University Press.
Cohen, R., 1997. *Global diasporas.* Seattle, WA: University of Washington Press.
Davila, A., 2001. *Latinos, Inc.* Berkeley, CA: University of California Press.
Freidman, T., 2005. *The world is flat.* New York: Farrar, Strauss, Giroux.
Gillespie, M., 1995. *Television, ethnicity and cultural change.* London: Routledge.
Gilroy, P., 1993. *The Black Atlantic.* London: Verso.
Glenn, E.N., 2002. *Unequal freedoms: how race and gender shaped American citizenship and labour.* Cambridge, MA: Harvard University Press.

Glick-Schiller, N., Basch, L., and Blanc-Szanton, C., 1992. Transnationalism: a new analytic framework for understanding migration. *In:* N. Glick-Schiller, L. Basch and C. Blanc-Szanton, eds. *Towards a transnational perspective on migration.* New York: New York Academy of Sciences, 1–24.

Grillo, T., 2001. Baptist book spurs march by Hindus. *The Boston Globe,* 22 November 1999, Monday, Third Edition, Magazine, Pg. B4.

Hall, S., 1990. Cultural identity and diaspora. *In:* J. Rutherford, ed. *Identity, community, culture, difference.* London: Lawrence and Wishart, 222–237.

Halter, M., 2000. *Shopping for identity: the marketing of ethnicity.* New York: Schocken Books.

Hebdige, D., 1988. *Hiding in the light: on images and things.* London: Routledge.

Howard, P., 2006. *New media campaigns and managed citizen.* Cambridge: Cambridge University Press.

Huntington, S., 1998. *The clash of civilizations and the remaking of world order.* New York: Simon & Schuster.

Ignacio, E., 2005. *Building diaspora: Filipino community formation on the web.* New Brunswick, NJ: Rutgers University Press.

Joshi, K., 2006. *On America's sacred ground.* New Brunswick, NJ: Rutgers University Press.

Kibria, N., 2002. *Becoming Asian American: second generation Chinese and Korean identities.* Baltimore, MD: John's Hopkins Press.

Kistivo, P., 2001. Theorizing transnational immigration: a critical review of current efforts. *Ethnic and Racial Studies,* 24, 549–577.

Kymlicka, W., 1995. *Multicultural citizenship.* Oxford: Clarendon Press.

Levitt, P., 2001. *The transnational villagers.* Berkeley, CA: University of California Press.

Levitt, P. and De La Rahesa, R., 2002. Transnational migration and the redefinition of the state: variations and explanations. *Ethnic and Racial Studies,* 26, 587–611.

Lury, C., 1996. *Consumer culture.* New Brunswick, NJ: Rutgers University Press.

Luban, D., 2005. Eight fallacies about liberty and security. *In:* R. Wilson, ed. *Human rights in the 'War on Terror'.* Cambridge: Cambridge University Press, 242–256.

Majumdar, S., 2008. Challenging the master frame through Dalit organizing in the US. *In:* A. Narayan and B. Purkayastha, *Living our religions: Hindu and Muslim South Asian American women narrate their experiences.* Stirling, MD: Kumarian Press, 265–280.

Marshall, T.H., 1964. Citizenship and social class. *In:* S. Lipset, ed. *Class, citizenship, and social development: essays by T.H. Marshall.* Chicago: Chicago University Press, 92–93.

Mandal, S., 2007. Oh Calcutta! the new Bengal movement in diasporic Indian English fiction. *In:* A. Singh, ed. *Indian diaspora: the 21$^{st}$ century migration, change and adaption.* Delhi: Kamla-Raj Enterprises, 9–23.

Narayan, A., 2005. *Gendered transnational identities: the case of Hindu student organizations in the US and UK.* Unpublished PhD dissertation, University of Connecticut.

Narayan, A., and Purkayastha, B., 2008. *Living our religions: Hindu and Muslim South Asian American women narrate their experiences.* Stirling, MD: Kumarian Press.

Peach, C., 1994. Three phases of South Asian emigration. *In:* J.M. Brown and R. Foot, eds. *Migration: the Asian experience.* London: St. Martins Press, 38–55.

Portes, A., 1997. *Globalization from below: the rise of transnational communities.* Available from: http://www.transcomm.ox.ac.uk/ [Accessed 5 July 2003].

Portes, A., ed. 1995. *The new second generation.* New York: Russell Sage Foundation.

Purkayastha, B. and Narayan, A., 2009. Bridges and chasms – orientalism and the making of Indian Americans in New England. *In:* M. Chiu, ed. *Asian Americans in New England.* Lebanon: University Press of New England.

Purkayastha, B., 2005. *Negotiating ethnicity: South Asian Americans traverse a transnational world.* New Brunswick, NJ: Rutgers University Press.

Purkayastha, B., 2008. Conclusion: human rights, religions, gender. *In:* A. Narayan and B. Purkayastha, *Living our religions: Hindu and Muslim South Asian American women narrate their experiences.* Stirling, MD: Kumarian Press, 285–295.

Rex, J., 1995. Ethnic identity and the nation state: political sociology of multicultural societies. *Social Identities,* 1, 6–20.

Robinson, M., 2005. Connecting human rights, human development and human security. *In:* R. Wilson, ed. *Human rights in the 'War on Terror'.* Cambridge: Cambridge University Press, 308–316.

Singh, A., ed., 2007. *Indian diaspora – the 21st century migration, change and adaption.* Delhi: Kamla-Raj Enterprises.

Soysal, Y., 1998. Towards a postnational model of membership. *In:* G. Shafir, ed. *The citizenship debates.* Minneapolis, MN: University of Minnesota Press, 189–220.

Tatla, D.S., 1999. *The Sikh diaspora: search for statehood.* Seattle: Washington University Press.

Tuan, M., 2001. *Forever foreigner or honorary Whites?* New Brunswick, NJ: Rutgers University Press.

UDHR, 1948 *The Universal Declaration of Human Rights.* Available from: http://www.unhchr.ch/udhr [Accessed January 2008].

Vertovec, S., 2001. Transnational challenges to the 'new' multiculturalism. Paper presented to the ASA conference, University of Sussex, 30 March-2 April 2001. Available from: http://www.transcomm.ox.ac.uk/ [Accessed 5 July 2003].

Vertovec, S., 2002. Transnational networks and skilled labour migration. *Working Paper, WPTC-02-02,* Oxford: Transnational Communities Programme. Available from: http://www.transcomm.ox.ac.uk/ [Accessed 5 July 2003].

Waters, M., and Levitt, P., eds., 2002. *The changing face of home: transnational lives of the second generation.* New York: Russell Sage.

Zakaria, R., 2008. Muslim women between dual realities. *In:* A. Narayan and B. Purkayastha, *Living our religions: Hindu and Muslim South Asian American women narrate their experiences.* Stirling, MD: Kumarian Press, 249–264.

Zukin, S., 1995. *The cultures of cities.* Cambridge: Blackwell.

# Revisiting the UK Muslim diasporic public sphere at a time of terror: from local (benign) invisible spaces to seditious conspiratorial spaces and the 'failure of multiculturalism' discourse[1]

Pnina Werbner

*School of Sociology and Criminology, Keele University, Keele, UK*

Public exposés of hidden spaces where diasporic Muslims allegedly enunciate extreme anti-Western rhetoric or plot sedition, highlight an ironic shift from a time, analysed in my earlier work, when the Pakistani diasporic public sphere in Britain was invisible and local while nevertheless being regarded as relatively benign: a space of expressive rhetoric, ceremonial celebration and local power struggles. Suicide bombings on the London underground and revelations of aborted conspiracies have led to a national media debate in which Muslim 'community' leaders for the first time have come to be active participants. They respond to accusations by politicians and journalists that multicultural tolerance has 'failed' in Britain, and that national Muslim organisations are the prime cause of this alleged failure. Addressing this 'failure of multiculturalism' discourse, the paper questions, first, whether talk of multiculturalism in the UK is really about 'culture' at all? Second, the paper explores why Muslim integration into Britain – the so-called success or failure of multiculturalism – has come to be 'tested' by Muslim national leaders' willingness to attend Holocaust Memorial Day commemorations. The public dialogue reflecting on these issues in the mainstream and ethnic press, the paper proposes, highlights a signal development in the history of the UK Muslim diasporic public sphere: from being hidden and local to being highly visible and national, responsive to British politicians, investigative journalists and the wider British public.

## Preamble

This paper is based on a reading of selected documentary sources since 2004, drawn from the diasporic ethnic press and the mainstream British press and media. Among these are articles reporting on court trials of foiled British Muslim terror plots and clandestine media recordings of hidden, allegedly subversive, diasporic Muslim rhetoric. But the aim of the paper is not to highlight tabloid-style scaremongering against Muslim immigrants. Instead, the paper's central project is to trace a developing public dialogue between British politicians and leaders of the Muslim community published in the mainstream and ethnic press and media. Its ultimate purpose is to highlight the impossibility of thinking of multiculturalism as business-as-usual at a time of global terror.

## Revisiting the diasporic public sphere

In 1992, I presented a paper bearing the title 'On Mosques and Cricket Teams: Nationalism and Religion among British Muslims'[2] that became the basis for a lengthy exploration of what I called the diasporic public sphere. Published as 'Fun Spaces' (Werbner 1996)[3], it anticipated the more detailed discussion of the diasporic public sphere in my book, *Imagined Diasporas among Manchester Muslims* (Werbner 2002). Following Habermas (1989 [1962]), the stress was on the local face-to-face, imaginative and creative aspects of the hidden, invisible public arenas diaspora Pakistanis create for themselves. At the time, the Pakistani community in Manchester, UK, the subject of my study, was encapsulated and inward looking, concerned with its own affairs, while being law-abiding and moderately pious. In the book I traced the process of 'visibilisation' of this arena of identity, fun, local factional politics and personal rhetoric in outraged response to the publication of Salman Rushdie's *Satanic Verses* in 1988 and the first Gulf War in 1991. Against Habermas's critique of the mass media as subverting the early bourgeois sphere, the book highlighted the way that diasporic Pakistani women and youth draw on the aesthetics of South Asian popular and mass culture to mobilise in autonomous arenas of their own, in resistance to male elders.

This was before the 9/11 bombings of the twin towers and the 'war on terror'. Following those cataclysmic events, I argue in the present paper, Muslim diasporic spaces changed both in the public perception and in their scale; what had been invisible but nevertheless benign, autonomous local spaces of debate, even if at times they were critical of the West, came increasingly to be regarded as conspiratorial. At the same time, the scale of debate shifted from the local to the national, with the diasporic public sphere now constituted by a series of polemical accusations and counter-responses by British politicians and Muslim national leaders, published in the national broadsheet and ethnic press. This painful dialogue concerned the invisible but allegedly seditious spaces and agendas diasporic Muslims were secretly fostering, and the implications of their 'revealed' existence for 'multiculturalism' in Britain.

## The pluralisation of the public sphere

The 1990s was a period in which Habermas's notion of a unified (national) public sphere was subjected to scrutiny by feminist and diaspora theorists, who argued for the need to conceptualise the pluralisation and complexity of the public sphere. In an edited volume that reconsidered Habermas's concept (Calhoun 1992), Nancy Fraser (1992) argued that women and other marginalised groups historically created a counter-civil society to the official, hegemonic public sphere. A truly functioning democracy, Fraser argued, requires such 'subaltern counterpublics' in which oppositional interpretations of 'identities, interests, and needs' are formulated (p. 123). Similarly, Seyla Benhabib (1992, p. 94) proposed that the increasing porousness and complexity of the public sphere allows women and other marginalised groups to set new agendas. Rather than a single public arena, the point made by these feminist theorists was that such separate and diverse spaces are essential for subalterns to thrash out their own perspectives on public policies and the public good.

If the public good, according to Habermas, was defined through public debate between rational citizens, later conceptualisations took account of its aesthetic and affective dimensions as well (for an overview see Dahlberg 2005). Paul Gilroy (1993), for example, had spoken of a black 'alternative' public sphere of 'story-telling and music-making' (p. 200). Fraser (1992) argued similarly that 'public spheres are not only arenas for the formation of discursive opinion. In addition, as 'arenas for the formation and enactment of identities' (p. 125), they are in some sense a 'theatre' (p. 110). This accords also with Alberto Melucci's (1997) view that the work of identity is one of first discovering and then negotiating shared identities. Dahlberg cites Young's argument that rational-critical discourse fails to take into account that 'meaning is always in excess of what can be understood discursively, spilling over beyond the symbolic' (Dahlberg 2005, p. 115; citing Young 1987). Public assemblies, Bruno Latour proposes, are as much about 'things' as people or the politics of representation (Latour and Sánchez-Criado 2007). In her theorisation of public arenas in India, Sandria Freitag (1989), it will be recalled, argued that processions and public rituals encompass both the 'political' and 'religious', the formal and informal, elite and popular concerns (p. 14). My study of the local Pakistani diasporic public sphere similarly highlighted its poetics – the way that political passion and rhetoric allow speakers to reach out persuasively to their audiences.

In the light of these arguments, the public sphere may be defined as constituted by ten key features: (1) Public good, defined through (2) Public debate between rational citizens, in a (3) Plurality (of subaltern counterpublics and spaces), characterised by (4) Porousness; (5) Performance; (6) Poetics; (7) Passion; leading to (8) Political mobilisation; (9) Protest; and (10) Proliferation of organisations within civil society.

Clearly, a recognition of the pluralised nature of the diasporic public sphere allows for a theorisation of diaspora, community and culture not as homogeneous, unified, monolithic, harmonious forms of sociality but as heterogeneous and conflictual. Among British Pakistanis, the debate has been not only between the religious and less pious but between democrats, socialists, and nationalists, women and men, young and old, with each group positioned differently and having its own partial, meroscopic political viewpoint.

Most diasporas engender a wide range of voluntary organisations which represent different interests and perspectives. Thus Khachig Tölölyan (2000) speaks of a 'diasporic civil society', constituted by a myriad of voluntary organisations. In the case of Pakistanis in Britain, who are both South Asians *and* Muslims, the historical migratory process of incorporation into British society *as Muslims* has been marked by internal diversification and a shift towards increasing religiosity, which can be traced through a series of stages:

- Profliferation (of religious spaces)
- Replication (of South Asian Islam's sectarian and ideological diversity)
- Diasporic encounter (with Muslims from the Middle East)
- Confrontation and dissent (following the Rushdie affair)
- Identity-led religiosity
- Adoption of Muslim diacritical ritual practices and attire in public
- Voluntary 'self-segregation'
- The politicisation and racialisation of Islam in Britain
- Confrontation and dissent (following the wars in Afghanistan and Iraq)

As South Asians, however, Pakistanis have followed an entirely different trajectory, and this has lead to the emergence of two distinct diasporic public spheres in which British Pakistanis participate situationally – one, of 'hybridity', fun and mass popular South Asian culture, the other 'pure' and Islamic. Both, in a sense, are politicised but their politics differ and are expressed in different media. The South Asian popular cultural sphere is expressed publicly through diasporic novels, films, television, news-papers, and classical and popular song and dance groups; its politics are focused above all on the familial politics of gender, class, consumption and intergenerational rela-tions, and secondarily, on racism within British society.

The Muslim public sphere, by contrast, has been characterised in Britain by intensified religiosity and reformist, puritanical preaching, part of a worldwide discourse generated partly in response to intractable international political conflicts in the Middle East, Iran, Afghanistan, Bosnia, Chechnya and Iraq. The diaspora has not been immune to this pervasive global radicalisation of political Islam, popularised and vernacularised in theological texts and in increasingly restrictive lifestyle options, and encouraged, perhaps, also by increased levels of literacy among young Muslims worldwide, the rise of an extra-terrestrial Islamic media, the extensive use of the internet by radical Islamic groups, and – in Pakistan – the huge expansion of neo-fundamentalist madrasas and training camps.

Despite the fact that they lived in Manchester, that is, in the diaspora, first gener-ation, local-level Pakistani leaders rarely addressed issues of local concern such as racism in their public events. Instead, they tended to orate about national events back home and international events such as the Middle East crisis and the plight of Pales-tinians. Within the invisible spaces of debate and ceremonial celebration they had created, these lay speakers, usually local businessmen or aspiring working class big men, assumed a larger than life dramatic presence, and their rhetoric was heroic and often millennial and apocalyptic (Werbner 2004). The critique of the West and along with it, of the failure of Islam or of Arab regimes, drew on a familiar globalised Muslim rhetoric.

After the Rushdie affair, with its public protest and marches, Muslims' visibility in Britain died down temporarily. It resurfaced once again in protest against the wars in Afghanistan and Iraq in the aftermath of 9/11. The emergence of an estab-lished Muslim national press at about the same time did not, of course, mean the disappearance of local arenas of diasporic debate. But as local organisations came together in national umbrella organisations, so too they were superseded at the national level by a more unified leadership and a 'mediatised' Muslim diasporic public sphere. Moreover, from being invisible and benign, the hidden spaces of the old diasporic public sphere came to be redefined by the British media and politicians as hidden and conspiratorial. The conclusion drawn was that multiculturalism had there-fore failed. This shift in public rhetoric and perception is the subject of the present paper.

## Public arguments: Islam and the media

### Uncovered plots

The debate about the diasporic public sphere in Britain today has to be seen in the context of international politics and the 'war on terror'. It took some time after 9/11 to discover that there were British citizens fighting in Afghanistan or on the side of the Taliban. Since then, the number of suicide bombers who were British citizens or residents of Britain has increased: there were two in Tel Aviv and following them, Richard Reid, the shoe bomber; the four suicide bombers of July 7; six others, three Somali and an Ethiopian, unsuccessfully attempted suicide bombing a fortnight later (sentenced in 2007). With a little over 1.5 million Muslims living in Britain, almost 1000 have been arrested on suspicion of terror, and while most have been released without charge, more than fifty have been charged and many have now been sentenced. One set of terror plotters, mainly Londoners, used a warehouse to store more than half a tonne of ammonium nitrate fertiliser chemicals to make a large car bomb, allegedly to blow up a London nightclub. Seven men aged between 19 and 34, six of them with family roots in Pakistan, went on trial at the Old Bailey in February 2006 for this offence (Sciolino and Grey 2006). One Algerian resisting arrest shot a policeman in Manchester. In East London, a policeman shot one Bangladeshi terror suspect in the shoulder. The suspect and his brother were later released, a case apparently of mistaken information by a 'reliable' informant, but not before their home, names and faces were publicised in a major media event. As early as 2002, a Wahhabi/Salafi preacher of violent jihad, 'energetic promoter of incendiary videos across the country to Muslim groups, inciting them to kill Jews, Hindus and other infidels' was arrested, and was tried in 2003 (Lewis 2007, pp. 130–131).

In August 2006, an alleged plot to blow up 12 aircraft above five US cities was foiled after a massive surveillance operation. 24 young British Muslims, mostly British-born Pakistanis, were arrested in dawn raids in Birmingham, High Wycombe and London. Others were arrested in Pakistan. The dawn operation caused travel chaos at airports. British Airways cancelled 400 flights out of Heathrow. Passengers have been prohibited since from carrying liquids on board. John Reid, the Home Secretary, echoing the London Metropolitan police deputy commissioner, Paul Stephenson, said: 'This was intended to be mass murder on an unimaginable scale' (Laville et al. 2006), 'Worse than 9/11'. 'Let us have no doubt that we are probably in the most sustained period of severe threat since the end of the Second World War', Mr. Reid is reported to have said (Whitaker et al. 2006). The British Pakistani Al-Qaida nexus had by now, according to The Independent, been firmly established (Whitaker et al. 2006). Yet the jury in the court trial of the suspects which took place at the Old Bailey in September 2008 remained deadlocked on the prosecution's central allegation (The Times, 9 September 2008, front page).

This type of scaremongering by security personnel and politicians has persisted, conveying the clear message that all British Muslims are potentially hidden terrorists. In February 2007, nine suspects were arrested in another mediated dawn operation for allegedly being involved in a plot to behead a Muslim soldier serving in the British army. A further man was later arrested and five were charged and stood trial at the Old Bailey on 23 February 2007. Three were released, one of whom accused Britain of being a 'police state'. In November 2006, MI5 (the British equivalent of the FBI) claimed in a front-page article in The Guardian (Norton-Taylor 2006) to have identified '30 major terrorist plots being planned in Britain', and to be 'targeting 1,600 individuals actively engaged in promoting attacks here and abroad'. These 30 plots 'are the most serious of many more planned by some 200 British based "networks" involved in terrorism' (!). Most plotters were said to be British-born and connected to Al-Qaida in Pakistan. Young teenagers were being 'groomed to be suicide bombers'. According to opinion polls cited by MI5, 'more than 100,000 British citizens considered the July 2005 attacks on London were justified' (Norton-Taylor 2006). This gloomy assessment by the head of MI5 at the time, Dame Eliza Manningham-Buller (she subsequently retired early) was backed up by increasingly histrionic statements by politicians and media reports on surveillance of university students (Dodd 2006). A further conspiracy was by young (foreign-born) Muslim doctors who planted a series of car bombs, two of them in London's West End. One crashed his car into Glasgow airport. This plot too was foiled and the men involved arrested.

### Media exposés and an emergent national public debate

Media investigative reports highlighted the connection of apparently respectable Muslim organisations with extremist anti-Western sects, or their secret links with fundamentalist organisations in Pakistan. Hence, according to a *Guardian* report (Lewis 2006) *Tablighi Jamaat* (the 'Fellowship of Preaching/Proselytising') is being monitored 'after it emerged that seven of the 23 suspects under arrest for allegedly plotting to blow up transatlantic airliners were affiliated to this movement' (Bajwa 2006c). In their response in the ethnic press, the organisation's leaders denied the allegations and reaffirmed the non-political nature of their movement, including its rejection of Wahabbism (supposedly a sign of their extremism).

A *Tablighi* leader, Emdad Rahman (2006), claimed in *The Muslim Weekly* that the organisation is 'one one of the most avant-garde Islamic movements in the world, a non-political group, shunning violence and engrossed in nothing more than proselytising and calling Muslims to return to Islam'. In an article that protested the transparency and openness of this now global organisation, one member is cited as asking: 'People who go to Church carry out atrocities. Does this mean that the Church is a terrorist body?' (Rahman 2006, p. 13). Nevertheless, the lengthy trips that Tablighis engage in, with young people often spending more than a month on the road in Pakistan, and the movement's strong links to the Deobandi, a religious tendency linked to the Taliban, has made such protestations about a peaceful past less convincing to the growing cohort of expert 'Islam watchers'.

A second media exposé was of the roots of the Muslim Council of Britain's leadership in *Jamaat-i-Islami* (the 'Muslim Fellowship'), an early fundamentalist organisation and political party founded in British India by a journalist, Mawlana Mawdudi, who first espoused the Islamisation of the state (Bright 2005).[4] Despite its mixed history of incitement against groups like the *Ahmadiyya,*[5] *Jamaat-i-Islami,* somewhat like Hamas, has a reputation for sobriety and honesty, and is remembered for delivering services to the needy and aid to refugees at the time of the Partition of British India. Nevertheless, the movement is also associated with the Pakistani army's violent massacres in Bangladesh during the civil war in 1971, and the extreme violence on campuses of its militant student wing, *Islami Jamiat-i-Tulabah* ('students') during the Zia years (President Zia was a member of JI) (Nasr 1994, p. 69). According to various websites the JI, like other Islamic Pakistani movements, indirectly sponsors camps training young men to fight in Kashmir through its militant wing, *Hizb-ul-Muhajideen,*[6] though its camps have not been the main training grounds for young British Pakistani jihadists. The British organisation created by the movement, UK Islamic Mission (UKIM), which is centred in Leicester, along with its various youth wings and offshoots (see Hussain 2007), claims to be a separate organisation, distancing itself from the parent movement and aiming to integrate into all walks of British society (ur-Rahman 2007a). The success of some of its members in founding the UK umbrella organisation, the Muslim Council of Britain (henceforth MCB), may be related more to their organisational capacity than their political views. Nevertheless, leaders are accused of dividing humanity into believers and unbelievers (*kaffir*) (Bright 2005) and their puritanical ideology is also manifested in their public attack on homosexuality in Britain and their attempts to censure Muslim cultural festival celebrations allegedly transgressing strict Islamic codes of conduct. Such emergent divisions among Muslims reveal the validity of a post-Habermasian approach that stresses the pluralisation of the diasporan Muslim public sphere in the UK. Diaspora Muslims include a wide range of nominally non-violent groups that are nevertheless violently opposed, at least rhetorically, to any Muslims they regard as transgressive or deviant.

Whereas there is no doubt about the media exposés, the timing of the shift in Government opinion is less clear. Chetan Bhatt (2006) claims that as late as 2006, the Home Office and Foreign Office defined 'reformist Islam' including Jamaat-i-Islami and the Muslim Brotherhood, as 'moderate' (p. 98). By contrast, tracing the history of the emergence of the MCB and its relations with Government, Jonathan Birt (2005) reports that as early as October 2001, 'Number 10 stopped returning MCB's calls', following the organisation's failure to endorse the war in Afghanistan (p. 96), and by 2002 its links with extremist organisations were publicly recognised by the Foreign Office (pp. 98–99). Against that, Sean McLoughlin, who also traces the process of the organisation's emergence partly on the basis of its own magazine, *The Common Good*, views the MCB and its affiliates as more positive, constructive organisations, less beholden to their subcontinental roots (McLoughlin 2002).[7]

Like the present paper, these scholarly accounts rely heavily on the media. The extent to which a genuine dialogue in the public sphere was emerging in Britain between British Muslim organisations and a critical press and media became evident after a media exposé of a range of Muslim national organisational leaders. A hard-hitting BBC *Panorama* programme, 'A Question of Leadership', exposed the *Jamaati* roots of representative members of the Muslim Council of Britain and the often vitriolic, anti-Western, anti-Semitic and intolerant views expressed by a range of different British Muslim leaders and Saudi visitors preaching at public meetings, gatherings and mosques, beyond the public eye.[8] Responses by Muslim leaders to questions about suicide bombings, religious intolerance and the politicisation of Islam by the programme producer could be construed as fudged and evasive. Following the airing of the programme (Panorama 2005), the Muslim Council of Britain refuted the accusations against it in a detailed letter which the broadcaster published on its website, alongside the producer's reply (BBC NEWS 2005). In the back-and-forth correspondence that ensued, one somewhat ironic development was that the website became a forum for a theological debate about the arcane historical views of the movement's founder, Mawdudi, with the MCB and BBC citing, in turn, book, chapter and verse - phrases, sentences and counter-sentences - to prove or disprove the allegedly 'fascist' aspects of Mawdudi's vision of an Islamic state (BBC News 2005). Throughout this dialogue, MCB leaders refused to condemn the founder of the movement.

In a later article in *The Muslim Weekly*, the MCB President denied the programme's accusation that the *Jamaat* and its British affiliate, the UK Islamic Mission (UKIM), are opposed to 'plurality, multiculturalism, universal human rights and peaceful co-existence' as 'false and mischievous' (ur-Rahman 2007b). 'In Islam', he says, 'the idea of human rights, cultural diversity and plurality of the human family, long predated anything similar in modern political thought' (ur-Rahman 2007b). He points out that the Koran describes Christians and Jews as People of the Book, Ahl al-Kitab (though he fudges the extent to which they nevertheless remained second-class citizens in the medieval Muslim world).

A third British media exposé, this time by Channel 4, reported on another Pakistani movement, *Ahl-e-Hadith* ('People of the Prophet's Sayings'), a Pakistani group close to Wahabbism espousing a Saudi brand of Islam. The programme reported that the organisation allegedly hosted travelling clerics preaching hatred of the West at various UK mosques, including the Birmingham mosque headquarters of the movement (Bajwa 2007a). Most shocking about the sermons broadcast on Channel 4 was the constant references to '*kaffir*', '*kuffar*' and '*kufaristan*' – unbeliever or infidel, the land of unbelief – as defining features of Britain and its citizens.[9] Some preachers seemed to be preaching the ultimate Islamic takeover of the British state.[10] In defence, Muslims organisations said they rent their premises out without necessarily endorsing the opinions of visiting preachers, and that, in any case, sentences were taken out of context (Bajwa 2007a). Nevertheless, the unbridgeable chasm between 'us' and 'them' exposed by the infidel rhetoric shocked British observers and was seen as a clear signal of Muslims' refusal to integrate.

Against these accusations, in a letter in *The Muslim Weekly,* a local Birmingham anti-war association defended *Ahl-e-Hadith* mosque leaders 'for their faith and community work' while its *imam* was said to work 'closely with peace organizations and government authorities'. In another major response, also published in *The Muslim Weekly*, Shouaib Ahmed (2007, pp. 12–13), the General Secretary of *Ahl-e-Hadith*, denied the alleged Saudi link, along with responsibility for anything the 100 visiting speakers had said in their sermons. He stressed the organisation's inter-faith work and described '*kaffir*' as a 'neutral term' (p. 13), opposed to '*mu'min*' (believer), applied to anyone who 'rejects Allah and his message'. He blasted the media for highlighting 'a few theoretical statements about hypothetical jihads and hypothetical Islamic states, while keeping silent about the hundreds of thousands of innocent civilians, predominantly Muslims, who have been slaughtered (not in theory but in actuality) in recent years in the Middle East, usually in the name of "liberation from oppression" and "establishing a democratic state" and never at the express invitation or request of this silenced (by death) majority' (p. 13). He ended by invoking eras of Islamic tolerance, and claimed to be a member of a law-abiding, peaceful community, that works closely with the police and government services.

*Ahl-e-Hadith*'s general secretary's article in *The Muslim Weekly* was followed by three other articles rebuffing accusations by the media: one by the UK Islamic Mission, written by its President, Shafiq ur-Rahman (2007a, pp. 14–15), one by Dr Ahmed Al-Dubayan, Director General of the London Islamic Cultural Centre and Central Mosque (*The Muslim Weekly* 2007a, p. 15), and one by the Muslim Council of Britain (*The Muslim Weekly* 2007b, p. 15). The first article speaks of an 'open season of Muslim-bashing and Islamophobia', and of Jihad as 'the greatest red herring of our post-modern Islamophobic discourse' (ur-Rahman 2007a, p. 14), which in fact is a 'holistic concept' that refers to the 'duty to do goodness and forbid evil'. He distinguishes 'military jihad' (*Qital*), the 'lesser jihad', which can only be 'waged in a just and noble cause', with rules 'clearly laid down', from civil struggle, the 'greater jihad' (*Jihad-e-Akbar*), which is 'lifelong'. ur-Rahman claims, somewhat ambiguously, that 'in our own British context, British Muslims are under no Islamic obligation to take part in any conflict or struggle overseas', but adds: 'It would not be Jihad should someone tried [try] to commit violence or indulge in any unlawful, let alone a subversive activity on the British soil' (p. 14). In the same newspaper, the London

Islamic Cultural Centre denies its Saudi connections (*The Muslim Weekly* 2007a, p. 15), while the MCB accuses Channel 4 of an 'attempt at promoting sectarianism among British Muslims'. At the same time, it vows not to allow 'divisive agendas' or 'unacceptable and inflammatory language' from mosque pulpits or on DVDs.

As with Mawdudi's writings, in this case too Muslim theological concepts have become, post 9/11, matters of public debate in Britain. Muslims are compelled in their defence against accusations of nefarious agendas to spell out more liberal interpretations of commonly used Koranic and Arabic concepts, terms and ideas, in order to prove to a sceptical English public and media how they may be construed as acceptable and tolerant.

### Seditious spaces?

At the start of the post-9/11 debate on Muslim radicalisation, it was assumed by politicians and the media alike that mosques were the main sites of incitement – that young Muslims were inflamed by 'ignorant', uneducated clerics coming from abroad. This was a notion Pakistani leaders, generally disdainful of their clerics, were happy to promote. The notorious Finsbury Park mosque, raided spectacularly by helicopter, seemed to confirm this image. Led by Abu Hamza al-Masri, a radical Egyptian Palestinian preacher sentenced to deportation in 2007, it appears to have been the home of many of the early suicide bombers, who were clearly influenced by his rhetoric. Abu Hamza was ultimately arrested, having gone into hiding for more than a year, and jailed for seven years in 2006 on six charges of soliciting murder, incitement to racial hatred, possessing 'threatening, abusive or insulting recordings' and a document useful to terrorists. When evicted from the mosque, he preached to crowds in front of it in the street for several months.[11] In February, 2007, *The Independent* and *The Times* reported the arrest on charges of 'encouraging terrorism' of a radical cleric, Abu Izzadeen, 31, born Trevor Brookes to Jamaican parents, and once the bodyguard of Omar Bakri Muhammad, leader of the now-banned *Al-Muhajiroun* group and later spokeman for *Al-Ghurabaa* and leader of the Saved Sect, also now banned. He was the subject of an exposé by ITN, the Independent Television Network, in a video made in 2004, in which he described the Secretary of State for Defence at that time, John Reid, as an 'enemy of Islam' and the British government as crusaders 'come to kill and rape Muslims'. In the video he is reported to have said that 'Whoever joins them – he who joins the British Army, is a mortal *kaffir*, and his only *hokum* [punishment] is for his head to be removed' (Morris 2007, p. 10). The cleric was said to have also participated in the protests outside the Danish embassy and had reportedly praised the suicide bombers of 7 July (Morris 2007, p. 10).

In response to the moral panic surrounding mosques and hate preachers, a new body was launched in Britain: MINAB, the Mosques and Imams National Advisory Body, comprising 1,600 British mosques and Islamic centres that, according to the ethnic press, 'aims to stop mosques being used by fundamentalist extremists by helping to reduce their reliance on using ministers of religion from abroad' and increase the skills of local imams (Khanna 2006a, p. 5). Imams are described as 'coming from nowhere and spreading hatred'. The new organisation received publicity even in the national press. It was founded by four Muslim umbrella associations: the Muslim Council of Britain (MCB), the Muslim Association of Britain (MAB), the British Muslim Forum and the Al-Khoei Foundation (representing moderate Shias in Britain) – 'as part of the Home Office's Tackling Extremism Together programme', though founding members denied government 'intrusion'. MINAB's stated aim is to identify best practice, release a Good Practice Guide for British imams and mosques, provide advice on imam accreditation, and organise training courses (no byline, *The Muslim Weekly*, 30 June 2006, p. 2).

One by one, new spaces of sedition have been uncovered or discovered by the British state and media. Added to the list of extremist mosques have been new Islamic bookshops, allegedly selling hate literature and so-called martyrdom DVDs. The 7/7 suicide bombers met in an Islamic bookshop, having been expelled from their mosque's basement. In a Birmingham raid in 2007, the police targeted an Islamic bookshop, as well as a cybercafé and a food shop.[12] In the public imagination, new sites of sedition seem to be multiplying in places where, previously, benign cultural or religious celebrations were held.

Young peoples' organisations have also become increasingly suspect. Two splinter groups of *Al-Muhajiroun*, *Al-Ghurabaa* (The 'Strangers') and the Saved Sect, were banned by the Home Office in July 2006, on the grounds that they openly promoted violent jihad aimed at creating a worldwide Islamic state. Most protesters outside the Danish embassy in London, as reported in court trial proceedings, were members of *Al-Muhajiroun* or its offshoots. Despite pressure from the government of Pakistan to ban it, the claims of another UK splinter organisation, *Hizb ut-Tahrir* (HT, 'Party of Liberation') to be non-violent were provisionally accepted by the UK government. One dissenting Muslim voice in the press argued, however, that 'Anyone involved in Islamic *da'wah* (call to Islam) for the past 25 years knows that HT is an organisation that foments revolution and bloodshed. That's why they had posters up and down the country saying that leaders [of Muslim countries] must be removed, must be overthrown' (Bajwa 2006b, p. 3). In November 2006, *Newsnight* and *File on Four* alleged that HT in Croydon was 'promoting gang violence by making recruits commit crimes to test their loyalty and teaching them that non-Muslims were "worthless"', an allegation denied by an HT spokesman (Bajwa 2006b, p. 5).

After HT, FOSIS, the Federation of Student Islamic Societies, which represents 90,000 university students (Lewis 2006, p. 11), was the next to be criticised, partly for its defence of HT, which is banned on campuses by the National Union of Students (NUS). In April 2006, FOSIS was 'widely accepted as a moderate organisation', according to Paul Lewis of *The Guardian*, and 'praised for its promotion of interfaith dialogue and campaigns against Islamophobia.' The organisation achieved a large presence in the NUS and yet it has been constantly suspected of radical tendencies. In rejecting the reinstatement of HT, the NUS president-elect, Gemma Tumelty described HT, according to the press, as 'homophobic, sexist and racist' (Lewis 2006, p. 11). FOSIS has claimed it is being spied upon by police, although this was denied (Badshah 2006).

The flood of media exposés of alleged Muslim radicalised organisations and spaces has become a veritable cascade. It is almost impossible to open a British news-paper without finding some new revelation. While it is obvious that in reality, few of the sites where British Muslims gather are places of conspiracy, by now adult and youth organisations, mosques, bookshops and cybercafés, have all been identified by the police, the courts and the media as diasporic spaces of conspiracy and anti-Western hatred. Following these, Islamic schools and even youth camps in the Lake District have been added to the list of dangerous sites. One school, the *Jameah Islamiyah* School in Essex, was accused of allowing terrorist training in its extensive grounds. It was finally closed in February 2007. A Saudi-funded private school, the

King Fahd Academy in Acton, was warned to remove books that describe Christians as 'pigs' and Jews as 'Monkeys', and was accused of fomenting hatred in the class-room. The Schools Minister announced that 45 independent schools, including Islamic institutions, had been closed since 2004 by government order (Frean 2007, p. 7). Perhaps most disconcerting was news in the national media that recruiting camps for potential terrorists were regularly held in the Lake District. Five suspects in the 21/7 failed suicide plot in London were identified in one such camp (Laville 2007). There were reports of Islamist rafting trips in North Wales, and terrorist training on farms in Kent and the Brecon Beacons. What could be more English than camping trips in Wordsworth's English countryside among thousands of other carefree holiday-makers? The Englishness of many of the young Muslim conspirators, the majority Pakistanis born and bred in Britain, has been one of the most remarked-upon findings to emerge. Young men involved in terror plots or suicide bombings appear to be quite ordinary. Most come from relatively well off, lower-middle class homes, rather than poverty-stricken inner cities. Most are not particularly marginal, being students, teach-ers or small businessmen, and quite a few are mature, in their late twenties and early thirties, married, some with children. There is nothing to distinguish them, on the surface, from the vast majority of British Pakistani South Asian Muslims. The lead suicide bomber on July 7 played cricket with English friends the night before the bombing. Even the culprits' piety has not been self-evidently unusual.

In the light of almost daily revelations, the Sisyphean task facing national Muslim organisational leaders, that of counteracting the widespread public image of pervasive, hidden, Islamic terror, is huge. Instead of lobbying for and promoting Islamic inter-ests, they find themselves and their organisations condemned by politicians and the media alike for their radical roots and failure to promote diasporic Muslim integration and multiculturalism.

## Multiculturalism in an age of terror

Given these revelations, the 'failure of multiculturalism' discourse has taken root in Britain, promoted by politicians, the media and academics, and is a central aspect of the debate between Muslim leaders and British politicians.[13] In scrutinising this discourse, one needs first to deconstruct its implicit assumptions. Hence, in a recent paper published in *Sociological Review* (Werbner 2005), I argue for the need to go beyond the usual arguments against state-sponsored multiculturalism, and to consider multiculturalism as played out in historical moments of crisis and confrontation, in which culturally intractable oppositions and incommensurabilities surface. I labelled the theorising of such intractable dilemmas as 'multiculturalism in history', to distin-guish it from the more quotidian debates about state funding allocations for cultural activities, or special educational programmes and dietary or clothing dispensations affecting ethnic minorities. For the Muslims of Britain, multiculturalism-in-history was inaugurated by the Rushdie affair, following the publication of *The Satanic Verses*. Alleging blasphemy punishable by death, Muslims in Britain seemed deliber-ately to insist upon values alien to the majority population. They burnt books and demanded the death of the author. The July 7, 2005 London suicide bombings by young British Pakistanis were carried out in the name of Islam and as retribution for the sufferings of Muslims in Iraq, Afghanistan and the Middle East. Once again this seemed to underline an unbridgeable chasm between European values of citizenship and the rule of law, and Muslims' vengeful transnational politics. The Danish cartoon affair was yet another manifestation of seemingly incommensurable values, this time in the field of art and representation.

Diasporic Hindus and Sikhs have each in turn also sparked apparently intractable multicultural conflicts in Britain. In the Sikh case, the conflict surrounded a play, *Behzti* ('Dishonour'), written by a young Sikh woman, Gurpreet Kaur Bhatti, which depicted the rape and murder of a young woman by a priest in the *Gurdwara* (Sikh temple). Produced by Birmingham Repertory, the play was cancelled after Sikhs responded with a massive show of public outrage and threatened violence (Asthana 2004, p. 13). In the case of Hindus, the clash of values arose in response to a solo exhibition by one of India's most celebrated contemporary artists, Maqbool Fida Husain, whose one-man retrospective in London included portrayals of the Goddesses Durga and Draupadi in the 'characteristic nude imagery associated with his work' (Khanna 2006b, p. 2). Asia House Gallery withdrew the exhibition after highly vocal protests by Hindu Human Rights, the National Council of Hindu Temples and the Hindu Forum of Britain (Khanna 2006b, p. 2).

The notion of multiculturalism-in-history is intended to separate day-to-day tolerance of cultural diversity and arguments over minor state funding allocations from exceptional cultural clashes that seem irresolvable. Historically, such confrontations are usually never resolved; they only 'go away', entering the collective subconsciousness of a community as a bitter sediment. This was certainly true of the Rushdie affair. The 2007 award of a knighthood to Salman Rushdie, almost twenty years after the confrontation over *The Satanic Verses*, ignited once again the bitterness British Muslims felt over the affair, despite their muted public response.

One problem with the notion of multiculturalism is that it often leads to an intellectual cul-de-sac. Detractors of multiculturalism argue that culture is not identical with community; it is not a bounded or territorialised entity; it cannot be reified since it is constantly changing and hybridising, an 'open text'. While such deconstructive arguments are undeniable, they evade the question, first, of why certain issues evoke such passionate commitment and sharp disagreement, and, linked to that, is it accurate to speak of *culture*, when at issue are historical conflicts sparked by deeply felt *religious* feelings, in confrontation with liberal secularism or Western geopolitics? David Cameron, the leader of the Conservative Party (the largest opposition party) in Britain, was able to say in the same breath, we will support the Notting Hill carnival (a cultural event), we reject multiculturalism as a failed policy. The 'culture' he invokes is seemingly innocuous and non-polemical, exclusive of race, ethnic chauvinism, or religion; hence an acceptable idiom in which to describe 'difference' in neutral terms. But when talking about multiculturalism and its failures, more often than not the underlying attack turns out to be against diasporic Muslims' alleged self-segregation in social ghettoes or their 'extremist' defence of their religious commitments (there are countries, of course, in which language has the same effect). The fact that the underlying problematic of religion is not acknowledged publicly in Britain (as it might be in South Asia) so that 'culture' becomes a euphemism for religion or community, entangles government ministers and opposition leaders alike in strange contradictions of which they seem entirely unaware.

## Political hubris

The recent 'failure of multiculturalism' discourse enunciated by British politicians of the left and the right, reflects a political hubris which is shared by many academic critics of multiculturalism. The unreflective assumption of these critics is that the cultures of minorities, defined in the broadest sense of the term to include religion, can be made to disappear by fiat if politicians and policy-makers refuse to support them, either rhetorically, on official occasions, or with small dollops of cash. In reality, historically, the very opposite has often been the case. The cultures of minorities are strengthened by the need to mobilise internally for the sake of culture or religion in the *absence* of public funding. Singling out Muslim religious associations for censure as British politicians have chosen to do, arguably merely legitimises their representative status in the eyes of the public they serve. The censured organisations gain kudos for being powerfully independent, and not just yea-saying patsies who pusillanimously approve government policy. Ministers' critique of Islamic *religious* organisations rather than ethnic ones (for example, Pakistani or South Asian) implies, *ipso facto,* that for the British state, it is religion that reflects 'culture and community'.

There are very good reasons why diasporic Pakistanis in Britain, who are observant Muslims, choose to highlight their religious identity in civil society and the public sphere: first, because as pious believers this is their most valued, high-cultural identity; but importantly also, there are in Britain laws which set out entitlements for religious groups. Among these are the right to found voluntary-aided state schools, supported by government funds; the right to worship, to build places of worship, and so forth. Oddly enough, despite all the recent uproar about the failure of multiculturalism, there are no *laws* in the UK that enshrine the cultures of immigrants, though limited legal rights to cultural, political and territorial autonomy have been granted to Wales, Scotland and Northern Ireland.[14] In other words, multicultural citizenship in Britain, as elsewhere, recognises the rights of indigenous territorialised peoples and settled minorities, aboriginals, Native Americans and so forth, to a measure of self-rule, autonomy and formal representation in the public sphere. Only secondarily does multicultural citizenship apply to diasporic minorities and urban immigrants who are *not* settled territorially and make no territorial claims. The UK Race Relations Act protects ethnic and racial minorities – and this includes most Muslims. The recent law against incitement to religious hatred does not necessarily include what Muslims themselves regard as religious offence or vilification.[15] On purely pragmatic grounds, then, immigrants fighting to gain equal rights in the UK will choose to struggle in arenas where there already exist established rights, some of which are denied them. In such cases there is no need to establish the ground rules and principles; merely to insist on their universal application.

One perhaps less obvious implication of multicultural citizenship is that everybody, even the majority, has a culture. The old assimilationist melting pot nationalism assumed that the majority way of life was normal in a taken-for-granted, transparent way; it was not a 'culture' but just the rational way of being, ethically and morally. Majority culture and religion were, in other words, unmarked. Minorities had cultures and these were different, often irrational, and hence a problem. The sooner they got rid of these bizarre ways of living, the better. Unlike hegemonic nationalism, multiculturalism's innovation as a philosophical movement is that it applies to all citizens, even the majority.

This principle, of the equality of citizens' cultures, appears to have been abandoned by British politicians in the aftermath of the July 7 bombings. The hitherto accepted right of minorities to foster their unique cultures or traditions alongside the majority culture and religion is now being effectively questioned, with constant demand that minorities make a serious effort to abandon their separateness. In a further twist that highlights the ambiguity of the culture concept, young Muslims themselves are rejecting their parental culture and tradition, in a paradoxical move that seems to deny culture in the name of religion.

## The attack on multiculturalism

In his book, *Globalising Islam*, Olivier Roy (2004) argues that neo-fundamentalist global Islamic movements have deterritorialised themselves by denying their cultures and traditions. In many ways, this is not a new argument. What makes fundamentalist movements modern, contrary to appearance, is the fact that – like modernist movements – they deny the validity of historical continuity; in a word, 'tradition'. In referring to a sacred book allegedly enunciated by God Himself 1500 years ago, and to the sayings of the Prophet Muhammad from that distant, inaccessible period, such movements claim to purify themselves from unlawful accretions over the centuries. These accretions have, of course, been part of the localising of Islam, its embeddedness in different places and responsiveness to local cultural milieus. Paradoxically, Roy argues, this deterritorialised purification movement has led to the secularisation of Islam since so much of everyday life is left out of the Islamists' utopian vision of the past-as-future. In his view, the stress comes to be on personal, individual religiosity, perhaps a kind of Protestantism.

Whether or not Roy is right, his analysis raises an interesting question: can there be a religion that is not also cultural? Pakistanis have always reiterated to me that Islam is a whole, all-inclusive, way of life, and this indeed was the argument put by the Muslims of India in claiming a national homeland for the Muslims of the subcontinent. But if Islam is a whole way of life, then surely it refers to the customs and traditions of particular localities? In a sense, both claims are equally dubious: religion is not the same as culture, at least not in the modern world, but nor is it entirely separable from it. Islamism may reject the Pakistani-style chiffon headscarf, but it substitutes for it another head covering which becomes over time a uniform, i.e. a custom. This custom can, however, be shared by persons from different places and backgrounds.

Nevertheless, I believe that it makes sense to distinguish between culture and religion, in a way that an Islamist does. This is because, as discursive formations in certain fundamental senses they are not the same, and particularly so in the case of the three monotheistic religions. In these, religious belief is about a relationship with a transcendent being that demands conviction and commitment, experienced in highly emotional ways. It may be, as Durkheim (1915) famously argued in the *Elementary Forms of Religious Life*, that God is merely the embodiment of community; and it is probably true that culture, in the sense, first and foremost, of language, but also food, music, art, architecture, spices and perfumes, clothing and so forth, also embodies a community – though not necessarily the same one. But religion and culture are not the same for the simple reason that cultural practices are not hedged in a similar way with sacred taboos, dangerous no-go areas. Culture is not pitted against moral transgressions and ethical violations, although those who perform it awkwardly can be laughed at for their gaucheness. Religion is threatened by believers' internal doubt, which may or may not be fuelled by externally inspired scepticism. Culture is threatened by the physical destruction of objects or buildings, by forgetfulness, and perhaps more than anything in the modern world, by radical dislocations and changes in social organisation. A person may have multiple cultural competences, and switch between them situationally, or she may be a cultural hybrid, the product of even or uneven fusions of two or more cultural worlds. There have been periods in the history of religion when boundaries between, for example, Islam and Hinduism in South Asia, or Judaism and Christianity in the Near East, were blurred. But in the modern world it would seem odd to be a Muslim, a Jew and a Christian simultaneously, however syncretic one's faith.

The gap between culture and religion raises the question of what exactly is meant by multiculturalism in Britain? Whereas cultural 'traditions' may be open to negotiation in the diasporic context, religious customs anchored in Holy writ and said to originate in a transcendental covenant, may be conceived of as non-negotiable. When encapsulated religious minorities negotiate a place in their new nation with the majority society, the more pious among them insist on the religious basis of customs (such as veiling) that in reality may have evolved historically. Culture for them assumes the aura of divine commandment, impervious to politicians' invocations of 'community cohesion.'

The problematic tendency to conflate religion and culture in debates on multiculturalism and identity politics in the UK includes academics like myself as well - from defenders of multiculturalism as religion such as Modood (2005) or Parekh (2000) to their critics on the left (e.g. Yuval-Davis 1997). The 'mystification of culture' as Bhatt (2006, p. 99) calls it, conflating religious pluralism with identity politics, imperceptibly merges two quite separate, historically constructed discourses (Asad 2003). On the one hand, a discourse on religion which recognises that modern religions are institutionalised, bounded and textualised, subject to constant internal divisions and schismatic tendencies, more or less 'extreme', 'doctrinaire' or 'humanist-liberal'; 'pure' or 'syncretic', 'relaxed'; 'universalistic' or 'particularistic' interpretations; and, on the other hand, a discourse on 'culture' which recognises its fuzzy, historically changing, situational, hybridising and unreflective aspects. Arguably, issues usually regarded as a matter of multicultural policy, for example the dispensation to wear exotic headdresses to school or work (turbans, veils, skull caps) more rightly belong in the constitutional domain of religious pluralism. Cultural conventions on headdress, which do not carry that non-negotiable imperative quality, can be ignored.

The attack on multiculturalism in Britain since 2006 has been led by three prominent public figures, speaking for wider constituencies: Ruth Kelly, until 2007 Secretary of State for Communities and Local Government, and thus a representative of the Labour government, David Cameron, leader of the Opposition and of the Conservatives, and a third multiculturalist critic (not discussed here), Trevor Phillips, a British Guyanese, Chair of the Commission for Racial Equality, and since 2006 of the newly formed Commission for Equality and Human Rights.

Ruth Kelly began her campaign against multiculturalism by calling, in August 2006, for the closing of Islamic schools that promote 'isolationism and extremism', and for an 'honest debate' over whether multiculturalism 'encouraged separatism'. Her speech was occasioned by the launch of a 'Commission on Integration and Cohesion' (Bajwa 2006d, pp. 1–2). In October 2006, she told police and council leaders to target Muslim 'hot spots' – schools, universities, mosques and colleges, and, in an open letter to the MCB, accused the organisation of being 'passive in tackling extremism, yet expect[ing] government support' (Bajwa 2006d, pp. 1, 3). While criticising Muslim schools, the Secretary of State, a devout Catholic, emphasised that 'Muslims are entitled to the same rights as Anglicans, Catholics, Hindus and Jewish groups, which all have state schools' (Bajwa 2006d, p. 2). In February 2007, Kelly announced that state money would be switched from groups like the Muslim Council of Britain to 'local programmes backed by local councils,' particularly to 'work with those who may be excluded from colleges, schools and mosques and may be vulnerable to grooming by extremists' (thus denying the obvious truth that most persons charged with terror in Britain were (ex)students and not marginal) (Wintour 2007, p. 12).

In a series of investigative articles published on 20 October 2006 (Josephs and Peled 2006, pp. 3–4), the *Jewish Chronicle* analyses the fall from grace of the MCB and links it to one major single symbolic event: the organisation's continued refusal to attend Holocaust Memorial Day, calling for it to be renamed Genocide Memorial Day. The weekly claims that Kelly warned the organisation's leaders that they would lose Whitehall financial support if they continued to boycott the event. It analyses the strong support of the MCB leaders for the Palestinian struggle, various anti-Semitic comments made by its leaders, their support for Hamas (one leader had attended a memorial to Sheikh Ahmed Yassin), their anti-homosexual stance and anti-Rushdie comments, as 'cause for disquiet' – indicators of the continued conservatism 'verging on fundamentalism' of the national leaders of the MCB. The accusations highlight the blurring of boundaries between contingent political behaviour and religious extremism in the eyes of politicians and the media. Among the MCB's associate members, the paper tells us, is the Muslim Association of Britain which has consistently refused to condemn Palestinian suicide bombing. Nevertheless, the JC also recognises the MCB's inter-faith work.

Holocaust Memorial Day has become, then, the litmus test of Muslim willingness to 'integrate'. Unlike in the US, where the Jewish lobby is very powerful, in the British case it is the British government that established HMD and that has lead the demand that the MCB attend its state commemorations. For South Asian Muslims, it is perhaps not immediately obvious that to participate in the state HMD ceremony is to identify not only with Britain but with a free, democratic Europe. Whereas the MCB leaders represent their non-attendance as a gesture of protest on behalf of the Palestinians, for British leaders it implies a rejection of the nation's heroic historical act of liberating the camps and defeating fascism for Europe and the world. Perhaps most interesting sociologically is the clear understanding by British politicians that, above all, it is the public reconciliation *between two diasporas* – the Jewish and the South Asian Muslim – that signals existentially Muslim willingness to integrate into their new nation. Press reports of Jewish-Muslim inter-faith dialogue attest to an apparent rapprochement, if not in the Middle East, then in the diaspora. A headline in *The Muslim Weekly,* for example, reported that 'Judeo-Muslim groups unite to create European platform' in which a new organisation, the Muslim Council for Religious and Racial Harmony, surfaced for the first time, with *Alif-Alef* as its Jewish counterpart (*The Muslim Weekly* 2007c, p. 7). Among other participants was a reporter from Radio *Salaam Shalom*, the UK's first Muslim-Jewish radio station.

Financially, however, it is evident that there was no practical pressure that could be exerted on the MCB: the *Jewish Chronicle* reveals that at stake in the government's threatened gesture of non-recognition were relatively small sums of money granted to the MCB to support projects on citizenship and equality: £148,160 in 2005–6, £50,000 in 2006–7 (the group originally applied for £500,000). It also received £170,000 from the Department of Trade and Industry (Josephs 2006, p. 4).

'Multiculturalism' was revealed as a policy of paltry financial support for an organisation representing 400 Muslim umbrella organisations, networks and mosques.

Yet its leaders' alleged sin of non-attendance on Holocaust Memorial Day was not entirely deviant or out of line with wider public sentiment in Britain: a YouGov poll for the *Jewish Chronicle* showed that a third of the general public supported renaming Holocaust Memorial Day Genocide Day with 14 per cent wanting it dropped altogether (Bajwa 2007b, p. 3). So too, the Palestinian struggle (if not suicide bombings) is widely supported in Britain, where Israel is increasingly seen by many as a rogue state, while the war on terror in Iraq and (to a lesser extent) Afghanistan are widely condemned.

In an open letter to Ruth Kelly in *The Muslim Weekly* in October 2006, a copy of which was sent by the Secretary General of the MCB, Muhammad Abdul Bari, to all mosques, local, regional and national Muslim organisations across Britain, Mr. Bari defends the organisation's democratic structure and 'successful initiatives in schools, prisons, hospitals, mosques and local communities'. He reminds the Minister of a series of top ranking British dignitaries and commissions that saw a direct link between British foreign policy and the rise of home grown terror. On Holocaust Memorial Day he says:

> Your suggestion that the MCB is not fully committed to religious tolerance and community cohesion merely on the basis of a single criterion of non-attendance at the HMD is both inaccurate and absurd. Since when has the achievement of community cohesion been dependent on attending the Holocaust Memorial Day? (*The Muslim Weekly*, 20 October 2006, p. 12)

He continues, 'We cannot accept that some people are more worthy of remembrance than others', and claims that 'a particular political interest group and certain allied journalists have tried to intimidate the MCB into remaining silent about the ongoing injustice and human rights abuses perpetrated against the Palestinian people'. Nevertheless, the MCB is 'absolutely committed to working together to maintain good relations with Britain's Jewish community'. The successful London Olympic bid, he says, drew upon 'London's record of diversity and confident faith... made because of the extensive network of partnerships forged by the formidable Mayor of London, Ken Livingstone, and faith bodies like the MCB'. He goes on to remind the minister of the MCB's record of calming violence following the various global terror attacks, encouraging voting, liaising with the police, distributing leaflets and guidance on 'rights and responsibilities', all in an effort to combat extremism. Hence, the decision to terminate funding indicates that only those organisations that 'support your government can expect to receive public funds' (*The Muslim Weekly*, 20 October 2006, p. 13). Such funding in any case was only for specific projects, not 'core funding', particularly justified because of the high levels of Muslim deprivation nationwide. He ends by accusing the government of fostering and promoting 'new Sectarian Muslim bodies with barely concealed links to US neo-cons' (the reference is probably to the sudden emergence of the Sufi Muslim Council of Britain), engaging in a 'merry go round' to find Muslims that agree with it while stigmatising the entire community in 'drip-feed' ministerial pronouncements.

### The emergence of a national mediated Muslim public sphere in Britain

This powerful public letter, like the others cited here, highlights the ability of a centralised Muslim umbrella organisation to reach its constituency nationwide, through the press and other media (including the mail). It also highlights the sense of secure citizenship felt by the Muslims of Britain, who do not fear confrontation with the government, and are not intimidated by threats of funding withdrawal.

The condemnation of the MCB underlines the difficulty for an organisation of transforming itself from being a lobby for the Muslims of Britain, aimed at defending them against discrimination and Islamophobia, to being the community watchdog, controlling the radicalisation of some members and the rhetoric of the majority at a time of global crisis.[16] The organisation's public relations seem virtually non-existent. For example, the Secretary of the MCB omits to mention in defence of the Muslim community in Britain, mostly of Pakistani origin, that the Muslims of India under the leadership of Muhammad Ali Jinnah, founder of Pakistan, openly supported the Allied Forces' battle against Nazism and Fascism in Second World War. Constituting more than a quarter of the Indian army, by the end of the war Muslim soldiers numbered almost half a million, and they were among the 160,000 total casualties of the Indian army, buried in war cemeteries in fifty countries extending from the Pacific Islands to Europe and the UK, according to the Commonwealth War Graves Commission. Several Muslims were awarded the Victoria Cross (see Husain 1998). Nor does Mr. Bari point to the fact that the Holocaust had been politicised by Israel and the Jewish diaspora, their victimhood stressed as a way of justifying the oppression of Palestinians. Neither of these strong arguments in defence of the MCB's unwillingness to attend the commemorations has ever been raised, possibly pointing to the organisation's continued *Jamaati* hard-liner views.[17]

On the other hand, the double standards used in British public policy are surely not lost on British Muslims either. Not long after her rejection of multiculturalism as a failed policy, Ruth Kelly was involved in a failed attempt, said to be backed by Tony Blair, to exempt the Catholic and Anglican churches from new rules on gay adoption, on the grounds that it would require the adoption agencies 'to act against the principles of Catholic teaching' (Woodward and Carrell 2007, p. 1), or that 'freedom of conscience cannot be made subject to legislation' (Archbishop Sentamu on Radio 4's Today programme, 24 January 2007). Kelly's failed attempt appears to send out a message that multiculturalism is fine for Catholics but not for Muslims.

David Cameron, the Tory opposition leader, also joined the tirade against multiculturalism. In a public speech in the Birmingham Lozells area which had recently been torn by interethnic violence between blacks and Asians, he echoed academic writings in arguing that, although it sounds like a good idea, multiculturalism, instead of promoting the 'right of everyone to be treated the same despite their differences', divides, often treating ethnic or faith communities as 'monolithic blocks rather than individual British citizens', and allocating housing along ethnic lines. He went on to list Muslim organisations viewed as extremist, including the Muslim Council of Britain, FOSIS, the Muslim Association of Britain, the Islamic Society of Britain, the Islamic Human Rights Commission, *Hizb ut-Tahrir*, and *Tablighi Jama'at* (Neville-Jones 2007, pp. 30–31). Yet his pronouncement of the failure of multiculturalism, which referred only to religious organisations, blurred the boundary between culture and religion and glossed over the reality that religious communities in Britain already have established rights, underpinned by legislation.

Like the media and Labour politicians, Cameron too accused the MCB of bad faith. FOSIS, the Muslim students' umbrella organisation was under suspicion, as we have seen, for links to the Muslim Brotherhood and for supporting the right of *Hizb ut-Tahrir* to operate on university campuses, while the UK Islamic Human Rights Commission (IHRC) in 2006 had challenged the government in the High Court for allowing US aircraft carrying bombs to Israel to stop at UK airports during the Lebanese war, which the organisation defined as an 'act of terrorism'. Its attempted injunction to halt such stopovers was rejected (*The Muslim Weekly*, 1 September 2006, p. 2).

Instead of Muslim organisations, Cameron announced that the Conservative party would reach out directly to 'individuals', bypassing organisations altogether. His speech drew on a report in January 2007, based on a widely criticised poll, that found that 37 per cent of Muslim 16- to 24-year-olds said they would prefer to live under *Sharia* law; 86 per cent said religion was the most important thing in their lives; nearly a third thought that those converting to another religion should be executed. On the other hand, 84 per cent said they had been well treated in British society. Munira Mirza, author of the report said, 'The government should engage with Muslims as citizens, not through their religious identity' (Bates and Agencies 2007, p. 5). This commendable notion of reaching out to 'individuals' was exemplified by Cameron's spending a night with an ordinary Pakistani family in Birmingham, with much media coverage. But his attack on multiculturalism hides the reality that national Muslim organisations *do not need* government endorsement to continue with their activities. *They cannot be made to disappear.* Instead, the rejection of multiculturalism is merely read by an already alienated Muslim diaspora as an attack on Islam. This is the dilemma faced by the British government. Moreover, with its move towards ad hoc funding of local groups, the British government and the opposition appear to be returning to the earlier, unsatisfactory reality of local multiculturalism – the local-level scrabble by local associations for small dollops of cash, poorly monitored. Ironically, this direct funding of groups at the local level is likely to cost far more than the funding of a single umbrella organisation like the MCB.

Tory criticism of Muslim organisations, including the MCB, was contained in a conservative policy report entitled 'Uniting the Country'. The report condemned what it calls 'identity politics' and drew a comparison between the extreme right British National Party and separatist Muslim organisations that promoted *sharia* law and demanded special treatment, claiming they are a 'mirror image' of the BNP (Neville-Jones 2007; see McVeigh and Woodward 2007, p. 12).[18] This followed an earlier report by a right-wing think-tank, Civitas, that claimed that 'Multiculturalism fosters racial divides and even hatred' (no byline, *The Muslim Weekly*, 19 May 2006, p. 3).

In their response in *The Muslim Weekly*, the MCB describe the claim that their organisation espouses the institution of *Sharia* law as a 'red herring' while FOSIS argued it was 'disproportionate', given that there is not a single mainstream Muslim organisation calling for the implementation of *Sharia* law. The MCB described the report as 'ill informed', defended the organisation's record and claimed it only lobbies for 'parity in the application of the law and equal respect' (Bajwa 2007c, pp. 1, 3).

Nevertheless, the continuous pressure and criticisms of the MCB appeared to have taken their toll, with reports of disagreements among senior Muslim leaders over HMD attendance. In a 'secret meeting', a third of its senior figures reportedly voted to cease the boycott, which was upheld by 23 to 14 votes (Dodd and Muir 2007, p. 12). There were, however, speculations that 'the current momentum would see the MCB's position reversed by next year' (Dodd and Muir 2007, p. 12). Several leaders thought the organisation should not be seen to 'cave in' to government pressure, while others described the boycott as an unnecessary 'self-inflicted wound' (Dodd and Muir 2007, p. 12). *The Muslim Weekly* reported a decision to hold a wider consultation with its

400 plus affiliate bodies (Bajwa 2007b). This came, according to the newspaper, because 'Holocaust Memorial Day this year acknowledged and remembered other acts of genocide and terror with particular emphasis this year on Darfur'.[19] Hence the MCB, in a letter to HMD's acting Chief Executive, admitted that 'common grounds were being reached' (Bajwa 2007b). On her part, the CEO emphasised that Holocaust day was an 'opportunity to reflect on more recent genocides…and it is our duty to stand up to those groups and individuals who encourage division and hatred in our communities' (Bajwa 2007b).

As early as 2005, vocal Muslim critics of the MCB like Dr Ghayyasuddin Siddiqui of the Muslim Parliament, accused Iqbal Sacaranie, Secretary General of the MCB, in an article in the Asian weekly *Eastern Eye*, of 'living in a dreamworld if it [the MCB] thinks just because it has different ideas, Holocaust Day will be scrapped. Why do our representatives always take a negative position?' he asks. 'We should recognise what happened to the Jews in Germany. …Just because Palestinians are suffering should not mean the suffering of Jews in the Holocaust should not be remembered. …Let's work together to create another day' (Verma 2005, p. 2).

In 2007, Shahid Malik, outspoken Labour MP for Dewsbury,[20] condemned the MCB in a column in the *Times* of London: 'Whether they like it or not their current position looks like anti-Semitism… the old guard is stuck in a timewarp' (Dodd and Muir 2007, p. 12). In his commentary, the MP recalls his keynote speech at the National Holocaust Centre's memorial event, with some 20 young Muslims in the audience. He defended the police as doing a good job fighting terror in tragic circumstances, before stating baldly that Ruth Kelly 'has set down the rules for engagement with government. Attending Holocaust Day is a prerequisite.' (!) Rather than extremist, the MCB in his view 'has chosen the easy, populist path of solely "defending" Muslims'. Rather than introspection, it had reinforced the 'victim narrative' that dominates Muslim discourse. Justifying the introduction of a £5 million budget to empower Muslims at local level, Malik (2007, p. 23) argued that the government should 'never again' be dependent on one group. Later that year the MCB approved its attendance of Holocaust Memorial Day, but withdrew it in 2009 following Israel's bombing in Gaza (Brickman 2009).

This exchange between representatives of different British Pakistani constituencies (moderate Muslims, Labour supporters and more radical Islamic groups) outlines the emergent contours of a pluralised Pakistani national diasporic public sphere in Britain. It is an open space of dialogue, in the sense that debates take place in public, in the press and media, and can be joined by British politicians and columnists as well. Although conducted in rational terms, the tone of the dialogue betrays the painful and highly emotive issues at stake. The argument *within* the Muslim diasporic sphere has gathered pace, as Philip Lewis (2007) documents, with monthly magazines like *Q News*, and newsletters, reports, pamphlets, novels and blogs by women's groups, community activists, moderate religious leaders, all involved, along with travelling preachers like Hamza Yusuf, who mobilise very large audiences promoting a less separatist, more open and tolerant Islam.

## Conclusion: intractable dilemmas and the diasporic public sphere

The present paper has documented the engagement and serious dialogue that has emerged in Britain since July 2005 between British politicians and leaders of the Muslim community through the media, ethnic and mainstream press. It highlights, I have argued, the impossibility of thinking of multiculturalism as business-as-usual in a time of global terror, a theme I have reiterated elsewhere as well. Politicians would naturally like the Muslims of Britain to be contained within the envelope of the nation-state, to live scattered among the wider population and to be concerned mainly with religious education and pastoral care. They reject not only the intense religiosity of many Muslims, including the second generation, but their living in an enclave and their diasporic commitments – not just to their country of origin but to Muslim communities elsewhere, especially Palestine, but also Iraq. *They demand a non-politicised religion, which they label 'culture'.* And because Muslims in Britain are far more pious than most other British citizens and are equally emotional about their transnational loyalties, then it seems multiculturalism has not only failed but supposedly foments hatred and division. Of course, at another level everyone – Muslims and non-Muslim alike – shares the knowledge that intractable international conflicts are impinging on the consciousness of young Muslims in Britain and encouraging a few of them towards – in their own eyes – heroic deeds of self-sacrifice, which to everyone else appear as unacceptable atrocities. How to reach these young people is a predicament shared by all British citizens, including Muslims. Attending Holocaust Memorial Day is not on the surface going to make any difference to these youngsters. Indeed, one may argue that as a form of peaceful protest, a way of expressing alienation non-violently, politicians should welcome this show of defiance as preferable to suicide bombings. Against that, however, it may be said that the British state has stumbled inadvertently onto a crucible of citizenship: to attend Holocaust Memorial Day in shared commemoration alongside the Queen, the Prime Minister, the Archbishop of Canterbury and other dignitaries, under the canopy of Jewish prayers, led by the Chief Rabbi of Britain; to share momentarily the memory of Jewish suffering, is tantamount to committing oneself to an inclusive British and European identity, to a primary allegiance that takes precedence over divisive conflicts elsewhere and which denies the anti-Semitism prevalent in the Muslim world today.

In a sense, too, it may well be that politicians feel on safer ground when they criticise religion, even if they label it 'culture'. They know from their own experience of European history that religion can be more or less extreme, more or less tolerant, more or less politicised. Second, the term culture is also used to imply 'community': ethnic communities are expected by British politicians to exert moral control over their members. The failure of the Muslim community in Britain to control some of its youngsters is a failure of community and hence also of culture and multiculturalism.

Clearly, it is absurd to believe that the paltry sums of money given by the government to Muslims organisations whose members are, after all, tax payers, can shake the foundations of Muslim faith in Britain. Muslims raise vast sums of money in voluntary donations, running into millions of pounds each year, for charitable causes and communal projects like mosque building. For the latter, they also sometimes access overseas donations. Ruth Kelly cannot determine the fate of Islam in Britain. The only use multi-cultural and multi-faith state or local-state funding can have is positive: to require that organisations service a wider range of ethnic minority users than their own internal fund-raising would demand; to create alliances, to enter into dialogue with unlikely partners, to engage in joint efforts with other groups in order to provide help and services to the needy. Rather than fomenting hatred, top-down state multiculturalism is designed to attenuate divisions between ethnic and religious groups and propel them into dialogue. But no amount of state funding can stop groups from asserting their diasporic loyalty and sense of co-responsibility vis-à-vis diasporas beyond the nation-state in which they have settled. World politics, not religion *per se*, are at the heart of the current multicultural debate.

In this context, the 'failure of multiculturalism' discourse can also be seen to constitute an implicit postcolonial, post-imperial warning by British politicians to South Asian immigrants, perhaps recalling the long history of subcontinental communal violence. The message transmitted is that the reach of the state and media into hidden diasporic spaces is inescapable. Millennial, incendiary divisive rhetoric against the state, the West, Christianity, Judaism etc., of a kind potentially leading to violence will not be tolerated. This is also the basis for the clause on 'glorification of terrorism' in the recent British Terrorism Bill (Bajwa 2006a, p. 5). The 'failure of multiculturalism' discourse is thus meant to remind minorities that in future there will be no no-go areas within the diaspora that are closed to the press and media. Double talk – one message for them, one for us – is unacceptable from now on. Increasingly, information on secretive extremist or terrorist organisations is becoming widely available. *The Islamist*, a book by an ex-HT supporter, Ed Hussain (2007), documents in detail his six-year journey through a wide range of hard-line Islamist groups, including jihadist ones. It describes government policy as a 'disastrous combination of laissez faire and political correctness'. Madelaine Bunting, journalist at *The Guardian*, points out that the book may be used to attack Islam (Bunting 2007), but in my reading it is evident that Hussain is deliberately pointing the finger at particular Muslim organisations and individuals and disclosing their hidden agendas.

The political thrust, then, is towards an open, *transparent* multiculturalism, legitimising press undercover reporting or engagement with spaces hidden from the public eye, and cultural-cum-religious debates with minorities on their own ground, sometimes on quite arcane issues, such as the writings of Mawdudi. The question is whether this constant digging beneath the surface, the day-to-day media reporting on Muslim seditious plots and plotters, Muslim opinion polls that reveal out-of-line opinions and conspiracy theories, tirades by politicians against so-called multiculturalism, or the invocations by politicians on the need to 'learn' to be good citizens, is in any way conducive towards a more positive integration of Muslims into British society? Such rhetorical attacks on a daily basis, many via the media, surely lead to a sense of siege and alienation among the vast majority of law-abiding Muslims, whatever their political sentiments.

It is unclear whether the dialogue recorded here between politicians and the organisational leaders of the Muslim community in the broadsheets, pitched in relation to the Jewish, Asian and Muslim ethnic press *is*, in fact, a dialogue. *The Muslim Weekly* claims a circulation of 40,000. Do the politicians read the lengthy defences penned by Muslim organisational leaders, which are addressed to them? A hint that they might indeed be doing so can be found in a quite lengthy article by Ruth Kelly herself, addressed to the Muslims of Britain on the pages of *The Muslim Weekly*. And since then the dialogue has continued, with an article in the *New Statesman and Society* eliciting a response in *The Muslim Weekly*.

Talal Asad makes the point that given that the public sphere is not an 'empty space for carrying out debates', but expresses the 'memories and aspirations, fears and hopes – of speakers and listeners'. If this is so, then the introduction of new religious discourses disrupts 'established assumptions structuring debates in the public sphere'. It 'threatens the authority of existing assumptions' (Asad 2003, p. 186). In the case of the war in Iraq, a secular war against a secular dictator has been redefined by Muslims and some Christians (including, ironically, President George W. Bush himself) as a religious war. The attack on multiculturalism may be conceived of as a rejection by British politicians and the media of this invasion of the British public sphere by religious discourses. If the public sphere is defined as a space of rational argumentation, economics and politics, then faith and passion do not, it is implied, belong there (Asad 2003, p. 187). Nevertheless, it could also be argued that the reasoned responses of Muslim leaders, utilising the national platform of their own ethnic press, has carved out a space of civility in which the responses of these leaders to expositions of their alleged extremism are expressed passionately and yet rationally.

## Notes

1. Versions of this paper were presented at Lancaster University, the University of Western Sydney and the Pakistan Workshop. I would like to thank the participants in these forums for their comments. I am also particularly grateful to Khachig Tölölyan for his acute and extremely helpful comments on an original draft of the paper.
2. The paper was presented at a conference on 'European Islam, Societies and State' in Turin, Italy, sponsored by the Agnelli Foundation.
3. Arjun Appadurai (1996) also uses this term. My paper was originally submitted to *Public Culture.*
4. Mawdudi's many books have been extremely influential in fundamentalist circles, even beyond Pakistan.
5. A heterodox sect in Pakistan whose leader claimed to be a true Prophet, profaning the idea that Muhammad was the last Prophet of Islam.
6. According to an article in the *Asia Times,* under the supervision of the ISI, the Pakistani intelligence services, a JI member apparently commanded the al-Badr facility in Khost Province, Afghanistan, where he commanded an international cohort of Arab jihadis, including the founders of Hamas. He later abandoned the JI and threw his fortune in with another Islamist group, opposed by the Taliban, who later took over the facility (Shahzad 2004).
7. Bhatt castigates the Left as well as the Government for joining forces in the Stop the War Coalition with conservative nationalist religious groups such as the Muslim Brotherhood, represented in the UK by the Muslim Association of Britain (on this see also Birt 2005). A different view would be, however, that the creation of channels for effective legal public protest was important in order to deflect young British Muslims from attempting to take the law into their own hands. I attended the largest million strong demonstration in London, arriving in one of the coaches from Manchester. What struck me most saliently was the absence of organised groups marching in solidary separateness, and the mingling of young Asians and Muslims as individuals with Guardian-reading CND types.
8. Initially, mosques were seen by outsiders as the main Muslim public forum, but as this paper demonstrates, there were many other Muslim spaces of debate which surfaced over time.
9. Philip Lewis (2007, p. 34) reports that the no less a luminary than the Grand Mufti of Saudi Arabia advised a British Muslim that Jews and Christians were *kuffar* who would be cursed, and go to hell.
10. A revisit by Channel 4 Dispatches of this earlier programme in September 2008, 'Undercover Mosque: the Return', found equally damning lectures inspired by Wahhabbi teaching at the Regent Park Central Mosque women's teaching circle. This too led to sharp responses in the Muslim press.
11. Most recently, in August 2008, the European Court of Human Rights stayed Abu Hamza's extradition to the United States.
12. The pressure group Liberty condemned the publicity surrounding this police round-up of suspects in a plot to behead a British Muslim soldier, expressing its 'grave concern' that journalists were briefed by Home Office advisors in advance of the raid (no byline, *The Muslim Weekly*, 30 June 2006, p. 2; see also Portillo 2007, p. 19). On Islamic bookshops see also Lewis (2007, p. 133).
13. Bagguley and Hussain describe this as a 'wholesale rejection of the discourse of multiculturalism' (2008, p. 159). Their focus is primarily on the local level and accusations that

local communities are refusing to integrate into British society. Hence the political call was for 'community cohesion'.

14. The amended British Nationality Act, 2005 requiring persons seeking naturalisation to have a minimal knowledge of English may be classed as a 'multicultural' law perhaps.

15. The blasphemy law, part of common precedent law, is reserved for Anglicans only. This was an issue highlighted by the Rushdie affair, when Muslims demanded equal protection before the law. Despite talk of abolishing it, the law was never abolished.

16. On the demand for 'responsibilisation' see Michael (2006).

17. It seems extremely unlikely that Mawdudi and the Jamaati Islami supported the British and Allied war effort. Nasr (1994) makes no mention of Mawdudi's views on this matter. Mawdudi opposed Muslims being part of an army under the control of a non-Muslim power. When he founded the Jama'at in 1941, its constitution clearly stated that pure Muslims must boycott the institutions of a non-Islamic polity, including the army and legislature. For Mawdudi, the westernised leadership of the Muslim League's vision of a Muslim state was against Islam (personal communication from Irfan Ahmad, ISIM, Leiden). The Muslim Brotherhood in Egypt was sympathetic to the Nazis.

18. The Report makes fascinating reading. Like the BBC Panorama site, it cites key passages from the writings in English of Mawdudi, Qutb and Qaradawi, to prove the incompatibility between their ideologies and those of liberal democracy, and associates their rigid advocacy of a Sharia-based Islamic state and, in the case of Qaradawi, endorsement of Palestinian suicide bombers, death sentence for homosexuals and other extremist views, with the MCB and other Muslim organisations who 'promulgate the teachings of Maudoodi and Qutb' (the MCB praised Qaradawi as a moderate). See in particular Neville-Jones (2007, pp. 7–8). In contradistinction, Muhammad Ali Jinnah is quoted as a beacon of democracy and liberal values (p. 10). Its comments on the need to promote a moderate democratic vision of Islam are thoughtful (pp. 12–13).

19. Apparently, an Armenian attempt to be included was rejected.

20. In 2007, he was appointed Minister for International Development in Gordon Brown's first government.

## Notes on contributor

Pnina Werbner is Professor of Social Anthropology at Keele University. She is the author of *The Migration Process: Capital, Gifts and Offerings among British Pakistanis* (Berg, 1990 and 2002); *Imagined Diasporas among Manchester Muslims* (James Currey and SAR, 2002); and *Pilgrims of Love: the Anthropology of a Global Sufi Cult* (Hurst Publishers and Indiana, 2003). Recent edited collections include *Anthropology and the New Cosmopolitanism* (Berg, 2008), and a special issue of the journal *Diaspora* on 'The Materiality of Diaspora' (2000). She is currently director of two research projects, an ESRC large grant, 'New African Migrants in the Gateway City: Ethnicity, Religion, Citizenship', and an AHRC large grant, 'In the Footsteps of Jesus and the Prophet: Sociality, Caring and the Religious Imagination in the Filipino Diaspora'.

## References

Ahmed, S., 2007. Jamiat Ahl-e-Hadith response to dispatches. *The Muslim Weekly,* 19 January 2007, p. 13.

Appadurai, A., 1996. *Modernity at large: cultural dimensions in globalization.* Minneapotis, MN: University of Minnesota Press.

Asad, T., 2003. *Formations of the secular: Christianity, Islam, modernity.* Stanford, CA: Stanford University Press.

Asthana, A., 2004. Tempest of rage shakes Sikh temple. *The Observer,* 26 December 2004, p. 13.

Badshah, N., 2006. Police lean on Muslim students. *Eastern Eye,* 3 November 2006.

Bagguley, P. and Hussain, Y., 2008. *Riotous citizens: ethnic conflict in multicultural Britain.* Aldershot: Ashgate.

Bajwa, H.A., 2006a. UK anti-terror laws 'contrive human right'. *The Muslim Weekly,* 3 March 2006, p. 5.

Bajwa, H.A., 2006b. Extremist groups banned, Hizb ut-Tahrir spared. *The Muslim Weekly,* 21 July 2006, p. 3.

Bajwa, H.A., 2006c. Tablighi Jama'at linked to 'Wahabbism'. *The Muslim Weekly,* 25 August 2006, p. 3.

Bajwa, H.A., 2006d. *The Muslim Weekly,* 1 September 2006, pp. 1–2.

Bajwa, H.A., 2007a. Channel 4 blasted for demonising Muslims. *The Muslim Weekly,* 19 January 2007, front page and p. 2.

Bajwa, H.A., 2007b. Common grounds towards Holocaust Memorial Day. 2 February 2007, p. 3.

Bajwa, H.A., 2007c. Stop scaremongering, Mr. Cameron. *The Muslim Weekly,* 2 February 2007, pp. 1, 3.

Bates, S. and Agencies, 2007. More young Muslims back sharia, says poll. *The Guardian,* 29 January 2007, p. 5.

BBC News, 2005. Response to MCB complaints. 30 September 2005. http://news.bbc.co.uk / 1/hi/programmes/panorama/4297490.stm.

Benhabib, S., 1992. *Situating the self: gender, community and postmodernism in contemporary ethics.* Cambridge: Polity Press.

Bhatt, C., 2006. The fetish of the margins: religious absolutism, anti-racism and postcolonial silence. *New Formations,* 59, 98–115.

Birt, J., 2005. Lobbying and marching: British Muslims and the State. *In:* T. Abbas, ed. *Muslim Britain: communities under pressure.* London: Zed Books.

Brickman, S., 2009. Hamas speech at HMD event. *Jewish Chronicle,* 30 January 2009, p. 5.

Bright, M., 2005. Radical links of UK's 'moderate' Muslim group. *The Observer,* 14 August 2005.

Bunting, M., 2007. 'We were the brothers', interview with Ed Hussain. *The Guardian,* 12 May 2007, p. 33.

Calhoun, C., ed. 1992. *Habermas and the public sphere.* Cambridge, MA: MIT Press.

Dahlberg, L., 2005. The Habermasian public sphere: taking difference seriously?. *Theory and Society,* 34 (2), 111–136.

Dodd, V., 2006. Universities urged to spy on Muslims. *The Guardian,* 16 October 2006, front page.

Dodd, W. and Muir, H., 2007. Senior Muslims used secret meeting to urge rethink over Holocaust Day snub. *The Guardian,* 27 January 2007, p. 12.

Durkheim, E., 1915. *The elementary forms of religious life.* London: George Allen & Unwin.

Fraser, N., 1992. Rethinking the public sphere: a contribution to the critique of actually existing democracy. *In:* C. Calhoun, ed. *Habermas and the public sphere.* Cambridge, MA: MIT Press, 109–142.

Frean, A., 2007. Minister calls for tolerance after closing terror-raid school. *The Guardian,* 10 February 2007, p. 7.

Freitag, S., 1989. *Collective action and community: public arenas and the emergence of communalism in North India.* Berkeley, CA: California University Press.

Gilroy, P., 1993. *The Black Atlantic.* London: Verso.

Habermas, J., 1989 [1962]. *The structural transformation of the public sphere.* Translated by Thomas Burger. Cambridge: Polity Press.

Husain, N.A., 1998. The role of Muslim martial races of today's Pakistan in [the] British Indian army in World War II. Paper presented at the International Conference on 'The British Commonwealth and the Allied War Effort 1939–1945', St. Anthony's College, Oxford, UK, 6–8 April 1998 (available online).

Hussain, E., 2007. *The Islamist.* London: Penguin Books.

Josephs, B. and Peled, D., 2006. In search of the MCB's Agenda. *The Jewish Chronicle,* 20 October 2006, pp. 3–4.

Josephs, B., 2006. Muslims attack Kelly in Holocaust Day row. *The Jewish Chronicle,* 10 November 2006, p. 4.

Khanna, A., 2006a. Muslim body to stop hate preachers. *Eastern Eye,* 7 July 2006, p. 5.

Khanna, A., 2006b. Naked gods are found!. *Eastern Eye,* 19 May 2006, p. 2.

Latour, B. and Sánchez-Criado, T., 2007. Making the 'Res Public'. *Ephemera,* 7 (2), 364–371.

Laville, S., 2007. Suspects under surveillance in campsite in Lake District. *The Guardian,* 18 January 2007.

Laville, S., Norton-Taylor, R., and Dodd, V., 2006. A plot to commit murder on an unimaginable scale. *The Guardian Unlimited* (online), 11 August 2006: http://www.guardian.co.uk/uk/ 2006/aug/11/politics.usa1.

Lewis, P., 2006. Adding their voice to the debate. *The Guardian,* 4 April 2006, p. 11.

Lewis, P., 2007. *Young, British and Muslim.* London: Continuum.

Malik, S., 2007. Stop whingeing and show leadership. *The Times Comment,* 10 February 2007, p. 23.

McLoughlin, S., 2002. The state, new Muslim leaderships and Islam as a resource for public engagement in Britain. *In:* J. Cesari and S. McLoughlin, eds. *European Muslims and the secular state.* Aldershot: Ashgate, 55–70.

McVeigh, K. and Woodward, W., 2007. Tories accused of anti-Muslim bias. *The Guardian,* 31 January 2007, p. 12.

Melucci, A., 1997. Identity and difference in a globalized world. *In:* P. Werbner and T. Modood, eds. *Debating cultural hybridity: multi-cultural identities and the politics of anti-racism.* London: Zed Books, 58–69.

Michael, L., 2006. Securing civic relations in the multicultural city. Paper presented at the Conference on 'Citizenship, Security and Democracy', Istanbul, Turkey, 1–3 September 2006.

Modood, T., 2005. *Multicultural politics: racism, ethnicity and Muslims in Britain.* Edinburgh: Edinburgh University Press.

Morris, N., 2007. Cleric who called for Muslim soldiers to be killed is arrested. *The Independent,* 9 February 2007, p. 10.

Nasr, S.V.R., 1994. *The vanguard of the Islamic revolution: the Jami'at-i Islami of Pakistan.* London: I.B. Taurus.

Neville-Jones, P., 2007. Uniting the country: interim report on national cohesion. Launched 30 January 2007.

Norton-Taylor, R. 2006. MI5: 30 Terror plots being planned. *The Guardian,* 10 November 2006.

*Panorama,* 2005. A question of leadership (including video). BBC Panorama, 16 September 2005. http://news.bbc.co.uk/1/hi/programmes/panorama/4727513.stm.

Parekh, B., 2000. *Rethinking multiculturalism.* London: Macmillan.

Portillo, M., 2007. Britain isn't a police state, but it's close to being a liar state. *The Sunday Times,* 11 February 2007, p. 19.

Rahman, E., 2006. Inside the real Tablighi Jama'at. *The Muslim Weekly,* 21 August 2006, pp. 12–13.

Roy, O., 2004. *Globalised Islam: the search for a new Ummah.* London: C. Hurst & Co.

Sciolino, E. and Grey, S., 2006. British terror trial centers on alleged homegrown plot. *The New York Times* online, 26 November 2006.

Shahzad, S.S., 2004. Cracking open Pakistan's jihadi core. *Asia Times Online,* 12 August 2004, http://www.atimes.com/atimes/South_Asia/FH12Df03.html.

*The Muslim Weekly,* 2007a. London Islamic cultural centre and central Mosque's response. 19 January 2007, p. 15.

*The Muslim Weekly,* 2007b. MCB respond to 'dispatches' documentary. 19 January 2007, p. 15.

*The Muslim Weekly,* 2007c. Judeo-Muslim groups unite to create European platform. 27 April 2007, p. 7.

Tölölyan, K., 2000. Elites and institutions in the Armenian transnation. *Diaspora,* 9 (1), 107–136.

ur-Rahman, S., 2007a. UKIM vehemently rejects all media allegations. *The Muslim Weekly,* 19 January 2007, pp. 14–15.

ur-Rahman, S., 2007b. Undercover mosques - letter from Shafiq ur-Rahman. Available from: http://www.sacc.org.uk/index.php?option=content&task=view&id=351&catid=44.

Verma, H., 2005. Calls to scrap Holocaust Day slammed. *Eastern Eye,* 23 September 2005, p. 2.

Werbner, P., 1996. Fun spaces: on identity and social empowerment among British Pakistanis. *Theory, Culture & Society,* 13 (4), 53–80.

Werbner, P., 2002. *Imagined diasporas among Manchester Muslims: the public performance of Pakistani transnational identity politics.* Oxford: James Currey; and Santa Fe: SAR.

Werbner, P., 2004. The predicament of diaspora and millennial Islam: reflections on September 11, 2001. *Ethnicities,* 4 (4), 451–476. Also SSRC website on September 11: http://www.ssrc.org/sept11/essays/werbner.htm.

Werbner, P., 2005. The translocation of culture: migration, community, and the force of multiculturalism in history. *Sociological Review,* 53 (4), 745–768.

Whitaker, R., Lashmar, P., Goodchild, S., Carrell, S., Woolf, M., and Huggler, J., 2006. Apocalyptic: bigger than 7/7? Worse than 9/11? Piece by piece, the plot unravels. *The Independent* (online), 13 August 2006, http://www.independent.co.uk/news/uk/crime/apocalyptic-bigger-than-77-worse-than-911-piece-by-piece-the-plot-unravels-411660.html

Wintour, P., 2007. From welfare to C02, Blair keeps the policy initiatives coming. *The Guardian,* 7 February 2007, p. 12.

Woodward, W. and Carrell, S., 2007. Cabinet rejects exemption on gay adoptions. *The Guardian,* 25 January 2007, p. 1.

Young, I.M., 1987. Impartiality and the civic public: some implications of feminist critiques of moral and political theory. *In:* S. Benhabib and D. Cornell, eds. *Feminism as critique: essays on the politics of gender in late-capitalist societies.* Cambridge: Polity Press, 56–76.

Yuval-Davis, N., 1997. Ethnicity, gender relations and multiculturalism. *In:* P. Werbner and T. Modood, eds. *Debating cultural hybridity: multi-cultural identities and the politics of anti-racism.* London: Zed Books, 193–208.

# 'My language, my people': language and ethnic identity among British-born South Asians

Rusi Jaspal[a] and Adrian Coyle[b]

[a]Department of Psychology, Royal Holloway, University of London, UK; [b]Department of Psychology, University of Surrey, UK

This study explores how a group of second generation Asians (SGA) understood and defined language, focusing upon the role they perceived language to have played in their identity. Twelve SGA were interviewed and the data were subjected to qualitative thematic analysis. Four superordinate themes are reported, entitled 'Mother tongue and self', 'A sense of ownership and affiliation', 'Negotiating linguistic identities in social space' and 'The quest for a positive linguistic identity'. Participants generally expressed a desire to maintain continuity of self-definition as Asian, primarily through the maintenance of the heritage language (HL). An imperfect knowledge of the HL was said to have a negative impact upon psychological well-being. There were ambivalent responses to the perception of language norms, and various strategies were reported for dealing with dilemmatic situations and identity threat arising from bilingualism. Recommendations are offered for interventions that might aid the 'management' of bilingualism among SGA.

There is a substantial amount of empirical and theoretical work on the relationship between language and ethnic identity (Fishman 2001, Harris 2006, Omoniyi and White 2006), as well as some important contributions from social psychology (Giles and Johnson 1987, Lawson and Sachdev 2004, Bourhis, El-Geledi and Sachdev 2007, Chen and Bond 2007, Jaspal and Coyle 2009). However, there has been little social psychological work on language and ethnic identity specifically among British South Asians, the largest ethnic minority group in the UK, although some attention has been paid to questions of ethnic identity in general (Ghuman 1999, Robinson 2009, Vadher and Barrett 2009, Jaspal and Cinnirella 2010). Nonetheless, sociolinguists have exhibited some interest in language and ethnic identity specifically among second generation Asians (SGA), but this research has focused mainly upon youth culture and upon the notion of 'new ethnicities' (Rampton 1995, Harris 2006) primarily in school settings with adolescent participants (Rampton 1995, Moore 2003, Harris 2006). Here it is argued that a social psychological perspective constitutes a fruitful point of departure, given the discipline's long tradition of studying both the micro and the macro levels of identity, including categorisation and identity processes as well as intergroup processes (Verkuyten 2005). The present paper offers such a perspective.

The study of language and ethnic identity among SGA is particularly interesting, as their linguistic repertoire often features English (the 'dominant' language), the language associated with their ethnic culture, which is termed the heritage language (HL) and, in many cases, a liturgical language associated with religious identity (Jaspal and Coyle 2010). Such multilingualism is constructed in the media both positively (as 'bilingual Asian children do better' in school – Casciani 2003) and negatively (as an obstacle to integration – Blunkett 2002). Today SGA outnumber the foreign-born first generation and their HLs continue to be widely used (Harris 2006). Theoretical generalisation across different cultures is problematic in this domain because not all cultures have the same relationship to language (Myhill 2003), which partly constitutes the rationale for the present study.

Taken-for-granted terms such as 'native speaker' and 'mother tongue' form part of the way that individuals think and talk about language (Myhill 2003). An individual might consider their 'dominant' language to be the language they speak most fluently (Fillmore 2000), although it would not be surprising for someone of Pakistani descent, for instance, to claim that their native language was Urdu, a language associated with Pakistani identity, on the basis of ethnic identity. This discrepancy in interpretation demonstrates the arbitrariness of terms such as 'native speaker' and 'mother tongue' and thus doubts arise regarding their acceptability in research.

A related issue is the relationship between language and ethnic identification, which has been addressed in research on bilingualism, albeit with other ethnic groups (Baker and Jones 1998, Cho 2000). It has been argued that through the HL, ethnic identity can be 'expressed, enacted and symbolised' (Baker and Jones 1998, p.113). Myhill (2003) discusses the 'language-and-identity ideology', which assumes an inherent emotional connection between an individual and their language. Proponents of this ideology suggest that in order 'to be a better, more authentic, more loyal, more committed' member of the group, one must speak the language associated with it (Fishman 1972, p. 46). Language is thus conceptualised as a marker of ethnic identity.

Conversely, the work of some sociolinguists problematises the role of language as an essential component of ethnic identity. Myhill (2003), for instance, makes the contentious claim that, for many diaspora Jews, their 'native language' is merely a 'tool' owing to the convenience of speaking the dominant language of the host country natively. Furthermore, Daller (2005) postulates that language may not necessarily be an intrinsic property of ethnic identity but that it can provisionally serve as an instrument with which a given group asserts its distinctiveness. Language allegedly performs this function when group identity is felt to be threatened and it might be abandoned when it no longer serves this function. Moreover, research undertaken by May (2000) shows that Welsh people who do not speak Welsh can nonetheless exhibit a strong sense of Welsh identity. Given the ambivalent role of language in ethnic identity, this research seeks to explore the meanings and perceived functions of the HL among SGA. Research into the social psychological implications of a lack of proficiency in their HL is lacking, although it is often suggested that only proficiency in the HL allows complete access to the ethnic group (You 2005).

There exists some research on the use of 'Black English' among British black youth (Hewitt 1986, Alexander 1996). The present research acknowledges the possible presence of varieties of 'Black English' in SGA participants' linguistic repertoires and more generally in their psychological worlds, since some sociolinguistic research has identified possible Asian appropriation of this language variety (Rampton 1995, Harris 2006). Such outgroup appropriation of 'Black English' has been described in the literature as 'language crossing', that is, the use of a given language by an outgroup member (Rampton 1995). It allegedly reflects an anti-racist practice and the desire of youths to redefine their identities. The act of using a variety that 'belongs' to another group contests racial boundaries, so this perhaps reflects self-representation based upon the adoption of a 'linguistic' self-aspect associated with the outgroup (Simon 2004). Rampton's (1995) work on language crossing appears to reiterate the notion that it is primarily language that enables identification at the expense of other dimensions of identity. The present research explores this notion through reflective accounts from a group of SGA.

In contrast to the largely quantitative survey-based social psychological research into language and identity (Lawson and Sachdev 2004), the present study explores how a group of young SGA individuals subjectively understand and define language and identity and associated terms and concepts (e.g. 'mother tongue'). It is believed that a qualitative approach will complement existing quantitative research in this area by offering holistic and contextual analyses, which consider the subjective meanings attached by participants to language and ethnic identity in a largely exploratory fashion (Coyle 2007). Furthermore, in-depth qualitative research is likely to inform future quantitative studies of language and identity specifically within this population. Through the analysis of participants' reflective accounts, this research endeavours to discern the role of language in ethnic identity. Since language is generally understood as a context-dependent phenomenon (Meyerhoff 2006), this study explores the role of (linguistic) socialisation upon individuals' sense of self. As a logical continuation of this, participants' evaluative attitudes towards languages are investigated. These complex issues are explored qualitatively through the analysis of participants' first-hand accounts of their experiences.

## Method

### Participants

A sample of 12 participants was recruited from the South Asian Community in a city in the East Midlands of England. The study focused solely upon the experiences of SGA of Indian and/or Pakistani heritage in order to recruit a more homogeneous sample, which was deemed important due to the small sample size.

A snowball sampling strategy was employed, with the initial participants recruited through the first author's social networks. Of the 12 participants recruited, seven were male and five female, with a mean age of 21.6 years (SD: 1.3). Six participants were university students, one had a Master's degree and the remaining five had GCSE/A-levels. Nine of the participants were of Punjabi origin, two were of Gujarati origin and one was mixed race (one parent was from the Punjab and the other was white British). Five participants identified as Muslim, four as Sikh and three as Hindu.

### Procedure

Participants were interviewed using a semi-structured interview schedule consisting of 11 exploratory, open-ended questions. The schedule began with questions regarding self-description and identity, followed by questions on home and school socialisation, the construction of participants' ethnic identities, the role of the HL and other languages in their lives, the management of their linguistic repertoires and reflections upon linguistic experiences. Five participants were interviewed in their homes, three in the interviewer's home and the remaining four at a youth centre. Interviews lasted between 60 and 90 minutes. They were digitally recorded and transcribed verbatim.

### Analytic approach

The data were analysed using qualitative thematic analysis as described by Braun and Clarke (2006). This approach was considered particularly useful since it allows the researcher to draw upon relevant theoretical concepts in order to add theoretical depth to the data analysis. Furthermore, this approach enables the analyst to engage with both the phenomenological and rhetorical aspects of participants' accounts. Borrowing strands from interpretative phenomenological analysis (IPA; Smith and Osborn 2008), the study also aimed to capture participants' attempts to make sense of their personal and social worlds, with a particular focus on identity.

The study employs a critical realist approach to the analysis of participants' accounts. The realist approach has been subject to criticism from a social constructionist perspective on account of its assumption about the representational validity of language and its inattention to the constitutive role of language for experience (Willig 2007). While the present study is located within a critical realist rather than a social constructionist epistemology, the analysis considers the use of discursive categories and the functions performed by participants' accounts as part of a pluralist interpretative endeavour alongside more phenomenological analyses. It is hoped that such epistemological experimentation will allow for a richer and more thorough analysis of participants' reflective accounts of language and ethnic identity (see Frost 2009 for more about the value of a pluralist interpretative endeavour in psychological research).

Turning to the analytic procedures, the transcripts were read repeatedly in order for the researcher to become as intimate as possible with the accounts. The right margin was used to note emerging theme titles which captured the essential qualities of the accounts. This procedure was repeated with every interview transcript. Four superordinate themes representing the 12 accounts were then ordered into a logical and coherent narrative structure, at which point relevant theoretical constructs were drawn upon as a means of theoretically enriching the more phenomenological interpretations.

In the quotations from participants that are presented in the next section, three points indicate where material has been omitted and material within square brackets is clarificatory.

## Analysis

This section reports some of the most important themes, which elucidate the nature of SGA individuals' experiences of language and the repercussions of these experiences for their identities. These themes are entitled 'Mother tongue and self', 'A sense of ownership and affiliation', 'Negotiating linguistic identities in social space' and 'The quest for a positive linguistic identity'.

### Mother tongue and self

The following section guides the reader through participants' meaning-making in relation to self and the mother tongue in their bilingual environment.

*'My mother tongue needs to make me feel like me'*

Participants widely expressed their desire for the mother tongue to represent 'me', that is, individual identity. Raheela's account of her understanding of her mother tongue, Urdu, was unambiguous in its prioritisation of individual identity:

> With me my mother tongue needs to make me feel like me. I sleep and think and dream in it and I use it when I get happy, sad and when I talk to myself.

Raheela's 'mother tongue' seems to be constructed in terms of a psychological trait or cognitive category which serves to process information and knowledge of self (Simon 2004); it is categorised as an instrument of communication with the self. Dreaming and talking to oneself most convincingly reflect the personal importance of the mother tongue in Raheela's process of self-interpretation. Although her account indicated harmony between self and mother tongue, this was by no means a universal commonality. Some participants' accounts indicated a sense of incompatibility between self and mother tongue. For example:

> I'm not one hundred per cent fluent in it [Punjabi] so it feels like my thoughts and my feelings are ruled by a language [English] that isn't really my own. (Baljit)

It was not uncommon for participants to express feelings of anxiety because of their perceived lack of proficiency in their HL, which echoes the idea that ethnic minorities can experience feelings of regret and guilt owing to their lack of fluency in their HL (You 2005). This perhaps implies that knowledge of the HL increases the possibility for minorities to develop a more positively evaluated ethnic identity. Accordingly, participants generally expressed the opinion that the HL was an important shared self-aspect, as a result of which collective (ethnic) identity emerged (Simon 2004). From a sociolinguistic perspective, participants' reported lack of proficiency in the HL may be explained in terms of language shift, since the English language achieves social and ideological priority subsequent to school enrolment (e.g. Fishman 1991).

Participants' 'confessions' that they were less than proficient in their HL sometimes caused dilemmatic 'tension points' in the interviews. Baljit, for instance, having defined herself as Punjabi and having identified Punjabi as her mother tongue, recognised that she was not 'one hundred per cent fluent in it'. It became apparent that Baljit followed her commonsensical conceptualisation of the mother tongue as a language 'learnt at the mother's knee', which she can claim as her own (Fishman 1991). The psychological dilemma arises as Baljit senses that her lack of proficiency in her mother tongue contradicts her commonsensical conceptualisation. Possibly to remedy this, she reports her lack of control over the matter by constructing English as a language she is compelled to use, perhaps as a last resort. Her use of the verb 'ruled' is of particular interest because of its connotations of a higher authority exerting its control over her, which suggests that she is the passive recipient of a language with which she does not identify. Baljit defines herself as a native speaker of Punjabi and the fact that she is compelled to acknowledge that her knowledge of this language is deficient may undermine her self-interpretation as a native speaker. Some participants faced similar dilemmas in the interviews but appeared to develop strategies to deal with them.

*Mutability of the mother tongue*

Two participants expressed what appeared to be coping strategies for potentially dilemmatic positions *vis-à-vis* the mother tongue. These entailed the amendment of their conceptualisation of 'mother tongue' in order for it to accommodate their own linguistic situations. This represents one of the many possible coping strategies that individuals may develop in response to threat to their (linguistic) identity. The following extract illustrates this:

> *Tanveer*: Like mine is like Tagalog. I mean, that was my mother tongue once.
> *Interviewer*: It was? Isn't it any more then?
> *Tanveer*: Well, it's changed now of course, because I don't remember Tagalog anymore. I was really young. It quickly changed to Punjabi and then it changed to English.

Having lived in the Philippines during childhood, Tanveer considers Tagalog his first mother tongue. Although he no longer speaks it fluently, it has retained a level of symbolic importance in his life narrative (Hudson 2001). He subsequently 'acquired' Punjabi as his mother tongue, since this language was most prevalent in his community. However, Tanveer's mother tongue changed once again upon entry into an English school. His account indicates his perception of the mother tongue as a context-dependent, mutable concept; for him it is by no means static and uniform. The social context appears to govern Tanveer's understanding of what his mother tongue actually is. While some participants retained their 'original' mother tongue, which, in most cases, had been inherited from their parents, Tanveer was more pragmatic in his conceptualisation of it. This appeared to resolve the potential psychological dilemma which arose from conflict between his commonsensical interpretation of 'mother tongue' and the language to which he ascribes that role. He re-conceptualises the mother tongue so that, in his psychological world, it is deemed to be mutable and thereby adjusts to the social context. This elucidates one of the psychological strategies employed by individuals to cope with language shift (e.g. Fishman 1991), which may require changes within the identity structure (Breakwell 1986).

An alternative strategy for coping with such dilemmas is outlined in Saeed's account:

> I guess you don't necessarily need to have one. You can have mother tongues in plural too.

Research has highlighted the sequential acquisition of the HL (at home) and English (primarily, at school) (Baker and Jones 1998). Therefore, it perhaps seems logical, in the psychological worlds of participants, to lay claim to both languages to the extent that they would consider both to be their 'mother tongues' ('in plural'). The gradual abandonment of biological heredity as a prerequisite for mother tongue status is particularly interesting. The language in which people write, think and dream is also eligible, according to participants' personal criteria. However, one aspect of the mother tongue debate appears to remain constant, namely the necessary sense of ownership over it and psychological affiliation to the speech community.

### A sense of ownership and affiliation

Participants quite readily offered evaluative comments about languages; there were frequent prescriptive remarks regarding what they felt constituted 'good' language use. Crucially, the data revealed that participants' perceived sense of ownership of a given language played an important role in the social psychological repercussions of their attitudes towards the language.

## 'Us' and 'them': evaluating linguistic identities

It seemed that those individuals who positively evaluated their ethnic identities generally exhibited a positive view of their HL. Participants generally referred to the 'correctness' and inherent eloquence of their ingroup language and some made reference to etymological and philological factors in order to justify the high status they attributed to it. The following extract demonstrates this:

> Gujarati Muslims are brought up to think that our Gujarati is better and nice and beautiful because we are the descendents of the upper class in Gujarat, we're clever, educated and stuff. (Saeed)

There is wide consensus among social psychologists that individuals generally seek positive self-evaluation (Tajfel and Turner 1979) and it is likely that participants' tendency to evaluate their own linguistic variety positively is perhaps tantamount to their search for overall positive self-evaluation. Conversely, Negy *et al.* (2003), in a study on ethnocentrism, found that the more individuals embraced their ethnicity, the more negative views they held towards people who did not belong to their respective ethnic group. This is exemplified by the account offered by Raheela, a Muslim speaker of Gujarati:

> Our language [Muslim-Gujarati] is beautiful ... . With Hindu-Gujarati, it's funny at home, and when I speak it, it makes everyone laugh. ... We take the mick. I know that sounds so bad. I shouldn't do it. (Raheela)

Some contextual information is useful in interpreting the significance of this extract. The Indian state of Gujarat has a Hindu majority (89%) and a sizeable Muslim minority (9%) (Census of India 2001). Linguists generally delineate the linguistic varieties of Gujarati in accordance with the geographical zones, in which they are habitually spoken, rather than on the basis of religion (Cardona and Suthar 2007). However, Raheela and others appeared to differentiate between the variety of Gujarati perceived to be spoken by religious ingroup members (i.e. Muslim-Gujarati) and that perceived to be spoken by religious outgroup members (i.e. Hindu-Gujarati) particularly in comparative contexts (see also Jaspal and Coyle 2010).

As exhibited in the above-cited account, in the home environment, the outgroup language (i.e. Hindu-Gujarati) becomes an object of amusement. By virtue of Raheela's perceived affiliation to the Muslim-Gujarati speaking group and not the Hindu-Gujarati one, she herself views her derision of the outgroup language as unjust; there is an awareness that her jocular use of the outgroup language could cause offence to a Hindu-Gujarati. Crucially, her positive evaluation of her HL *vis-à-vis* her derision of the outgroup HL could be tentatively interpreted as a means of enhancing the collective self-esteem of her religious ingroup. More specifically, this is achieved through the socio-psychological strategy of downward comparison; the ingroup HL is perceived to be 'better' than that of the outgroup (Tajfel and Turner 1979, Wills 1981).

The complexity of this became particularly evident as many participants, who exhibited less ethnocentrism, were critical of their own HL:

> I take the piss [out of the HL] but they [white Scottish people] are different, they are like white and er it's not like the same thing. With the Indian accent, you know that you mean no harm and that, so you just can. (Neha)

Neha's account reveals that she sometimes uses the HL comically and imitates the Indian accent in order to evoke amusement among her peers and family. In contrast with Raheela's account above, Neha sees this as unproblematic, since she herself claims affiliation to the ethnic group that she parodies and thereby claims ownership of and entitlement to the HL. This notion is also expressed in Veer's account of the same phenomenon:

> My language, my people, so yeah, I take the piss, just messing around like.

Participants appeared to equate the HL with ethnic identity; they were perceived as an entwined compound of two inseparable elements (Baker and Jones 1998). The examples that have just been presented suggest that some participants see themselves in a 'privileged position' to criticise and mock their own HL by virtue of their perceived ownership of the language. Neha's comparison between white Scottish people, a group she would be sceptical about criticising, and Indians, against whom she could 'mean no harm', manifestly exhibits her perceived right to use the HL in this way. However, this in itself raises the question of precisely *what* constitutes an authentic group member and *who* may 'rightly' claim ownership of a given language.

## Questionable authenticity

The question of authenticity was frequently invoked by participants. Several discussed Asian appropriation of 'Black English' which they unanimously referred to as 'Slang'. Their accounts revealed who, they felt, had the right to use it. In the following extract, Tanveer contemplates how he might respond to a white British male (an atypical speaker) addressing him in Slang:

> I'd find it kind of surprising. It'd be barbaric but it'd make you think, 'Hang on, is it because of the way I look that he's talking to me like that or does this guy genuinely talk like that?' To a person like that I wouldn't talk back in Slang because it would make me think that this guy is taking the piss. I couldn't take him seriously. I'd like try talking back in proper English and see if that like made him change his opinion of me being a typical Asian.

This demonstrates the important role of authenticity in language crossing. Tanveer's use of the adjectives 'surprising' and 'barbaric' demonstrates the perceived surreality of an outgroup member (in this case, a white middle-class British male) using Slang, which in turn engenders feelings of insecurity (note the use of rhetorical questions). This hypothetical person is not viewed as an authentic speaker of Slang and cannot possibly be accepted into the speech community to which Tanveer feels affiliated.

Invoking Fishman's (1972) criteria for group membership, the analysis of participants' accounts regarding outgroup use of their language reveals that *some* outgroup members are unlikely to be given the opportunity to 'prove themselves' as potentially authentic, loyal and committed group members, since the very act of language crossing is generally viewed with suspicion and engenders fear of persecution or ridicule. It is, in many cases, considered perhaps as a criticism of or attack against Asians, owing to the stereotype reported by many participants that 'a lot of Asians think they're black'. Consequently the only rational response, from Tanveer's perspective, is to use a 'neutral' language, which acts as the *lingua franca* of different social/ethnic groups. This implies that the use of an outgroup language by 'non-authentic' speakers can appear somewhat abrupt and incongruous, with potentially negative consequences for interpersonal/intergroup relations.

The analysis also explored authenticity at an intragroup level, namely within the same ethnic group. Participants referred to SGA who are unable to communicate in their HL:

> You see other British people go there [to India] ... . Complete coconuts – brown on the outside but white on the inside, and they don't know the language ... . These people are white, they aren't true Indians. (Manjinder)

Many participants were fairly unsympathetic towards SGA who had little knowledge of their HL, since it was generally constructed as a prerequisite for ethnic identity:

> Knowing the language is really the first step to being Indian. (Saeed)

Monolingual SGA were often constructed as inauthentic members of the ethnic group; they were derogatorily referred to as 'coconuts', for instance. While Myhill (2003, p. 78) is highly critical of the language-and-identity approach because of its danger of creating 'an atmosphere of suspicion towards members of certain ethnicities', it would appear that this ideology is indeed echoed in the accounts of many participants in this study. Monolingual Asians are viewed as inauthentic members of the ethnic group and the pervasiveness of this attitude is best exemplified by the use of derogatory labels against monolingual SGA such as 'coconut'. In this case, both ownership of the language and affiliation to the ethnic group are questioned by HL-speaking group members.

This would come as no surprise to many proponents of the language-and-identity ideology, since the HL is conceptualised as the dominant shared self-aspect, which gives rise to collective identity (Simon 2004). However, the matter is further complicated by the accounts of several participants, who indicated that one's *level* of proficiency in the HL is also a governing factor in authenticity. Baljit, who claimed to be a fluent speaker of her HL, Punjabi, recounted a telephone conversation with an uncle from India in which she committed a linguistic error which could potentially have caused offence:

> He was just laughing his head off ... . He didn't take any offence at what I said because he's like 'Oh she's from England and she doesn't know what she's on about'. That is kind of putting you down.

Participants frequently reported feelings of inferiority ('putting you down') because of their perceived lack of competence in the HL. Although there is no doubt that Baljit is able to converse in Punjabi, the fact that she makes unconventional use of the HL, commonly associated with bilingualism (Ellis 1985), calls into question her authenticity as a legitimate group member. Participants were aware of their 'questionable authenticity' and this frequently gave rise to feelings of confusion. It is commonly assumed that 'retention' of the HL is a sufficient means of ensuring that individuals develop a positive ethnic identity (Fillmore 2000, You 2005) but these data suggest that mere retention is perhaps not sufficient; a lack of proficiency in the HL possibly poses a threat to the individual's self-interpretation as a legitimate member of the Punjabi ethnic group.

From the perspective of identity process theory (Breakwell 1986), the resulting feelings of confusion and helplessness in participants' accounts might perhaps be attributed to attacks on the value dimension of identity and consequential threat to self-esteem. Those lacking proficiency in their HL may be led to believe that they are inferior, inauthentic members of the group, who 'don't know what they're on about'. However, participants were mindful of the role of social space in others' interpretation of them as fluent or non-fluent speakers.

### Negotiating linguistic identities in social space

Participants readily reflected upon their use of language in various social contexts and their accounts exhibited an awareness of 'language norms', which are social representations of 'appropriate' linguistic behaviour (Hudson 2001, see also Moscovici 1988).

### Clearly defined language norms in social space

There was a general awareness of 'appropriate' language choice/use according to social context. Neha's account exemplifies this:

> When I'm wearing my work suit, I'm just automatically professional in talking. As opposed to like abbreviating words, I will say full sentences and correctly; instead of saying 'Isn't it?' I'll say 'Is it not?' ... Professional in the office environment does not include speaking any language other than English.

Although many participants expressed pride in their HL, some clearly felt embarrassed about using it in predominantly English-speaking contexts. Neha referred to the apparently negative connotations of her HL; for her, Punjabi represents a rural language, used primarily to denote names of food which are untranslatable into English. Theoretically, her reluctance to associate the HL with her work environment is perhaps explicable; her HL constitutes a cognitive category or self-aspect which is shared with members of her extended family (and ethnic group) and self-interpretation on the basis of this self-aspect gives rise to a collective (ethnic) identity (Simon 2004). However, the account above indicates that this identity is deemed to be incongruous with life at work; it would perhaps hinder the formation of a collective identity with work colleagues who, from Neha's perspective, would share other self-aspects associated with 'being professional'. Thus, it might be argued that Neha's abandonment of her HL (even with other Asians) at work represents a strategy to deal with a potentially threatening situation. She justifies the removal of her HL from the social context by deprecating its importance and emphasising its potential disadvantages. Crucially, Neha constructs this idiosyncrasy as a socially accepted norm, as if it were not *her* view that the HL is incongruous in the office environment but society's view.

As a possible consequence of perceived language norms, participants widely reported having been 'forced' to speak a particular language in a given context, which may have contributed to the psychological internalisation of these norms. For example:

> When we were younger ... my dad made us speak Punjabi and was like 'Ghar sirf punjabi bolni chahidi' [you should only speak Punjabi at home]. (Baljit)

She [mum] didn't believe in completely turning us English. ... If we spoke in English, sometimes she'd just say 'I'm not listening' and then we knew that we had to talk Punjabi. (Amardeep)

These examples demonstrate the imposition of language norms during socialisation at home. Many participants reported parents' attempts to render the home environment a HL-speaking context; participants attributed this to the perceived fear among parents that their children would metaphorically 'turn white' if English were permitted at home.

Well, they [my parents] didn't want me to grow up a white man. (Raj)

In fact, these rules regarding desirable language use were so stringent that English, in some cases, ceased to be an adequate instrument of communication at home as a result of parents' rejection of it, thus thrusting individuals in the direction of the HL, the perceived desideratum. Parental imposition of the HL at home may be viewed in terms of an attempt at language maintenance *vis-à-vis* their perception of language shift among the second generation (see Fishman 1991). Interestingly, this seemed to be counteracted in the school environment, in which participants observed the imposition of English and, by implication, discrimination against use of the HL:

One thing that used to piss me off was like if I'm chatting to a mate in Punjabi, like an apna [literally 'one of our own'], white teachers would just butt in and be like 'Oh, talk English, you're in England' and we'd get in trouble for it. Such racists. (Daljit)

Participants generally referred to this as racism, possibly because of the widespread belief in the intrinsic relationship between HL and ethnic identity (Fishman 1991; Baker and Jones 1998). In any case, the strict norms of language use, both at home and in the school environment, appeared to have contributed to the establishment of a binary structure in their language use. Daljit uses the metaphor of crossing a geographical frontier to illustrate this dichotomisation:

At home we'd always speak Punjabi and English at school so it was a bit like the minute I got home I was like walking through a frontier into a different frontier.

## Challenging language norms in social space

For most participants, it became increasingly difficult to negotiate or explore their linguistic identities in different social contexts, since the imposed norms seemed to hinder this. The desirable state of affairs was for them to use the HL in informal situations, such as the home environment, and English for official purposes such as school and later the world of work. One might argue that for many participants a quasi-diglossic situation developed whereby one language was reserved for 'high' functions (such as education) and the other for 'low' functions (such as food) (Ferguson 1959):

Basically I'll just use Punjabi to talk about Indian food and stuff. ... Uni and work is talked about in English. (Neha)

Although participants generally perceived linguistic boundaries delimiting different social contexts, this is not to suggest that all participants were compliant. Participants subverted language norms in two principal ways, namely by speaking in Slang, a variety with which neither their parents nor teachers would identify, and also by challenging rules regarding 'appropriate' language choice. Amardeep offered his account:

> Being in England makes me more Indian and being in India makes me more English … .
> When I'm in England I insist on speaking loads of Punjabi in public as if I was in India.
> When I'm in India I always talk in English. … I suppose it's because I don't want to conform.

It has commonly been hypothesised that if an individual's choice of language is recognised as 'normal' for a given group, group membership will follow (Fishman 1991). Thus, arguably, language has a symbolic role, which was exploited by some participants who reported using language subversively; in the quotation above, this is unambiguously constructed as an attempt not to conform to societal norms. Sterling (2000) postulates that language can inspire deep group loyalties; it might be argued that his lack of 'loyalty' to English within English-speaking contexts demonstrates Amardeep's general disidentification with English culture. Many accounts appeared to indicate that this was an attempt to challenge the perceived hegemony of prescribers of 'appropriate' language use; participants intended to assert their own authority:

> I know my dad'll understand both English and Punjabi so why should I just speak whatever he wants me to speak? (Baljit)

Other factors might perhaps underlie this. It is claimed that individuals construct their identity through the choice of linguistic forms that will convey specific information that categorises them as part of a particular social group (Sterling 2000). Thus, in Britain, Amardeep refuses to be 'depersonalised' within English-speaking society and, conversely, in India he is averse to becoming part of the mass of Punjabi-speakers. It would appear that Amardeep seeks to maintain distinctiveness from others in both contexts. His act of challenging language norms in clearly defined linguistic contexts perhaps facilitates self-definition as a unique individual (Breakwell 1986). In this way, participants' accounts of their language use reflect the widespread desire for a positive identity, which constitutes the focus of the next section.

### The quest for a positive linguistic identity

Participants employed various strategies to ensure the development and maintenance of an identity, *inter alia*, the rejection of languages which were seen as stereotypical of the ingroup and downgrading the importance of the HL. The following section focuses upon the latter.

#### 'I'm not missing out on anything': downgrading the importance of the heritage language

Some participants acknowledged their lack of proficiency in the HL. Their accounts of this were generally constructed with an unambiguous tone of casualness, as depicted in Neha's statement:

> Punjabi? Not really a big factor because my parents speak English. … It's normal for kids my age [not to be fluent in their HL]. I mean it'll completely phase out in a few generations anyway.

The topic of language arose within the context of ethnic identity, which may have indicated that there was an implicit assumption that the two are linked in some way. Neha's response to this was to downgrade the importance of the HL. One of her initial comments about language and ethnic identity was that it was 'not really a big factor' for her as her parents are fluent in English, which perhaps implies that the HL is considered most important for those individuals whose parents are monolingual in their HL. This suggests that language is merely an instrument of communication and that English is the most desirable language for communication with her parents. Furthermore, these comments have interesting implications for cognitions towards social background: use of English at home symbolises sophistication, a privileged upbringing and a history of education in the family. For Neha, the HL is simply not *required* at the level of communication. Neha's case was not an isolated one; similarly, other participants constructed their linguistic repertoire as the norm for SGA in the UK:

> Punjabi's good to know, yeah, but truth is a lot of us don't know how to speak it that well. … That's the way it is nowadays. (Aamir)

Monolingual SGA generally constructed widespread use of the HL in the South Asian home as a rarity, although there is evidence that many SGA retain their HL (Harris 2006). Participants denied occupying a differential position by constructing themselves as the norm, possibly because acknowledging this might compromise self-definition as authentic Asians. Many of the same participants, in other less 'threatening' contexts, asserted that the HL is indeed an important aspect of their ethnic culture:

> I really want our children to speak fluent Gujarati and Punjabi. … That's important to me. (Neha)

This appears to represent a dilemmatic position. If Neha is adamant that her future children should know their HL, presumably she attaches some importance to these languages. This perhaps suggests that Neha's convincing argument that her own lack of knowledge of her HL does not pose any grave difficulties for her British Asian identity is the product of 'blurring' the boundaries between the conceptualisation of language as an instrument of communication and as a marker of identity. Indeed, as an instrument of communication, it can satisfactorily be argued that the HL is relatively unimportant, especially if one's parents speak English fluently. However, if language is conceptualised primarily as a marker of identity (Hudson 2001), this argument becomes less effective. It is contended that participants who advocate this argument in this context seek to maintain a positive identity through deprecation of their HL and by constructing it as unnecessary for their self-definition as British Asians.

## Discussion

The present paper elucidates some of the potential implications of language for SGA individuals' sense of self and it seeks to sensitise readers to the diversity of experiences within this small sample. The lack of generalisability of this research, due to the small sample, should not be viewed as a shortcoming, as its theoretical and practical implications may be considerable.

It is acknowledged that there is a growing body of theoretical and empirical work which suggests that British South Asians of Indian and Pakistani backgrounds should be viewed as separate populations due to observed differences in *inter alia* their ethno-religious experience and their relationships to British national identity (e.g. Robinson 2009, Jaspal and Cinnirella 2010). However, the results of the present study did not attest to any salient differences in participants' accounts regarding the role of the HL in ethnic identity construction on the basis of their Indian or Pakistani ethno-national identities. In research on language and *religious* identity, however, differences have been observed (Jaspal and Coyle 2010). Consequently, it seems appropriate to consider the identity experiences of SGA collectively.

In terms of identity, the present research demonstrates the pervasiveness of language at all levels of identity; it can be 'a reminder of who I am' in individual terms but also a symbol of group identity. This challenges previous research on language and identity, which has often conceptualised language primarily as a marker of group identity (Omoniyi and White 2006). The meanings and functions of language appear to vary according to the various levels of social inclusiveness.

Moreover this research challenges assumptions and terminology commonly employed in the literature. Both researchers and laypeople discuss the mother tongue as if 'we all know what we mean by this' (Myhill 2003, p. 78). Although such terms have been debated and problematised by others (Edwards 1985, Myhill 2003), these findings may be viewed as a contribution to the 'campaign' against uncritical, casual use of such terminology in academic discourse. Future academic writing must be more tentative in its use of such terminology or better still, it might re-conceptualise the 'mother tongue' as a more fluid, context-dependent, mutable notion, as participants' accounts have demonstrated.

Similarly, participants' accounts indicate that such rigidity should be avoided in practical terms; the strait-jacket of language norms in different social contexts appeared to have a negative impact upon participants. They expressed their awareness of (implicit and explicit) norms in the home and school/work environments and (the prospect of) any contravention of such norms gave rise to a variety of emotions, such as embarrassment (Fillmore 2000). While some participants appeared to have developed a problematic relationship with their heritage cultures due to a perceived tension between language and environment, others actively challenged such norms. This demonstrates participants' ambivalent responses to the perceived incongruity of language and environment.

It is unlikely that a degree of linguistic freedom in participants' school lives and elsewhere might pose a threat to the position of English (cf. Kirkup 2007). This is not to express support for bilingual education in British schools but rather this is a recommendation to allow greater freedom for individuals to explore the multiple roles and functions of language. Participants recounted parental attempts to coerce them into using their HL and reported being reprimanded for failing to do so. Greater linguistic freedom and a celebration of multilingualism appeared to be endorsed by participants. Such an endeavour might enhance psychological well-being rather than creating situations/contexts which give rise to negativism, that is, 'doing the opposite of what is required in a given situation' (Apter 1983, p. 79).

Crucially, the recommendation of 'linguistic freedom' does not necessarily signal support for or encouragement of language crossing (Rampton 1995) as this practice is problematised by the present research. The importance of phenomena such as authenticity, the language-and-identity ideology (Myhill 2003) and level of proficiency have been largely understated in contemporary research on language and identity. *Prima facie*, the use of outgroup languages might appear to improve intergroup relations but it is argued that such an endeavour must be undertaken with caution since, as the analysis reveals, languages can hold deep and emotional meanings for speakers. The use of a given language in a given social context by a seemingly 'inauthentic' member of the speech community could have a variety of social psychological repercussions in participants' social worlds, from feelings of euphoria at the prospect of an outgroup member speaking one's language to feelings of suspicion at the thought of an outgroup member trespassing upon ingroup territory.

Some accounts demonstrated that participants were averse to outgroup appropriation of their language, perhaps as a result of the widely perceived stigmatisation of it. Such stigma may perhaps pose a threat to the value dimension of identity (Breakwell 1986), given that language is seen as a vital aspect of one's ethnic identity. This work complements previous research whose findings have led to the general recommendation that educators ought to encourage linguistic diversity and avoid prescriptivism in language (Fillmore 2000).

The analysis signalled that prescriptive, evaluative comments about languages could have psychological repercussions for speakers. It has been argued that participants frequently seek to construct a positive identity by adopting or distancing themselves from certain languages. This included the denigration of languages with which they did not identify and the positive evaluation of languages with which they did. However, both the adoption and rejection of languages were reportedly met with resistance. Some participants claimed that there was an unambiguous sense of animosity towards SGA monolingual in English who could be positioned derogatorily as white. Such discrimination was unambiguously constructed as a consequence of participants' speech patterns, as opposed to any other trait.

In general terms, participants were unanimously positive about the implications of the interview discussions for their own sense of self; many reported never having reflected upon these issues but that having done so provided them with 'answers'. For instance, the accounts highlighted the difficulties that participants generally experienced in making sense of the 'boundaries' between the roles of language as an instrument of communication and as a marker of identity. Some accounts exhibited contradictions and dilemmas, while others demonstrated an initial lack of understanding of the dichotomy. Participants valued discussing such phenomena, as many felt able to make sense of their situations. The interviews undoubtedly constituted a dual learning experience: participants provided the researcher with a glimpse of their experiences but were also 'able to clarify their experiences and to become aware of the feelings underlying their words' in a quasi-therapeutic manner (Coyle 1998, p. 58). Furthermore, at a therapeutic level, if counsellors are aware of the potential challenges that bi-/multilingualism can pose for SGA, this might enable greater identification with clients and greater understanding of their (bilingual) backgrounds.

Bilingualism tends to be viewed positively, especially in terms of its cognitive advantages (Kirkup 2007). Although it is argued that linguistic freedom and widespread language learning should be encouraged, the social psychological approach has indicated how a 'mismanagement' of bi-/multilingualism might compromise psychological well-being. Future research must not conceal the potentially negative psychosocial issues associated with bi-/multilingualism and the possible repercussions for one's sense of self. Rather, it ought to create awareness of and engage with these issues in order to contribute to the developing picture of language and identity among SGA and to bring about positive social change.

## Acknowledgements
The authors would like to thank two anonymous reviewers for detailed and insightful comments on this article.

## Notes on contributors
Rusi Jaspal is a Social Psychologist at Royal Holloway, University of London. His research focuses upon the construction of national, ethnic and linguistic identities. He is particularly interested in socio-psychological responses to identity threat. Rusi has published in journals such as *British Journal of Social Psychology, Mental Health, Religion and Culture* and *Social Psychological Review.*

Adrian Coyle is a Senior Lecturer in the Department of Psychology at the University of Surrey. His research has addressed a wide range of topics, including identity, religion and spirituality, bereavement and various issues within lesbian and gay psychology and qualitative psychological research methods. He was co-editor of *Analysing Qualitative Data in Psychology* (with Evanthia Lyons, 2007, Sage).

## References
Alexander, C., 1996. *The art of being black.* Oxford: Oxford University Press.
Apter, M., 1983. Negativism and the sense of identity. *In*: G. M. Breakwell, ed. *Threatened identities.* Chichester: Wiley, 75–90
Baker, C. and Jones, S., 1998. *Encyclopaedia of bilingualism and bilingual education.* Philadelphia, PA: Clevedon.
Blunkett, D., 2002. Integration with diversity: globalisation and the renewal of democracy and civil society. *In:* M. Leonard and P. Griffith, eds. *Reclaiming Britishness.* London: The Foreign Policy Centre, 66–78.
Bourhis, R.Y., El-Geledi, S., and Sachdev, I., 2007. Language, ethnicity and intergroup relations. *In:* A. Weatherall, B. Watson and C. Gallois, eds. *Language, discourse and social psychology.* New York: Palgrave MacMillan, 15–50.
Braun, V. and Clarke, V., 2006. Using thematic analysis in psychology. *Qualitative Research in Psychology,* 3, 77–101.
Breakwell, G.M., 1986. *Coping with threatened identities.* London: Methuen.
Cardona, G. and Suthar, B., 2007. Gujarati. *In:* George Cardona and Dhanesh Jain, eds. *The Indo-Aryan languages.* London: Routledge, 659–697.
Casciani, D., 2003. *Bilingual Asian children 'do better'* [online]. Available from: http://news.bbc.co.uk/1/hi/education/3236188.stm [accessed 2 April 2008].
Census of India, 2001. Population. Available from: http://censusindia.gov.in [accessed 1 March 2010].
Chen, S. and Bond, M., 2007. Explaining language priming effects: further evidence for ethnic affirmation among Chinese–English bilinguals. *Journal of Language & Social Psychology,* 13 (4), 398–406.
Cho, G., 2000. The role of heritage language in social interactions and relationships: reflections from a language minority group. *Bilingual Research Journal,* 24 (4), 369–384.
Coyle, A., 1998. Qualitative research in counselling psychology: using counselling interview as a research instrument. *In:* Petruska Clarkson, ed. *Counselling psychology: integrating theory, research and supervised practice.* London: Routledge, 56–73.
Coyle, A., 2007. Introduction to qualitative research. *In:* Evanthia Lyons and Adrian Coyle, eds. *Analysing qualitative data in psychology.* London: Sage, 9–30.
Daller, H., 2005. *Language shift and group identity: mennonite immigrants from the former Soviet Union in Germany.* Available at: http://www.lingref.com/isb/4/043ISB4.PDF [accessed 28 May 2008].
Edwards, J., 1985. *Language, society and identity.* Oxford: Basil Blackwell.
Ellis, R., 1985. *Understanding second language acquisition.* Oxford: Oxford University Press.
Ferguson, C., 1959. Diglossia. *Word,* 15, 325–340.

Fillmore, L., 2000. Loss of family languages: should educators be concerned? *Theory into Practice,* 39 (4), 203–210.

Fishman, J., 1972. *Language and nationalism: two integrative essays.* Rowley, MA: Newbury House.

Fishman, J., 1991. *Reversing language shift.* Clevedon, Avon: Multilingual Matters.

Fishman, J., 2001. *Handbook of language and ethnicity.* New York: Oxford University Press.

Frost, N., 2009. 'Do you know what I mean?' The use of a pluralistic narrative analysis approach in the interpretation of an interview. *Qualitative Research,* 9(1), 9–29.

Ghuman, P.A.S., 1999. *Asian adolescents in the West.* Leicester: British Psychological Society.

Giles, H. and Johnson, P., 1987. Ethnolinguistic identity theory: a social psychological approach to language maintenance. *International Journal of the Sociology of Language,* 68, 69–99.

Harris, R., 2006. *New ethnicities and language use.* Basingstoke: Palgrave Macmillan.

Hewitt, R., 1986. *White talk Black talk: inter-racial friendship and communication amongst adolescents.* Cambridge: Cambridge University Press.

Hudson, R., 2001. *Sociolinguistics.* Cambridge: Cambridge University Press.

Jaspal, R. and Cinnirella, M., 2010. Ethnic identity construction among UK South Asians: insights from identity process theory. Manuscript submitted for publication.

Jaspal, R. and Coyle, A., 2009. Reconciling social psychology and socio-linguistics can have some benefits: language and identity among second generation British Asians. *Social Psychological Review,* 11 (2), 3–14.

Jaspal, R. and Coyle, A., 2010. 'Arabic is the language of the Muslims – that's how it was supposed to be': exploring language and religious identity through reflective accounts from young British-born South Asians. *Mental Health, Religion & Culture,* 13 (1), 17–36.

Kirkup, J., 2007. English a minority language in 1,300 schools. *The Daily Telegraph,* 18 December 2007.

Lawson, S. and Sachdev, I., 2004. Identity, language use and attitudes: some Sylheti–Bangladeshi data from London, UK. *Journal of Language and Social Psychology,* 23 (1), 49–69.

May, S., 2000. Accommodating and resisting minority language policy: the case of Wales. *International Journal of Bilingual Education and Bilingualism,* 3 (2), 101–128.

Meyerhoff, M., 2006. *Introducing sociolinguistics.* London: Routledge.

Moore, E., 2003. Learning style and identity: a sociolinguistic analysis of a Bolton High School. PhD thesis, University of Manchester.

Moscovici, S., 1988. Notes towards a description of social representations. *European Journal of Social Psychology,* 18, 211–250.

Myhill, J., 2003. The native speaker, identity and the authenticity hierarchy. *Language Sciences,* 25 (1), 77–97.

Negy, C., Shreve, T., Jensen, B., and Uddin, N., 2003. Ethnic identity, self-esteem and ethnocentrism: a study of social identity versus multicultural theory of development. *Cultural Diversity and Ethnic Minority Psychology,* 9 (4), 333–344.

Omoniyi, T. and White, G., 2006. *The sociolinguistics of identity.* London: Continuum.

Rampton, B., 1995. *Crossing: language and ethnicity among adolescents.* London: Longman.

Robinson, L., 2009. Cultural identity and acculturation preferences among South Asian adolescents in Britain: an exploratory study. *Children and Society,* 23 (6), 442–454.

Simon, B., 2004. *Identity in modern society: a social psychological perspective.* Oxford: Blackwell.

Smith, J. and Osborn, M., 2008. Interpretative phenomenological analysis. *In:* J. Smith, ed. *Qualitative psychology: a practical guide to methods.* London: Sage, 53–80.

Sterling, P., 2000. *Identity in language: an exploration into the social implications of linguistic variation* [online]. http://glasscock.tamu.edu/agora/winter00/sterling.pdf [accessed 10 March 2008].

Tajfel, H. and Turner, J., 1979. An integrative theory of intergroup conflict. *In:* W. Austin and S. Worchel, eds. *The social psychology of intergroup relations.* Monterey, CA: Brooks/Cole, 33–47.

Vadher, K. and Barrett, M., 2009. Boundaries of Britishness in British Indians and Pakistanis. *Journal of Community and Applied Social Psychology,* 19, 442–458.

Verkuyten, M., 2005. *The social psychology of ethnic identity.* London: Psychology Press.

Willig, C., 2007. Reflections on the use of a phenomenological method. *Qualitative Research in Psychology,* 4 (3), 209–225.

Wills, T.A., 1981. Downward comparison principles in social psychology. *Psychological Bulletin,* 90 (2), 245–271.

You, B., 2005. Children negotiating Korean American ethnic identity through their heritage language. *Bilingual Research Journal,* 29 (3), 711–721.

# The Sikh gurdwara in Finland: negotiating, maintaining and transmitting immigrants' identities

Laura Hirvi

*Department of History & Ethnology, University of Jyväskylä, Jyväskylä, Finland*

As recent studies suggest, religious institutions play a crucial role in shaping immigrants' identities. Drawing on fieldwork conducted in Helsinki, Finland among Sikh immigrants from Northern India, this article sets out to investigate the manner in which the gurdwara (Sikh temple) is involved in the process of negotiating, maintaining and transmitting immigrants' identities. By means of mapping out and analyzing the gurdwara's architectural as well as organizational structure, its foodways, and its role in transmitting religious as well as cultural traditions to Sikh youth, this article seeks to highlight the complex process underlying the (re-)creation of immigrants' identities in a diasporic context.

## Introduction

Immigrants who leave their country of origin behind in order to settle either temporarily or permanently in another country often have to face a new and unfamiliar cultural setting upon arrival. People may talk in a different possibly unknown language, may think another way about the upbringing of children or marriage, and drink perhaps coffee instead of tea. Coming to terms with such new cultural stimuli can be a tiring process that might cause immigrants to long for a community of people, who think, act, eat, talk and pray like they do, and with whom they can share their experiences and thoughts concerning their lives away from their original home country. Immigrant worship communities provide such a setting in which immigrants produce and share 'feelings of belonging' (Martikainen 2004, p. 226). In addition, it has been argued that they constitute meaningful sites for the preservation and transmission of immigrants' identities (see for example: Warner and Wittner 1998, Ebaugh and Chafetz 2000, Hall 2002, Foley and Hoge 2007). The purpose of this article is to cast greater light on the manner in which religious worship communities are involved in the process of negotiating, maintaining and transmitting immigrants' identities. For this case study, I look at Sikh immigrants from Punjab (India) living in Finland and explore what role the gurdwara (Sikh temple) plays in shaping their as well as their offspring's cultural and religious identities.

First, I will give a short overview of the background of Sikhs living in Finland followed by comments on how the key concept of *identity* is understood in this work. After introducing the data on which this article is based, I will scrutinize the activities and artifacts related to the gurdwara in order to achieve a better understanding of the manner in which Sikhs negotiate their identities in Finland.

The Sikhs have been chosen for this case study because of their distinctive religious traditions and because combined with other South Asians they are one of the fastest growing immigrant groups in Finland.[1] Furthermore, as this is in fact the first study carried out on Sikh immigrants living in Finland, I hope to add important knowledge to the global research body of Sikh diaspora studies.

The first Sikhs, mostly males without their dependents, started migrating to Finland in the beginning of the 1980s with the intention of improving their living standards. They came with work permits and many of those early settlers applied later on for Finnish citizenship. According to my informants, the first group consisted of around 10 Sikhs, but by 2008, out of 2716 Indians living in Finland,[2] already 632[3] people were listed as speaking Punjabi, which is the mother tongue of most Sikhs. A few Sikhs living in Finland also speak Hindi as their mother tongue, since they lived in Delhi prior to migrating to Helsinki. Based on these statistics and on my fieldwork observations, thus it can be assumed that there are currently about 500 Sikhs living in Finland. Most Sikh immigrants have settled down in the area of Helsinki and its neighboring city, Vantaa, and the majority work in restaurants, pubs or nightclubs, either as employees or as entrepreneurs.

## Data

This article draws on ethnographic fieldwork that has been carried out between February 2008 and August 2009 among Sikh immigrants living in the metropolitan area of Helsinki, Finland. During the fieldwork, I took part in various religious and cultural events as a participant observer. Numerous photographs have been taken, which assist in memorizing those events. In addition, data was collected through semi-structured interviews, conducted either in English or in Finnish, the latter of which I translated on into English. The interviews were conducted with established members, newcomers, youth, and expatriates whom I met at the gurdwara or found by the help of the Internet. Altogether, 26 Sikhs living in the Greater Helsinki area were interviewed for this study. Upon examining Table 1, it becomes clear that the group of informants consists of more men than women, and that the first generation constitutes the majority of the informants. It has to be noted that five of the informants were expatriates, who were not considered relevant informants for the last part of this article dealing with the transmission of religion and culture, due to their temporary stay in Finland and because none of them had children of their own.

The interviews lasted between 30 minutes and 2 hours, and were taped with the help of a voice recorder when possible. Following the Code of Ethics of the American Anthropological Association, I ensured the informants' anonymity by altering their name unless they explicitly expressed the wish to have their name mentioned in my work. Since Sikh names do not reveal gender, either 'F' for female or 'M' for male was added after each name. During my fieldwork, I clearly established the fact with

Table 1.   Profile of informants.

| Female | Male | Expatriate | 1. Generation | 1.5 Gen. | 2. Gen. |
|--------|------|------------|---------------|----------|---------|
| 10 | 16 | 5 | 13 | 4 | 4 |

those I interviewed or talked to that I was an anthropologist collecting material for my dissertation.

This study is part of a larger comparative anthropological research examining how Sikhs living in Finland and California negotiate their identities.

### The concept of identity

One of the key concepts of this article is *identity*, which has been of great interest within the field of migration studies. This is due to the fact that immigration provokes in many cases 'profound questions about identity' as Foley and Hoge (2007, p. 191) point out in their recently published study on the worship communities of the new immigrants in the USA. The reason for this might be explained by referring to the anthropologist Eriksen's (2002) argument that 'identity becomes most important the moment it seems threatened' (p. 68). The feeling of threat may be caused by the fact that immigrants are only part of a minority in the country they are living in and therefore have to face in many cases the majority's claims that they adapt, adjust, assimilate and/or integrate into the host society. Living under such circumstances seems to inevitably provoke the question 'Who are you (singular as well as plural)?' which transforms into the immigrants' self-focused question 'Who am I/are we?' *Identity* can be considered to be the constructed answer to these emerging questions. The manner in which a group or an individual will react to the question 'Who are you/am I/are we?' depends on many factors, including the historical background and the situational context in which the question is formulated, both on a symbolic as well as on a concrete level. In the following example, I asked a married couple whether they considered themselves to be Indians, rather than Finns or Sikhs:

| Ravneet (F): | Pure Sikhs we are not. |
| Bhagat (M): | No, we are not. |
| L: | The stronger identity is … |
| Ravneet (F): | Indian, yes. That is what we are externally and that is where we come from. |
| Bhagat (M): | If someone asks I can say Indian, and he may ask where and what is this, then I can say that I am a Sikh from North India. |

Thus, in the Finnish context, Ravneet, who has been living in Finland since her very early childhood, prefers to identify herself as Indian in the first place, based on her physical appearance as well as her parents' place of birth. Additionally, her husband Bhagat, who arrived in Finland in his twenties after having married Ravneet, identifies himself in the first place as Indian, and only reveals his religious as well as more specific ethnic identity when asked for this specific information. However, outside of Finland when meeting friends (who are possibly also Sikh immigrants from Punjab), they both would prefer to identify themselves as Finns, as the following excerpt shows:

| L: | If you would be in Italy for example, and you would visit friends, and someone would ask you where you are from, what would you say? |
| Ravneet (F): | Probably that we are from Finland. Totally from Finland! (*laughs*) |
| Bhagat (M): | From Finland, yes. If he asks more then I can say [from India] but first I say from Finland. |

This example seeks to demonstrate that context has an impact on the way identity is constructed and supports Hall's (1992) suggestion that the subject seems to assume 'different identities at different times' (p. 277). Consequently, identity cannot be perceived as a fixed unity that would always be the same, independent of its context, but rather identities are constructed in response to a given context. Bearing this in mind, the following article sets out to examine the gurdwara in Finland as a place where Sikh immigrants negotiate, maintain and transmit their cultural, religious, ethnic, and linguistic identities.

## Negotiating identity: the impact of context

The Sikh gurdwara community[4] in Finland has been registered as a religious community since 8 May 1998. In the beginning, Sikhs used to gather at rented public places for their religious gatherings once a month. However, around 2006, they had collected enough money to be able to purchase their own premises in *Sörnäinen*, a suburb of Helsinki, where the first and only gurdwara of Finland is located today. The suburb has the reputation of being a neighborhood where many immigrants, artists and students live, but it is also known for having its share of heavy drinkers. It can be described as a neighborhood with a very vivid multi- and subcultural atmosphere, in which the Punjabi letters above the gurdwara's door probably do not attract much attention. This might also be due to the fact that the gurdwara's architecture is quite plain and unimposing in its appearance and thus easy to miss, despite its central location on Sörnäinen's main street *Hämeentie*. As my informants told me, the building used to be an office and they had to do a lot of renovation work in order to make it suitable for their purposes. The renovation project was financed by offerings made by members of the congregation. In addition to financial donations, my informant Ranjit told me that many of the gurdwara community's members made donations in the form of material goods, such as paint and carpets. In his article dealing with Hindu immigrants in Norway, Jacobsen points out that 'sacred time and sacred space do not create themselves; they are produced by the hard work of the community' (2006, p. 163). Similarly, it can be stated that the gurdwara in Finland has been built solely by the hard work of the Sikh community, as they did not receive any sort of financial support, either from the Finnish authorities, or from Punjab, or other Sikh communities within the diaspora. Furthermore, it can be suggested that those Sikhs who took part in the process of financing and renovating the gurdwara expressed through their active participation an interest in preserving – and as we shall see later on also transmitting – their religious Sikh identity in the Finnish context.

Although the gurdwara in Finland cannot be compared to one of those purpose-built Sikh temples in the UK that Peach and Gale (2003) have termed together with mosques and Hindu temples as the country's 'new cathedrals' (p. 469), the mere physical existence of a gurdwara in Finland already reflects the fact that there are Sikhs in this country. Moreover, the temple in Sörnäinen could be considered to be Sikhs' tentative attempt to carve out a place for themselves in the religious landscape of an increasingly multi-cultural Finnish society.

However, the interest in displaying Sikh identity in the Finnish public is subject to Finnish regulations. Thus, when the Sikh community intended to erect a pole with the Sikh flag on top, which is called *Nishan Sahib*, in front of the gurdwara building, they had to contend with local authorities and Finnish bureaucracy. As they applied for permission to transform the former office into a gurdwara, the group that had started the temple already went successfully through a similar amount of paperwork. However, applying for permission to put up a *Nishan Sahib* in front of the temple seemed too troublesome and not worth the effort, as Ranjit explains:

L:            Do you have at your gurdwara the *Nishan Sahib*?
Ranjit (M):  In this gurdwara it is inside, a small one. The City of Helsinki did not give permission for one outside, I called them myself a couple of years ago and they said that you need this and you need that and you need this and you need that, then I thought, 'Is it even worth to put it outside'?

Thus, the physical setting and the external requirements drove the Sikh community to make a structural adaptation and as a result they decided to hoist the *Nishan Sahib* inside rather than outside the gurdwara. As the tenth Guru, Guru Gobind Singh, introduced the *Nishan Sahib* with the intention of visibly marking the building as a Sikh temple; this adaptation is significant. However, the Sikh community hopes that this is only a temporary adaptation and they are planning to apply for permission in the near future. This intention reflects that the *Nishan Sahib* is indeed an important symbol for the Sikh worship community in Finland.

Besides the *Nishan Sahib*, which is inside rather than outside the gurdwara building, there are also other ways in which the Sikh community in Finland has adapted to the conditions imposed on them as a result of diasporic circumstances. Other than in India, for example, the gurdwara in Finland is usually just open Sundays and sporadically during the week for an hour or two in the morning. In fact, it is only open for special occasions on Saturdays and evenings during the week when the temple has visitors from India, who give lectures to the children as well as the adults. The traditional food called *langar*, is however only served on Sundays.

One of my informants, who initially came as an expatriate from Delhi (India), describes his first encounter with the gurdwara in Finland as follows:

Charan (M):  It was … Saturday! It was Saturday and it (the gurdwara) was locked. So, I was too confused: How can a gurdwara be locked?!? Because back in India there is never a 'locked' word in the gurdwara, so they just never lock. It is open 24 hours, you can go in anytime.

The reason why the gurdwara is only open on Sundays, is partly of a financial nature: the community cannot afford to have the temple open all the time and provide for the living of a person staying at the gurdwara, as is the usual procedure in gurdwaras in India. Furthermore, it is also a question of necessity, since most Sikhs living in Finland reported in the interviews to be unable to go to the gurdwara during the week because of their busy work schedule and also owing to the distance between their home and the temple, which is often rather great in comparison to what they were used to in India. Most of them have to travel between 20 and 40 minutes in order to reach the gurdwara. Being able to go to the gurdwara is according to my findings a question of time for Sikhs living in Finland, and time seems to be more limited in the overseas context. As my informants explained to me, in India there was more time for socializing and for going to the gurdwara:

Charan (M):  … it is quite difficult, because I used to visit, at least I tried to visit the gurdwara each day there in India but it is difficult for me to go to the temple here everyday.
L:            Is it open here every day?

Charan (M):   Actually I have the key. But it is difficult for me ... here, because the journey is too far, it takes half an hour to go. So it is not possible to go every day.

The question of time is also one of the reasons why people cannot make it to the gurdwara on Sundays. As earlier and briefly mentioned, most of the Sikhs living in Finland work in pubs, restaurants or nightclubs. The disadvantages of this kind of work are long working hours, especially Saturday nights, and also working Sundays in restaurants during the daytime. For this reason, many Sikhs are either too tired to come to the gurdwara on Sundays or they have to work on that day. Trying to respond to this situation, the Sikh temple in Sörnäinen only starts its service around 2 pm so that those who have to work late Saturday night can get more sleep, as my informants explained. My additional fieldwork in Yuba City (California) suggests that this is a rather unique arrangement in the Finnish case, as all regular Sunday services in the four gurdwaras of Yuba City started in the morning, around 10 am.

It can be concluded from these accounts that Sikhs living in Finland partly adapted their organizational structure of the gurdwara to the specific challenges caused by their particular diasporic circumstances; moreover, within this process, they had to negotiate their collective Sikh identity as displayed in the Finnish public. In addition, Sikh worshippers' ability and readiness to adapt on an organizational level to the regulations of their host country, prove that certain aspects of religious traditions are far from being fixed, but in the hands of its practitioners are flexible and easily adjusted to extraordinary circumstances in order to survive (see also Warner and Wittner 1998, p. 20).

## Maintaining identity: the significance of food

The gurdwara in Sörnäinen consists of a small entrance hall, a kitchen and a prayer hall, which is the biggest room of the building. There is a carpeted floor covered by white sheets, where people sit on the floor during the ceremony. The *Sri Guru Granth Sahib* (Holy Scripture, treated as a living guru) is at the back of the room, resting on a platform, above which a canopy is hung. It is put to rest in a wardrobe on the wall behind it. Devotees leave their offerings in a box called *golak* in front of the Sri Guru Granth Sahib. On one side of the Holy Scripture is the place where people perform the *kirtan* (devotional music) and hold speeches. On the other side of the Guru Granth Sahib, is a little shelf for the *kara prashad*. The *prashad* is a sweet food, which is usually prepared by one of the Sikh women on Sunday mornings before the function starts. Once it is ready, it is brought in a kettle covered with a clean cloth into the prayer hall. When the ceremony comes to an end, some of the children go to get some napkins from the nearby kitchen and distribute them to the adults, so that people can clean their hands after having eaten the *prashad*. At the same time two people, usually men around thirty, get up to serve the *prashad* to the congregation sitting on the floor. But before it can be served, the *kirpan* (ceremonial sword) has to be plunged into the food to strengthen it symbolically. After that, everyone gets their share. The *prashad* is a sacred food, which is considered to be blessed by the guru and thus it should not be refused by anyone.

After the ceremony in the prayer hall is over, people sit down in the kitchen to receive a free meal, called *langar*. During this meal, all, regardless of their gender, caste, class or age, are according to the teaching of Sikhism invited to sit down next to one another on the floor. Thus, the principle of equality, which is an essential part of the Guru's teachings, is put into action.

Durkheim (1961) makes the following observation in his classic work, *The Elementary Forms of the Religious Life*, about meals taken in common:

> Now in a multitude of societies, meals taken in common are believed to create a bond of artificial kinship between those who assist in them. In fact, relatives are people who are naturally made of the same flesh and blood. But food is constantly remaking the substance of the organism. So a common food may produce the same effects as a common origin. (Durkheim 1961, p. 378)

In this quotation, Durkheim refers particularly to the significance of consuming *sacred* food like the *prashad* offered in a gurdwara. Consuming sacred food can be considered to create a bond between the worshipper and the divine (Durkheim 1961, p. 378). However, the free meal offered at the temple is also of great significance as it creates a relationship between the worshippers. Such relationships can produce a feeling of unity, which gains a special significance in the diasporic context as the following statement of Charanjeet, who stayed in Finland as an expatriate, seems to suggest:

L:            What significance, would you say, has the food and the Prashad you eat in the gurdwara here IN FINLAND for you? …

Charanjeet (M): The significance of having the *Prashad* and the food in the gurdwara remains the same as it was in India. Nothing changes one bit. Though over a period of time I have realized it brings a feeling of unity in the local community and helps socializing.

Occasionally, there are also a few non-Sikhs at the gurdwara, who take part in this meal. In such a situation, the offered food becomes a tool for displaying hospitality (Barthes 1997, p. 21). Barthes considers food to constitute 'a body of images' (1997, p. 21). Thus, we can ask what are the images conveyed by *prashad* and *langar* served in the gurdwara. For Sikh immigrants of the first generation, both *langar* and *prashad* could be interpreted as a concrete reminder of their past. The images connected to food stimulate a memory that helps to shorten the mental distance felt to the home they left in Punjab.

That food is a 'rich cultural symbol' (see Nesbitt 2000, p. 54), which also plays an important role in communicating and informing Sikh children about their parents' cultural background, becomes evident in the following quote made by one informant, who was born in Finland:

Jasnam (F):     … and food, I think food is a very important point of reference for the culture, because you eat it, then you know 'Aha, that it is Indian' that helps a lot.

Consequently, it could be suggested that consuming the sacred *prashad* as well as the traditional Punjabi food served as *langar* at the temple help to maintain and transmit a sense of religious as well as cultural identity among Sikh immigrants and their offspring. Moreover, this example supports the idea that the gurdwara is not only a place to strengthen religious identities but also cultural[5] identities. This argument is further strengthened by the fact that occasionally there are some Indian Hindus who visit the gurdwara. When asked, why she and her husband had decided to visit the gurdwara instead of the Hindu temple that existed in Helsinki, a Hindu woman explained that her husband was originally from Punjab and that:

> The husband had been in Finland for two years now and he had the wish to meet some people he would feel connected to. But when they went to the Hindu temple in Helsinki, there were only South Indians, and they felt that they did not belong to them. Therefore they decided to come to the Sikh temple, where they knew they would meet people from Punjab whom they would feel connected to. Here, she said, they would feel to be around their kind of people. (Field diary, 23 March 2008)

In other words, the gurdwara also provides a space in which people with other religious affiliations can strengthen their ethnic and cultural identities.

As the kitchen and the adjunct hall are too small to accommodate all the diners, the women and children usually eat first followed by the men. Again, the younger men of the community usually serve the food to the people seated on the floor, thus showing respect towards the women and the elder men. The food in the gurdwara is either prepared by a restaurant ordered from by the temple, or by one of the Sikh families, often with the help of some of their relatives or friends. In her study on Sikh children in Coventry, Nesbitt (2000) notes that such activities are very much respected in the Sikh community as they are considered to be *seva*, a voluntary service that the Gurus supported (p. 81). Similar to the shared meal, it could be suggested that preparing the weekly *langar* strengthens the bond between those who prepare the food together. When a family takes over the duty of preparing the weekly *langar*, they often do so in order to mark important events, such as birthdays, for example. After the meal, women as well as men often sit apart in the same sex group, where they socialize and discuss various matters. As Mahaan (M) says, 'We talk about everything, we talk about everything'.

In addition, it can be argued that food and its familiar taste as well as smell provoke certain memories that help to create a familiar atmosphere in the temple. Together with sounds, artifacts and activities, food contributes to an atmosphere in gurdwaras that is Punjabi in its flavor (see also Mann 2000, p. 268) thus turning them into meaningful places to maintain cultural identity. Especially for the first generation of Sikhs living in Finland, the gurdwara provides an important opportunity to bridge the mental distance felt between their old and their new homeland by offering them a place where they feel at home:

> Charan (M): ... because if you are somewhere abroad, you are fed up once, if not daily, with these things, just to keep on listening to alien sounds from the everyday, so once you are in the gurdwara, now, what you hear you can understand ... you can understand what they are talking, what these noises are all about and that is where you feel like home.

In other words, the gurdwara is for many Sikhs of the first generation a temporary escape from the Finnish culture into a familiar cultural and religious environment. This view is supported by Ebaugh and Chavetz (2000) who write 'Immigrant congregations are attractive to their members precisely because they reproduce the language and custom of the old country and thus create a comfort zone for their uprooted congregants' (p. 36). Further, the gurdwara is one of the few places in Finland where Sikh immigrants form a majority and can act as cultural insiders.

To summarize, it can be said that foodways at the gurdwara create a feeling of belonging and home among immigrants. By means of preparing, sharing and consuming the food served at the temple, Sikhs are able to maintain and transmit their religious, cultural and ethnic identities.

## Transmitting identity

As Warner points out in the introduction to his book, *Gatherings in the Diaspora: Religious Communities and the new Immigration*, a 'prime motivation for immigrants to found religious organizations is to pass on their heritage to their children' (1998, p. 25; see also Rayaprol 1997, p. 143). This is a statement also affirmed by many of my first generation informants:

| L: | And what was the motivation behind the idea that you wanted to have a gurdwara? |
|---|---|
| Mahaan (M): | The thing is, look, we all have children ..., that they would learn where they are from and our religion and all that, that they would not forget it. |

For the same reason, the key individuals running the gurdwara in Sörnäinen decided a couple of years ago to annually arrange a summer camp for the children at the temple. Bhai Ranjodh Singh, a teacher from Punjab who tours different diasporic Sikh communities around the world during the summer months, is invited each year to run this summer camp. The camp takes place at the gurdwara, and the event usually lasts one week in total. As Ranjodh Singh stated in an interview conducted with him, he usually starts his tour in the beginning of June and returns to Punjab in the end of August. On his tour, he also visits other Sikh communities in: Portugal, Germany, Sweden, Italy, Belgium, Greece and Australia, thus working truly transnationally. The visits from the Indian clergy are in so far significant that the daily classes arranged during this camp provide, in addition to home, a setting in which Sikh youth are encouraged to learn more about Sikhism. In the classes I attended during his visit in 2009, he told the 13 children among others about the origins of Sikhism, their Gurus, and showed them their Holy book. He also encouraged them to learn a hymn, called *shabad*, which they then had to recite in front of the congregation (see Figure 1).

Through presenting the *shabads* in front of the congregation, young Sikhs take on an active role in the Sikh community, and learn to be part of their parents' religion. This experience one could argue, provides them with a foundation on which they have the possibility to shape and negotiate their religious identities as Sikhs.

In addition, the summer camp offers Sikh youth living in Finland the unique opportunity to become instructed in spoken as well as *written* Punjabi (see Figure 2), of which the latter is neither taught in Finnish schools[6] nor at home. Being able to read Punjabi is important, as it would allow Sikh youth to acquire knowledge about their religious and cultural background by reading literature written in Punjabi. Sikh youth usually hear and learn *spoken* Punjabi in contexts in which Sikhs form a majority. This might be at home or at the gurdwara, for instance. Similar to Hall's (2002) study on Sikh youth growing up in the UK, for Sikh youth in Finland, Punjabi is also a language of intimacy which they use to communicate with their parents and other relatives. The importance of Punjabi becomes clear in the following excerpt taken from an interview conducted with a girl, who had been living in Finland her entire life:

| L: | What language do you speak at home? |
|---|---|
| Gurmeet (F): | Punjabi usually, all in the family talk Punjabi but the kids speak amongst each other Finnish that makes going to school easier but with the parents we talk Punjabi. ... |

Figure 1. Sikh children reciting a shabad in front of the congregation. Source: Author, 2009.

L:                    And what would you say is your mother tongue?[7]
Gurmeet (F):    I would say that *Punjabi* is my mother tongue, I do not consider Finnish
                     as my mother tongue, I can speak it well but I do not know, but I consider
                     Punjabi as my mother tongue, I speak it most of my time.

Being able to speak Punjabi may enhance among Sikh youth a sense of belonging to their parents' culture, since a common language 'defines the limits of community ... and leads to bounded ... ethnic solidarities', as Portes and Rumbaut (2001, p. 113) point out. Consequently, learning Punjabi at the gurdwara and at home has a great influence on the process through which Sikh offspring shape their ethnic and cultural identities.

However, besides reflecting a strong attachment to her parents' language, the informant's answer also reveals another interesting fact common to Sikh immigrants' offspring growing up in Finland. When talking to adult Sikhs such as their parents, they speak Punjabi, but within their peer group, which includes their siblings and friends, they usually prefer to speak Finnish. Thus, they are continuously switching between the languages and cultures surrounding them. Occasionally, they also engage in acts of 'translation' (Hall 1992), as reflected in the language use of one little boy I met at the gurdwara. Whenever he addressed his older sister, he would start the sentence by using the Finnish words for 'big sister'. This expression used in a conversation between a brother and a sister sounds strange to Finnish ears. However, within

Figure 2. Children learning the Punjabi alphabet in the Sikh temple. Source: Author, 2008.

the Indian cultural context, 'big sister', which is a translation of *didi* or *didiji*, is a term used to address respectfully a female person who is older than oneself, but not old enough to be called an *aunti* (=aunt) yet. By translating this expression, which is meaningful with respect to his Indian cultural background, into the Finnish language, the little boy faced the challenge of negotiating between the various cultural influences and 'cultural languages' in his life (Hall 1992; see also Hall 2002, p. 5).

But the actual strength of the gurdwara lies in its ability to make the abstract idea of religion and culture comprehensible[8] for young Sikhs with the help of activities and artifacts that they experience and see in this building. As one Sikh mother explained when asked about the challenge of educating her children in Finland: children learn with their 'eyes', they understand what they *see*, not what someone *tells* them. When visiting the gurdwara, children see and experience their parents' religion as well as culture with all their senses: by smelling and eating the *prashad*, by listening to the sounds produced by the *kirtan* players, by seeing the Holy Book and by touching the floor when bowing in front of it. As Hall states, 'The temple is a world filled with the sounds, sights, and scents of their parent's homeland' (2002, p. 173). Thus, it can be said that the gurdwara contributes to the process of shaping Sikh offspring's cultural as well as religious identities in Finland by reproducing a body of images representing their parents' religious as well as cultural heritage.[9]

## Concluding remarks

In the findings above, it has been argued that the gurdwara is for many Sikh immigrants living in Finland much more than only a place to worship. The religious institution offers them a place where they can find fellowship and a cultural environment that is similar to the home they had in Punjab.

While this is true for a great part of Sikhs living in Finland, it is important to note that there are also many Sikhs in Finland who avoid going to the gurdwara, mostly because of gossip and internal power struggles. Thus, it can be stated that for all Sikhs living in Finland the gurdwara is not a meaningful place to maintain and shape their identities. Moreover, not all Sikh parents turn to the gurdwara in search for what Foley and Hoge (2007) call 'cultural continuity and instruction for their young' (p. 196). However, as the findings presented in this article suggest, the gurdwara can be considered along with home as a 'primary site of transmission of religion and culture' (Hall 2002, p. 173) for those Sikhs living in Finland who choose to go to the gurdwara. The sum of artifacts and activities that are present at the gurdwara transform it into what Jacobsen and Kumar call a 'centre of religion and culture' (2004, p. xiii), and it is significantly involved in the process of maintaining and transmitting cultural, ethnic and religious identities.

Considering the future of the Sikh religious sites in Finland, it can be reported that the Sikh community in Finland has already bought an estate, and currently they are trying to save money in order to build the first purpose-built gurdwara in Finland. This chronology of developments of first renting a place once a week/month, then buying a building and converting it to their needs, and then building a temple tailored for their own purposes, seems to also be typical for Sikh immigrant communities in other countries (see for example, Mann 2000, Singh and Tatla 2006, Tatla 1999, as well as my additional fieldwork findings in California). Moreover, these phases also appear to be characteristic of the development of other immigrants' religious communities as studies like Vertovec's (2000) and Jacobsen's (2006) seem to suggest.

The simplified formula underlying this typical development within overseas Sikh communities, which in some cases seems to also apply to other immigrant worship communities, can be written as follows: the longer the migration history of an immigrant community and the bigger it is, the larger its financial resources and the better equipped the place of worship. As other studies suggest (e.g. Kalsi 1992, Ballard 2000, O'Connell 2000, Singh and Tatla 2006, Foley and Hoge 2007, as well as my additional fieldwork in Yuba City), it could be further argued that within Sikh diasporic groups it is rather typical that once the community has grown significantly in size, it is most likely to split as a result of divergent points of view. As I write this, I can report that my recently conducted fieldwork during summer 2009 revealed that some of the Sikhs in Finland have formed a group with the intention of setting up their own separate worship gatherings.

**Notes**

1. This information is based on a report of the Finnish Immigration Service, available at: www.migri.fi/netcomm/content.asp?path=8,2709,2740,2485,2739&article=3388&index= _&page=1 (accessed on 11 February 2009).
2. Finnish Immigration Service: www.migri.fi/netcomm/content.asp?path=8,2709,2717 (accessed on 1 April 2009).
3. Statistics Finland, see http://www.stat.fi (accessed on 1 April 2009).
4. The term 'community' refers throughout the text to the community constituted by those Sikhs actually visiting the gurdwara. See Baumann (1996) for a critical discussion on the term 'community'.
5. Min (2006) makes the same observation in his study on Hindu temples.

6. Hindi or Punjabi classes can be organized at Finnish schools provided that there are at least five students in one group, which seems to be rarely the case.
7. Most of the Sikh youth I talked to have to attend Finnish as *second* mother tongue classes. Even if their Finnish is good enough and the teacher allows them to take part in Finnish as the *first* mother tongue classes, they get a note in their school-leaving certificate indicating that Finnish is actually – according to the Finnish education system's classification – their second mother tongue.
8. In her case study of Hindu women in Pittsburgh, Rayaprol (1997) makes a similar observation when she writes 'Meeting as families in the temple helps parents concretize abstractions about Hinduism and Indian culture that they find difficult to explain to their children' (p. 67).
9. Chong (1998) had a similar finding in her study on Second Generation Korean Americans, and Min (2006) in his study on Indian Hindu immigrants in the USA.

## Notes on contributor

Laura Hirvi is a doctoral student at the Department of History and Ethnology at the University of Jyväskylä, Finland. Currently, she is a Fulbright visiting student at the Center for Sikh and Punjab Studies at UC Santa Barbara. Hirvi is working on her dissertation in which she focuses on the manner in which Sikh immigrants in Finland and in California negotiate their identities. She is the book review editor of the *Finnish Journal of Ethnicity and Migration*.

## References

Ballard, R., 2000. The growth and changing character of the Sikh presence in Britain. *In*: H. Coward, J.R. Hinnells and R.B. Williams, eds. *The South Asian religious diaspora in Britain, Canada, and the United States.* Albany: State University of New York Press, 127–144.

Barthes, R., 1997. Toward a psychosociology of contemporary food consumption. *In*: C. Counihan and P.V. Esterik, eds. *Food and culture: a reader.* London: Routledge, 20–27.

Baumann, G., 1996. *Contesting culture: discourse of identity in multi-ethnic London.* New York: Cambridge University Press.

Chong, K.H., 1998. What it means to be Christian: the role of religion in the construction of ethnic identity and boundary among second-generation Korean Americans. *Sociology of Religion,* 59 (3), 259–286.

Durkheim, E., 1961. *The elementary forms of the religious life.* New York: Collier Books.

Ebaugh, H.R. and Chafetz, J.S., 2000. *Religion and the new immigrants: continuities and adaptations in immigrant congregations.* New York: AltaMira Press.

Eriksen, T.H., 2002. *Ethnicity and nationalism,* 2nd ed. London: Pluto Press.

Foley, M.W. and Hoge, D.R., 2007. *Religion and the new immigrants: how faith communities form our newest citizens.* New York: Oxford University Press.

Hall, K.D., 2002. *Lives in translations: Sikh youth as British citizens.* Philadelphia: University of Pennsylvania Press.

Hall, S., 1992. The question of cultural identity. *In:* S. Hall, D. Held and T. McGrew, eds. *Modernity and its future: understanding modern societies – an introduction.* Cambridge: Polity Press, 273–316.

Hall, S., 2002. *Identiteetti.* Tampere: Vastapaino.

Jacobsen, K.A., 2006. Hindu processions, diaspora and religious pluralism. *In*: P.P. Kumar, ed. *Religious pluralism in the diaspora.* Leiden: Brill, 163–173

Jacobsen, K.A. and Kumar, P.P., eds, 2004. *South Asians in the diaspora: histories and religious traditions.* Leiden: Brill.

Kalsi, S.S., 1992. *The evolution of a Sikh community in Britain: religion and social change among the Sikh of Leeds and Bradford.* Department of Theology and Religious Studies: University of Leeds.

Mann, G.S., 2000. Sikhism in the United States. *In*: H. Coward, J.R. Hinnells and R.B. Williams, eds. *The South Asian religious diaspora in Britain, Canada, and the United States.* New York: State University of New York Press, 259–276.

Martikainen, T., 2004. *Immigrant religions in local society.* Pargas, Finland: Åbo Akademi University Press.

Min, P.G., 2006. Religion and the maintenance of ethnicity among immigrants: a comparison of Indian Hindus and Korean Protestants. *In*: K. I. Leonard, A. Stepick, M.A. Vasquez and J. Holdaway, eds. *Immigrant faiths: transforming religious life in America.* New York: Alta Mira Press, 99–122.

Nesbitt, E., 2000. *The religious lives of Sikh children: a Coventry based study.* Community Religions Project. Department of Theology and Religious Studies: University of Leeds.

O'Connell, J.T., 2000. Sikh religious–ethnic experience Canada. *In*: H. Coward, J.R. Hinnells, and R.B. Williams, 2000. *The South Asian religious diaspora in Britain, Canada, and the United States.* Albany: State University of New York Press, 191–209.

Peach, C. and Gale, R., 2003. Muslims, Hindus, and Sikhs in the new religious landscape of England. *Geographical Review,* 93 (4), 469–490.

Portes, A. and Rumbaut, R.G., 2001. *Legacies: the story of the immigrant second generation.* Berkeley: University of California Press.

Rayaprol, A., 1997. Negotiating identities: women in the Indian Diaspora. New Delhi: Oxford University Press.

Singh, G. and Tatla, D.S., 2006. *Sikhs in Britain: the making of a community.* London: Zed.

Tatla, D.S., 1999. *Sikh diaspora: the search for a statehood.* Seattle: University of Washington Press.

Vertovec, S., 2000. *The Hindu diaspora: comparative patterns.* London: Routledge.

Warner, R.S., 1998. Introduction – immigration and religious communities in the United States. *In:* R.S. Warner and J.G. Wittner, eds. *Gatherings in the diaspora: religious communities and the new immigration.* Philadelphia: Temple University Press, 3–34.

Warner, R.S. and Wittner, J.G., eds, 1998. *Gatherings in diaspora: religious communities and the new immigrant.* Philadelphia: Temple University Press.

# Communal networks and gender: placing identities among South Asians in Kenya

Pascale Herzig

*Department of Anthropology, University of Fribourg, Switzerland*

The analysis of the intra-ethnic relations of South Asians in Kenya has revealed that migration interlinked with networking form a key to successful social mobility. The caste system, which in South Asia is not only persistent in Hinduism but has also at least partly survived in Sikhism, Islam, and Christianity, appears in Kenya only in so-called communities. These communities are based on religion, language or place of origin and further divisions such as caste (*jati*), and they maintain their own community centres or places of worship. The 'established' Asians have developed a specific East African identity and they tend to dissociate themselves from recent South Asian immigrants. The creation of communities has assisted the migrants in feeling more at home – or in place – in their new environment. The aim of this paper is to illustrate and analyse communal networks of Kenyan Asians, by taking intra-communal divisions into account.

## Destination Kenya

There is a substantial number of people with South Asian origin living in Kenya. They belong to an urban, very heterogeneous and relatively wealthy minority (Herzig 2006). Most of the so-called Kenyan Asians originate from Gujarat and Punjab (India and Pakistan), a few come from the former Portuguese colony of Goa (Salvadori 1989). More recent migration attracted people from other places in India, Pakistan and Bangladesh. Before the division of British India they were referred to as Indians or *Wahindi* in Kiswahili. After 1947 the term *Asian* was commonly used in English (Nagar 1998), although the more precise specification would be *South Asian*. The category *Asian* is mainly an ascription used by the Europeans and by the Africans; the Asians themselves rather identify with their community. Nonetheless, today the South Asians in Kenya prefer the terms *Kenyan Asians* or *Kenyans of South Asian origin* (cf. Herzig 2006).

There have been migratory movements from the Indian subcontinent to East Africa for a long time, however, it was not before the second half of the nineteenth century that these movements intensified as a consequence of British imperialism (Gregory 1971). The Asians were conscripted as indentured labourers by the British in order to build the railway-line from the East-African coast to Lake Victoria (1896–1902). After the completion of the Uganda Railway, most indentured workers returned to British India (Ghai and Ghai 1971). Independent migratory activities set in soon as well. People started to migrate from India to East Africa on their own initiative and expenses, attracted to the prosperous colony by a host of job- and business-opportunities (Twaddle 1990, Kiem 1993). Apart from setting up their own businesses, many Asians served as teachers, medical personnel, bank-staff or worked for the administration of the colony, the police and the army. This second phase of migration, resulted in a mass migration, East Africa became 'the America of the Hindu' (Mangat 1969, p. 63). Asian men and women in Kenya do not share the same history: patterns of migration vary according to gender and other differences (Seidenberg 1996, Nagar 1998).

Between 1911 and 1999 the total population of Kenya increased from 1.8 million to 28.7 million people. In Kenya the Africans always made up the great majority of approximately 98%. The Asian minority population demonstrated an enormous growth from 11,800 in 1911 to 176,000 in 1962, followed by the exodus after independence when almost 40,000 Asians left Kenya within seven years (Herzig 2006, p. 30). In 1989 (newer figures are not available to the public), approximately 90,000 Asians lived in Kenya (which is 0.42% of the total population), almost half of them in Nairobi (cf. Herzig 2006, p. 28).

Most of the Kenyan Asians had a rural background in India. As a result of the changing patterns of occupation and because it was forbidden for Asians to own farmland, Asians in Kenya settled in the townships and became increasingly urbanised. This concentration in towns, in turn, facilitated the development of community associations and services (Salvadori 1989), the so-called communities. In order to cope successfully with the host- and colonial society, the Asian minority from the very beginning acquired knowledge and developed communal networks. The majority of the Kenyan Asians share the experience of social (upward) mobility. Life in a foreign social environment obviously had a significant impact on the South Asian cultures in East Africa.

In general, the organisation of migrants in communities enables them to maintain a strong network and solidarity. These organisations contribute to economic, social, and cultural reproduction. Therefore, the aim of this paper is to explore the role of the communities, and why and how they change over time. Additionally, I will identify and analyse the differences within the communities as well as the processes of identity and place. The paper consists of the following four sections: after the introduction, some theoretical and methodological aspects relevant to the topic are illustrated. In the next part of the paper community and the boundaries within are outlined, followed by a section about communal networks and communal places. Finally some concluding remarks are presented.

## Theoretical approach

The theoretical perspective which is taken up in this paper is based on recent conceptualisations of diaspora (Safran 1991, Cohen 1997, Vertovec 1997, Anthias 1998a, Werbner 2002, Safran et al. 2008) as well as on boundary theory (Barth 1969), which has been extended by feminist scholars (Anthias and Yuval-Davis 1983, Nagar 1995, Pratt 1999, Denis 2001) to other differences. In addition, I promote to focus on the relation between identities and place (cf. Silvey and Lawson 1999, Ehrkamp 2005).

### The concept of diaspora

In the 1990s, the concept of diaspora emerged as a major theme in the human sciences (Lie 2001). The concept offers an alternative way of thinking about transnational migration and ethnic relations in contrast to those that rely on 'race' and 'ethnicity' (Anthias 1998a, Wahlbeck 2002). In seeking a common theory for the diverse phenomena of human migrations, analysts have suggested that 'diaspora' captures the most common experiences of displacement associated with migration: homelessness, painful memories, and a wish to return. 'Some writers are reluctant to extend the term "diaspora" to migrant groups, insisting that a diaspora condition represents a unique and almost mythical experience of the Jewish exile' (Tatla 1999, p. 3). Others are less reluctant. Recently any social group who has also maintained strong collective identities define themselves as a diaspora, though they have never been active agents of colonisation nor passive victims of persecution (Cohen 1997, Vertovec 1997). Floya Anthias (1998a, p. 557) therefore argued that the term 'now constitutes kind of mantra, being used to describe the processes of settlement and adaptation relating to a large range of transnational migration movements'. However, the current over-use and under-theorisation of the notion diaspora among academics, transnational intellectuals and community leaders alike, threatens the term's descriptive usefulness (Cohen 1997, Vertovec 1997).

There are several works which intend to illuminate the diaspora discourse. Steven Vertovec (1997) wrote an essay on the different meanings of 'diaspora' and stated that recent writing on the subject conveys at least three discernible meanings of the concept. These are (1) diaspora as a social form, (2) diaspora as a type of social consciousness and (3) diaspora as a mode of cultural production. Diaspora as a social form is characterised by a 'triadic relationship' (Sheffer 1986) between a globally dispersed yet collectively self-identified ethnic group, the host countries and the country of origin (Vertovec 1999). The Asian diaspora in Kenya reflects most aspects as defined by Safran (1991). However, the Kenyan Asians lack a 'myth of return', at least within the long established families. The second meaning of diaspora – as a type of social consciousness – according to Vertovec (1997) has been developed relatively recently and puts greater emphasis on describing a variety of experiences, a state of mind and a sense of identity. Diaspora consciousness is a particular kind of awareness said to be generated among contemporary transnational communities. According to Anthias (1998a, p. 565) this conceptualisation represents diaspora in a post-modern understanding, which denotes 'a condition rather than being descriptive of a group'. The third meaning of diaspora – as a mode of cultural production – according to Vertovec (1997) is usually conveyed in discussions of globalisation. In this sense globalisation is examined in its guise as the world-wide flow of cultural objects, images and meanings resulting in various processes of creolisation, back-and-forth transferences, mutual influences, new contestations, negotiations and constant transformations. In this way diaspora is described as involving the production and reproduction of transnational social and cultural phenomena (cf. Appadurai 1991, Glick Schiller *et al.* 1992).

### *Diaspora as a field of intersectionality*

An additional way of dealing with diaspora is conceptualising it as a 'field of intersectionality' (argued mainly by Anthias (1998a) and Brah (1996)). Anthias (1998a) argues that unless attention is paid to difference and the material is presented to show that these differences are transcended by commonalities of one sort or another and in certain contexts, the idea of a community even as 'imagined community' cannot be sustained. According to her, there 'appears to be a general failure to address class and gendered facets within the diaspora problematic' (Anthias 1998a, p. 570).

Increasingly, critics are seeking to understand the ways in which diaspora itself is gendered and the role sexuality plays in the diaspora identity (Mirzoeff 2000). With regard to gender, the role of men and women in the process of accommodation and syncretism may be different. Women are key transmitters and reproducers of ethnic and national ideologies and central in the transmissions of cultural rules (Anthias and Yuval-Davis 1989). Therefore Anthias proposes that the issue of gendering the diaspora can be understood at two different levels:

> At the first level of analysis, it requires a consideration of the ways in which men and women of the diaspora are inserted into the social relations of the country of settlement, within their own self-defined 'diaspora communities' and within the transnational networks of the diaspora across national borders. ... The other level of analysis, regarding gendering the diaspora notion, relates to an exploration of how gendered relations are constitutive of the positionalities of the groups themselves, paying attention to class and other differences within the group and to different locations and trajectories. (Anthias 1998a, p. 572)

Anthias (1998a) asks for a diaspora notion that pays full attention to the centrality of gender on the one hand and to intersectionality on the other. In doing so 'it may be possible to see ethnicity, gender and class as cross-cutting and mutually *reinforcing* systems of domination and subordinations, particularly in terms of processes and relations of hierarchisation, unequal resource allocation and inferiorisation' (Anthias 1998a, p. 574, *original emphasis*).

The concept of diaspora enables us to analyse and understand social relations that encompass politics, economy and culture at the global level. It pays attention to the dynamic nature of ethnic bonds, and to the possibilities of selective and contextual cultural translations and negotiations. In contrast to Anthias (1998a) I understand gender as one boundary among others, which should not be understood as the apex of social differences. In my opinion, it is necessary to focus on boundary drawing processes in general, because the meaning of boundaries is context specific (Herzig 2006).

### Boundary theory and placing identities

Boundary theory was developed mainly in social anthropology with its main exponent Fredrik Barth (1969). By publishing the introduction to *Ethnic groups and boundaries*, Barth initiated the shift from a static to a flexible and interactional approach of ethnicity. Boundary theory puts the focus on the construction and maintenance of ethnic boundaries. Barth further emphasised that ethnic groups as a form of social organisation are based on ascription and self-ascription and gain their social relevance out of it. The main findings of this approach were that ethnic identities are not primordial but fluid and situated. In Barth's conceptualisation of ethnicity and boundary theory, one point can be criticised. Barth did not question why and how the fact of difference itself (as a result of boundary construction) becomes significant. In thinking about ethnicity Barth takes it for granted that difference matters. 'But difference does not always matter, nor do all differences matter' (Verdery 1994, p. 44). Difference does not always matter because the significance of differences depends on situations, e.g. the boundary 'ethnicity' is more relevant between ethnic groups than within. In addition not all differences do matter at all, such as differences without any social impact (Herzig and Richter 2004). For example, the size of the feet is not a basis for organising social relations. Nonetheless, everyday practices of boundary construction and maintenance result in intersecting memberships of different collectivities (Nagar 1998). The positioning of individuals or collectivities is based on self-ascription and ascription by others and is based on power relations (Anthias 1998b).

Migration implies not only spatial mobility but it has got social implications as well, and therefore it has an impact on identities. This means that the construction of identities is also connected with place. In general, many approaches dealing with difference do not refer to place explicitly. Rather, recent approaches of migration research have pointed to the deterritorialisation of transnational migrants. In contrast to these approaches I state that individuals appropriate space and therefore start identifying with certain places – they are connecting identity and place or in other words they are placing their identities (Herzig 2006). However, I assume that not only migrants but literally everybody transforms places of residence by 'placing their identities' (Ehrkamp 2005) that is, construct places of belonging and create local ties. 'Places, however,' Ehrkamp writes, 'are neither simply containers that serve as platforms for the construction of subject positions and identities; nor are places static. Being produced and reproduced in social processes and relations at different scales, place lies at the intersection of different spaces and moments in time' (2005, p. 349). Social processes and relations do not only create a place in a material sense, but they also produce meaning that people attach to places, evoking a sense of place (Massey 1993).

According to Jacobs and Fincher (1998) people's relationship with places help construct their identities like their relationship with class, gender and ethnic groupings. But the embeddedness to local lives shall not hide the complexity of spatial scales that flow through place. Local identities are always also constituted through non-local processes, or place-based identities are tied to the micro-politics of the home (Herzig 2006, Herzig and Thieme 2007). Identities and boundary maintenance are social constructions with consequences of inclusion and exclusion but 'identity will continue to be a matter of local (the place where people live), network (the ways people interact) and memory (the understandings which are sustained and re-created over time)' (Preston 1997, p. 167).

## Methodologies and methods

This paper is based on both fieldwork, which I carried out in Nairobi, and on an analysis of the existing literature, which includes primary sources as well as data from the scientific discourse. I spent in a total of seven months in Kenya (1997, 1998, 2000 and 2007) doing participant observation and collecting oral as well as written accounts of Asian women and men from different backgrounds about their lives, experiences, thoughts and feelings. It made it easier for many interviewees to talk with me, because I was considered as an outsider. The status as an outsider made people secure that I will not inform friends or relatives about the information they presented to me. From the female respondents I was considered also at least partly as an insider.

Since more than two thirds of all East African Asians live in Kenya and of these more than 50% live in Nairobi, I decided to carry out the fieldwork there. Several methods were used for collecting the empirical data in Nairobi. During my fieldwork I applied the following methods:

- Participant observation (1997, 1998, 2000, 2007);
- Semi-structured interviews (1997, 5 interviews; 1998, 55 interviews; 2000, 7 interviews);
- Questionnaire survey (2000): valid questionnaires, 400; returned but not valid, 10; missing system, 55; respond rate 86%;
- Personal communication (1997–2007).

The interviewees were selected according to the so-called snowball sampling. The participant observation and the semi-structured interviews, usually classified as qualitative, allow for a more subtle and detailed understanding of the present situation as we are also directly informed about views and motives of the Asians themselves. The questionnaire survey had the aim to develop some generalising data on the present situation of the Asian minority in Kenya. I decided to distribute the questionnaire in the three main shopping centres and in some other places where all Asians of all communities do their shopping. The reason why I chose the shopping centres and main Asian business streets was that there all Asian people mix freely regardless of their religion, language or community. Since these shopping centres are also places where people spend their leisure time such as in the cinemas or fitness centres, I distributed the questionnaires from morning till evening and seven days a week and through that tried to reach as many Asians as possible.

In Table 1 the frequencies of the key variables, gender and age group (cross-tabulated), are presented.

Regarding migratory generation the sample consists of 44 first-generation Asians (11%); 105 second-generation Asians (26%); 174 third-generation Asians (44%) and 76 fourth-generation Asians (19%). It is necessary to take into account the self-ascribed generation of the individuals. This means that, for example, the father of a respondent might be third generation and the mother is first. What holds for the respondent? In this case I applied a categorisation which is in accordance with the self-definition of the respondents. This is also why I do not agree with some authors who grouped the migratory generations according to their year of birth. An additional point against this static assumption is that migration has not stopped at a specific point, i.e. even today there are first-generation migrants arriving in Kenya. This means that all generations in all age groups can be found at the same time.

In Table 2 the proportion of the respondents in the survey 2000 as they ascribed themselves to a specific community is presented. Some very small communities were summarised as 'other Hindu' or 'other Muslim' communities.

Approximately 39% ascribe themselves to a Hindu community; approximately 20% are members of a Jain and 10% of a Sikh community, respectively. Twenty-one per cent of the respondents can be summarised as belonging to a Muslim community.

Table 1.   Variable gendered age group (survey 2000).

| Age group | Male | Female | Total |
|---|---|---|---|
| Young adults (14–25) | 30 (15.9%) | 79 (37.4%) | 109 (27.3%) |
| Middle-aged adults (26–49) | 117 (61.9%) | 112 (53.1%) | 229 (57.3%) |
| Elderly adults (50+) | 42 (22.2%) | 20 (9.5%) | 62 (15.5%) |
| Total | 189 (100%) | 211 (100%) | 400 (100%) |

Source: Author's research (survey 2000).

Table 2.    Variable communities (survey 2000).

| Community | Female | Male | Total |
|---|---|---|---|
| (Hindu) Patel | 29 (13.7%) | 26 (14.0%) | 55 (13.9%) |
| (Hindu) Brahmin | 17 (8.1%) | 13 (7.0%) | 30 (7.6%) |
| (Hindu) Lohana | 13 (6.2%) | 12 (6.5%) | 25 (6.3%) |
| Other Hindu communities | 19 (9.0%) | 25 (13.7%) | 44 (11.1%) |
| Jain | 51 (24.2%) | 30 (16.1%) | 81 (20.4%) |
| Sikh | 21 (10.0%) | 18 (9.7%) | 39 (9.8%) |
| Ismaili | 21 (10.0%) | 12 (6.5%) | 33 (8.3%) |
| Bohra | 8 (3.8%) | 8 (4.3%) | 16 (4.0%) |
| Punjabi Muslim | 8 (3.8%) | 8 (4.3%) | 16 (4.0%) |
| Other Muslim communities | 9 (4.3%) | 10 (5.4%) | 19 (4.8%) |
| Other | 4 (1.9%) | 2 (1.1%) | 6 (1.5%) |
| No community | 11 (5.2%) | 22 (11.8%) | 33 (8.3%) |
| Total | 211 (100%) | 186 (100%) | 397 (100%) |

Source: Author's research (survey 2000).

In addition the sample contains 2% 'other'. The category 'other' includes respondents from the Goan and Parsi communities. Some 8% state to be not a member of any community.

Boundary drawing and maintenance, as I have described in the theoretical concep-tualisation, does not only have implications for the research process in general but also for the analysis of the data in particular. Since the aim of the questionnaire survey was to arrive at a higher level of generalisation it was sufficient to analyse the data mainly with methods of descriptive statistics. In addition, many of the variables are in the nominal scale. The results are plotted in frequencies, cross-tabulation and scales, anal-ysed with the computer program SPSS. To receive statistically significant relations, the data was analysed with $\chi^2$-tests as well, and if necessary with Fisher's Exact test (significance level $\alpha = 5\%$). The analysis was made on the categories gendered age group, generation and community. To find out which boundaries play a significant role, additionally the data was analysed along other categories such as citizenship, person with/without children.

## Community in the Kenyan Asian diaspora

I don't know to which community I belong. My father was a Brahmin, my mother was a Kshatriya, both from Gujarat. Their families disowned them, that's the reason why they came to Kenya. I married a Punjabi Hindu, an Arya Samajist. I do not identify myself with any Community. If you asked my sons, they would say I'm a Kenyan – full stop! (Hindu woman, 52, interview 1998)

As I have outlined in the introduction, the Asian minority in Kenya is concentrated in the urban centres of the country. This concentration in the towns facilitated the devel-opment of community associations and services. Each major community established its own places of worship and its own schools. Community organisations help to develop and maintain the social networks which form the basis of economic, social, and cultural reproduction. In the diaspora, communal organisations are important sources where members maintain their social networks. The solidarity within the communities and the exchange of different forms of capital have been an important feature of the South Asian society in Kenya.

South Asians in Kenya are not a monolithic ethnic group, but they are differentiated by religion and region of origin – the so-called communities. The term 'community' refers to an organised social group, which is defined by religion (therefore by caste/*jati* or sect as well) and place of origin (Herzig 2006). While it is true that not all of the caste divisions in South Asia survived the journey across the Indian Ocean, linguistic and religious divisions were a persistent feature in the history of the Asian minority in East Africa. According to my interviewees (1998), the community is traditionally the primary frame of reference besides the family for the Kenyan Asians. In general, the Hindu communities are based on caste (*jati*), and Muslim communities are based on sect. A sense of community exists within these groups and not within the Asian minority as a whole. Only recently, with the rising level of education, the importance of communal networks has started to lose its significance. Major communities in Kenya are for instance: the Brahmins, the Patels, the Oshwals, the Ismailis or the Sikhs.

The communities serve the cultural and religious needs of their members and offer many economic advantages. They fulfil tasks typical for diasporas, namely fundraising, administration of and support for their social and cultural activities as well as their educational, religious, health and welfare organisations (Rothchild 1973, Voigt-Graf 1998). Communities are important group markers, which find their expression in communal places as well. Communal places provide the platform where people interact with each other and strengthen their communal networks in terms of social, cultural and economic reproduction. These communities provide places where migrants can feel 'in place' (cf. Cresswell 1996, Fredrich *et al.* 2007) or where migrants can maintain a feeling of home and belonging.

### Boundaries within

Broadly speaking, the key to 'free' migration was the ability to pay the ticket for the shipping (for this reason the term 'passenger migrant' emerged), which depends on the economic capital of the migrants' family and on the social network. Nonetheless, also lower class/caste Asians came to East Africa, mainly as domestic servants for upper class Asians during colonial times (Nagar 1998). The reason for leaving British India was to make a better life in East Africa, and many of them succeeded. In the Kenyan society as a whole the Asians are mainly members of the middle and upper classes.

> The Indians came here and were determined to make a good life. They understood this was a land of opportunity. We may have got a few, who went into farming but most of them were traders and a few professionals who came here to work and make a living and come up in life. They had come in with working in mind and succeeded. (Hindu man, 35, interview 1998)

Since for a long time the relations between Africans and Asians were limited to business relations (i.e. trader and customer), the myth of the *dukawallah* (shopkeeper) persisted. Internal fragmentation concerning communal organisation and occupation

Table 3. Occupations by ethnic group in 1968.

|  | African | Asian | European |
|---|---|---|---|
| Professionals, directors, managers | 2.4% | 28.8% | 60.7% |
| Skilled and semi-skilled | 42.6% | 69.9% | 38.3% |
| Unskilled labourers | 55.0% | 1.3% | 1.0% |
| Total | 100% | 100% | 100% |

Source: Tandon and Raphael (1978: 9).

were ignored, and the negative stereotype was assigned to all Asians in East Africa. The stereotype of the Asian *dukawallah* is undercut when the Asian minority is identified in terms of occupational categories (Table 3).

A number of observations can be made on the basis of Table 3. First, the figures are for 1968, which is five years after Kenya's independence (Tandon and Raphael 1978). The pre-independence situation was much worse for Africans, since only Africanisation has brought some Africans into leading positions. Second, the figures only relate to the modern sector of the economy and therefore leave out Africans working in the peasant subsistence sectors of the economy (Tandon and Raphael 1978). Therefore, if the whole workforce was taken into account, the proportions would be even more unequal. In addition, Table 3 shows that the majority of the Kenyan Asians were in occupations that do not earn extremely high salaries (but higher than the African majority).

The stereotype of the rich Asian entrepreneur is nourished by the economic success of some Asian business families. After the initial phase in East Africa, the Asian economic role steadily expanded; and after 1945, the Asian minority definitely turned into the richest group in East Africa. In urban areas, more than 75% of all buildings and real estate, and about an equal proportion of investments belonged to the Asians (Bharati 1964). The situation has not changed recently: 'A survey of 100 large-scale manufacturing firms in 1990, established that 75 percent was owned by Kenyan Indians. They also owned 86 percent of the firms valued over Ksh. 100 million' (Himbara 1994, quoted by Ranja 2003, p. 6). As I have set out in the introduction, in 1989, the Asian population contributed 0.42% to the total Kenyan population. Because of this, it is not surprising that the Asians' wealth is regarded with repugnance. However, there are only a few families who are extremely rich; the majority of the Asians can make a more or less comfortable living in Kenya (Herzig 2006). Consequently, the economic boundary not only divides African and Asians in the Kenyan society but also the Asians themselves. Stereotyping the Asians as an entity by the Africans (or the rich Asians by the poorer Asians) helps to understand the large disparities and injustice regarding income and wealth in Kenya. However, since independence the former correlating social boundaries of race and wealth increasingly drift apart and create new collectivities which are not based on the old colonial order anymore (Herzig 2006, p. 130).

On average, the level of education is considerably high among Kenyan Asians: 65% have attained a tertiary degree, 32% left school after secondary education and 3% have attended only primary education (survey 2000). The reasons for leaving school after primary or secondary education are mainly marriage (for young women), and joining the family business (for young men) (interviews 2000). In general, women are more likely to be educated at colleges, while men head for university degrees. Regarding

103

generation, the majority of first-generation Asians have attained a tertiary degree. This is also rooted in the fact that some of the recent immigrants are more educated than the immigrants at the beginning of the century. Second-generation Asians are less educated on average, while in the third and the fourth generation the proportion of tertiary education increases again. Nevertheless, the number of persons who finish their education after primary or after secondary school has decreased over the generations (survey 2000).

The Asian diaspora is heterogeneous as a whole, similarly are the communities. Within the communities there are hierarchies as well:

> If you talk about class, those Asians who are very classy people, they don't want to know people like us. They look at us like we are still down. ... I have been to England, I have been to India, they don't feel that way, only in Nairobi those people who are very rich they think that they have got very high class. They don't want to know people like us; they want to stay separate from us. (Sikh woman, 45, interview 1998)

The recognition of these hierarchies also depends on the social status of the individual or the family, and therefore they are not visible for everybody to the same extent.

> But when we get together in the community we don't look at it that this one is poor or that one is rich, ... . Everybody is equal. (Hindu woman, 31, interview 1998)

In general, the poor people constitute only a small part of the Kenyan Asians and frequently they are recently migrated first-generation Asians, the so-called 'rockets'. Most of the 'established' Kenyan Asians, in comparison, have struggled and worked hard for generations and have managed to achieve middle or upper class status (Herzig 2006).

In East Africa, the caste system was only reproduced concerning endogamy and worship. In addition, the other religions have reintroduced some elements of the Hindu caste system.

> Even in the older days we've never had any 'outcastes' as such! 'Untouchables' and all ... we've never had them here. Probably [it is] because the 'untouchables' never made it to this country. And for a lot of people then, who took birth here like somebody like me, never knew what 'untouchables' are, never understood that concept of 'untouchables'. So even if there were any here now, I'm sure they are all well to do, and nobody would notice. (Hindu man, 35, interview 1998)

According to Warah (1998, p. 49), the caste system 'is so ingrained in the psyche of the average Indian that even those religions which reject the notion of caste, such as Sikhism, have adopted a kind of caste system of their own'. Therefore the boundary of caste does not only affect Hindus. However, among more educated and cosmopolitan people the direct connection of community and caste is withheld more likely: they don't want to give the impression of being backward. Though, caste orientation is presented more openly by less educated individuals. The interviewees were unanimous in the question of outcastes (interviews 1998; see quotation above). The same interviewee adds about the rules of interaction:

> We have no water restrictions here, in fact the tradition followed here many years ago and even now, is the first thing they do when you go to anybody's place is, they offer water. It doesn't matter which house you're in or which caste you belong to and water would be offered straight away. And this is all over and since the beginning. ... A lot of

those [Indian] traditions never came here; they never made it to this country, which is a nice thing! It stopped a lot of traditions which we never understood. (Hindu man, 35, interview 1998)

Ritual purity and pollution were the reason why Hindu traders were discouraged to settle permanently in Zanzibar. However, in present-day Kenya purity and pollution are not a topic anymore (cf. Herzig 2006). However, as long as endogamy is performed along community lines, caste will not disappear totally.


## Communal networks

The community-based networks serve as one of the central elements for the success of South Asian communities not only in Kenya but world-wide. The aim of this section is to investigate the recent changes of the social networks of Kenyan Asians. The fundamental role of networks is to significantly reduce the risks associated with migration (Hugo 1996, Thieme 2006). By being attached to a strong and tightly integrated diaspora, family- and community-based economic transactions are made easier and safer (Cohen 1997).

> Drawing on personal, family, kin, friendship, community and ethnic links, networks provide potential migrants with information about destinations, contacts with gatekeepers, and sometimes funds for travel and brokers' charges. They may provide migrants with support en route. In destination countries, they may provide help with accommodation and finding employment. (Van Hear 1998, p. 257)

Provided that the migrants sojourn in the country of destination, it is necessary to maintain the networks with their countries of origin. According to Clarke *et al.* (1990, p. 18) the relative affluence of the Asian minority in East Africa allowed the members 'to maintain extensive ties with South Asia: marriage arrangements, kinship networks, property, and religious affiliations keep many migrants well-linked to the sub-continent, especially as a large number are still first-generation migrants'.

As soon as the communities were established in Kenya, the strong relation with South Asia was not as essential anymore. However, according to Mangat (1969), already after the Second World War, the ties with South Asia started to decline. The economic success and improvements in education contributed to the social progress of the Asian diaspora. The processes of settling down, of adaptation to British institutions, the extensive urbanisation of a social group emigrating from Indian villages, the rise of a new generation exposed to the influences of the Western education and to better economic standards, all these factors influenced far-reaching changes within the Asian diaspora (Mangat 1969). The second- or third-generation Asians regarded Kenya or East Africa as the place where the networks should be maintained. South Asia was increasingly regarded as a place of the ancestors, though many of the young Asians did not even know. Zarwan (1974, p. 141) also found that ties with South Asia were 'stronger during the earlier part of this century, than more recently'. He adds the following explanation:

> When the first people emigrated, they were unsure of their future. Naturally entire families would not leave at the same time. People domiciled in Africa would sometimes make social visits to India. ... As the population grew, however, it became less important to go to India. Marriages could be arranged entirely within East Africa. ... Eventually most of one's family would be settled in Kenya. (Zarwan 1974, p. 142)

There are families in Kenya who have never visited the Indian subcontinent (interviews 1998, 2000). Although an attachment to the previous home remained, the physical contacts with South Asia decreased while the number of the communities in Kenya increased. Therefore, the migration of whole family units as well as the establishment of strong communal networks in the diaspora leads to permanent migration and later on, it weakens the ties with the homeland. Networking is a matter of families and communities and not of the whole Asian diaspora (Herzig 2006).

> People have helped them [the new immigrants] with jobs. They are now in such a position that they can earn their own money and they can live a comfortable life. I think most of the Indian families; they all live a comfortable life in their own means. ... If they don't have money then the community or friends, Indian friends, do help but most of them wouldn't say that 'I gave the money for the people'. (Hindu woman, 31, interview 1998)

Networking does not only serve business matters, it also supports people when they face personal problems.

> It is as if the Oshwals were a different planet, everybody is a different planet, and nobody comes together. Networking is mostly within the community, because the communities are not intermarrying. (Jain man, 46, interview 1998)

The importance of marriage alliances is apparent, and therefore it becomes clear why parents who rely on these networks encourage community marriages. However, according to the informant quoted above, more recently a new form of 'cross-networking' is emerging, which is not based on community anymore but on the membership of the golf club or of a social club such as Lion's Club, Rotary Club and so on. These new forms of collective identities establish new insiders, which creates new boundaries. The boundaries, which are shifting from community to other social categories, such as level of education or occupation respectively, are emerging in other spheres of social life as well (Herzig 2006). This can partly be explained by the fact that businessmen socialise with each other regardless of race, religion, or caste. Participation in these social events is necessary because they are used for exchanging information or even doing business transactions (Voigt-Graf 1998).

The maintenance of transnational ties has been a long standing South Asian household strategy; during the first decades of presence in Kenya, though, the networks were focused on South Asia. This changed after independence in the East African countries as well as after Amin's expulsion of the Asians from Uganda (Kuper 1979, Okalany 1996, Van Hear 1998). An increasing number of Asians were forced, or chose, to migrate a second time, especially to the UK and to North America (i.e. Canada and the USA). These migrants are named 'twice-migrants' (cf. Bhachu 1985). More recently people started to migrate to Australia as well. After the expulsion from Uganda, the most highly skilled people tried to go to North America; the working family members headed for Britain (Bhachu 1985, Van Hear 1998). This could be termed as a strategy of transnational insurance (Herzig 2006). The tradition of family cohesion and assistance, which has been an important factor in the success-formula of the Asians in commerce and industry in East Africa, now was needed on a transnational basis. The community networks that once helped relatives to start their new life in East Africa were needed by the Kenyan Asians to start their new lives in the UK or North America. But again, the arrival of East Africans as family units, very often consisting of three generations, 'has led to their rapid settlement in the UK, alongside the reproduction of strong communication links established during their stay in East Africa' (Bhachu 1990, p. 6). This also meant that the social networks, which were established and maintained in East Africa, shifted to the new places of settlement. Especially in the UK, East African Asians were far more successful than the direct migrants (Bhachu 1985, Bhopal 1997). In my opinion, they did not only have the (embodied) cultural capital (Bourdieu 1985) with them but were also able to shift the (embedded) social capital from East Africa to the UK. Therefore, those Kenyan Asians who stayed behind shifted their orientations to the Western countries (Herzig 2006).

Since the 1980s, migration to Kenya has started again from South Asia and the West (i.e. the UK or North America). While the latter are considered as 'home comers' by the 'established' Kenyan Asians, the former are ascribed as outsiders. As I have mentioned before, the recent immigrants from India are abusively called 'rockets', because of their speed, and un-Africanised way of life. According to my interviewees (1998, 2000) they speak and walk too fast, and only want to make money in Kenya. Therefore a new boundary has risen and is now drawn within the communities. Communities are not united anymore, if they ever have been so.

> We don't have patience with them [the recent immigrants] anymore. They push themselves into everything, they want to lead everything. In times gone by we [the Kenyan Asians] offered our relatives from India jobs when they came to Kenya. We organised everything for them, and helped them where we could. But now we want them to leave. At least some problems with the 'rockets' are solved now. Some Kenyan Asians made the government deport the recent immigrant 'dancers' and 'bands'. ... I have stopped going to the community activities, because our community centre is crowded with rockets and I do not even know anybody anymore. What we achieved in hundred years, they want in ten to twenty years. (Hindu man, 37, interview 2000)

This topic was also discussed in the Kenyan Press. The following reader's letter by Brijal Patel from Nairobi serves as an example:

> Has a Minister in the President's Office ... forgotten his promise to investigate the large number of Asian expatriates in Nairobi? Anywhere one goes these days – Westlands, Parklands, Nairobi West, South B/C – one finds hundreds of foreign Asians. What are they doing here? It is worrying because this is getting out of hand. Does the government not know what is going on? ... As a Kenyan, I feel it's about time the government started doing something about this influx of foreigners. We are getting tired of broken promises. (*Daily Nation* 1998)

Obviously, Kenyan Asians have placed their identities in Kenya, many of them identify with Kenya as their place of home and belonging. Therefore there are social boundaries that run across a community which seem to be more relevant than the boundary of community itself.

## Communal places and gender

Communal places include community centres of different intra-ethnic groups (such as the Patel, the Oshwal or the Ismaili communities) as well as religious sites such as Hindu temples, Muslim mosques or Christian churches. Caste remains active mainly in two fields in Kenya: endogamy and worship. The latter can be recognised in the existence of the various separated community halls and temples. Each community maintains its own places of worship, which are important in the construction of social identities. Neighbourhoods, temples, community halls, clubs, and bars define the social worlds of the different sections of Asian communities (Nagar and Leitner 1998).

> These places play a major role in building and sustaining a deep sense of belonging to their caste, religion, ore sect among the people. Regularly held social and religious gatherings in these places enhance the centrality of the community in people's lives. (Nagar and Leitner 1998, p. 230)

Communal places of the Kenyan Asians can be looked at as semi-public. On the one hand community centres are open to the members of the specific community, but on the other hand they exclude members of the whole Kenyan society, even members of other Asian communities. Therefore communal places are differentiated by a social boundary that divides insiders for example the Brahmins from the outsiders, for example the non-Brahmins (Herzig 2007).

Neighbourhoods, temples, community halls and clubs define the social world of the Asian communities in Kenya. These places play a major role in constructing and sustaining a sense of belonging to their community or religion among the people. For the majority of the people, social and religious gatherings held in these places enhance the centrality of the community in people's lives. Relatives, friends, marital partners as well as business partners come usually from the same community. Therefore, these communal places are essential for the people to feel 'at home' in the new environment. But although communal places obviously have various advantages for the migrants, these communal places are also important in reinforcing existing power hierarchies (Nagar and Leitner 1998). To be a woman or a man affects most people in their daily life severely. The predominant gender roles in the South Asian context that are ascribed to, both, women and men, is a gendered division of work. Gendered division of work or housework respectively also results in a differentiated appropriation of space, not only in the public but also at home. Housework is clearly women's work and the kitchen is a space which is almost exclusively appropriated by women. But not only the home is segregated by gender but also the community centres (Herzig 2007). Different places are used by different groups: men or women, youth or the elderly people. For example one interviewee stated that:

> [my grandfather] didn't want the family to be involved with the community, so we just used to attend functions, but otherwise we had nothing much to do with the community. (Hindu woman, 31, interview 1998)

This means that the community centre (or parts of it) is appropriated by the elderly men; family members are welcome only for special occasions. Another woman, from a different community, told me:

> My grandparents came from India to Kenya in 1963, because they were getting old. ... My dad had brought them from India and they were staying with us. And I used to drop my grandfather at the community hall – he met other retired people there. (Jain woman, 45, interview 1998)

Again, an elderly man meets other men in the community hall. For two reasons we can assume that he met only men: firstly, day-to-day life among Kenyan Asians is gendered, and secondly, if there are also women in the community hall, the grandmother would have accompanied him. Elderly men appropriate the community places and with this process they feel more at home, or in place. Owing to the thorough gendered division of work, after retiring elderly men have no duties regarding the housework. Therefore, they need a place outside the home to meet other people. In comparison, elderly women don't have the opportunity to be retired because they are still engaged in the household. For that reason they meet with other women in different settings. Nonetheless, women may also be active in the community places, but more in an organised manner: they attend functions, or take part in cooking classes or other educational courses (Herzig 2006).

The appropriation of communal places represents the organisational structure of the whole community, or in other words, they represent the inherent power relations between men and women, but also between the different age groups or migratory generations. Figure 1 shows the amount of the communal activities on average per year. For this question, the sample size is 300 valid questionnaires. Communal activities include participation in women's organisations or children's clubs, meetings, gatherings and so on. The amount of activities is distributed more or less equally among the gendered age groups except elderly women and young men. The former are much more involved in communal activities than the other gendered age groups. This is not a contradiction to my statement above – elderly women are predominantly engaged in religious activities, for example they perform the daily puja. In fact, in many households, 'women are responsible for the spiritual side of the world, and men for the material side of the world' as several informants explained to me (interviews 1998, 2000). Because young men are largely engaged in work, they are less involved in communal activities. This is explains why young men are the least active group.

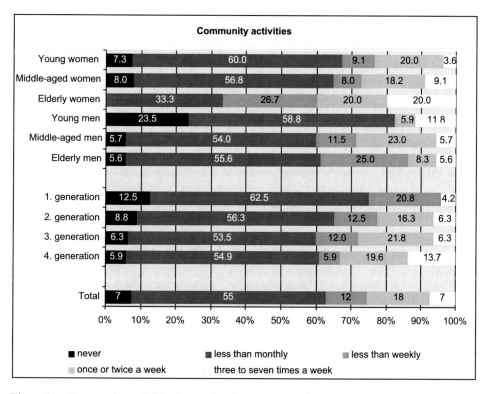

Figure 1. Community activities by gendered age group and generation. Source: Herzig (2006, p. 176).

Regarding migratory generation, it is apparent that first-generation Asians are least involved in community activities, and that the commitment increases from generation to generation. Combining it with the proportion of membership to the different communities, it makes clear, that the first generation is not as communalistic as often assumed. This is quite different to the common perception of social networks. However, I assume that since the first-generation Asians are involved in the struggle of making a living, they cannot spend the time for community activities. In addition, they still maintain a myth of return – especially the young men who migrated recently – which prevents them from investing too much to the communities. The communities don't need only economic capital, they need also commitment. The second, third and fourth generations are far more established in Kenya. Some families have no ties with South Asia anymore; their whole working and family life is in Kenya. For this reason it is essential for them to invest their different forms of capital in the communities and the communal places in Kenya (Herzig 2006).

This example shows how place and identity are mutually interlinked with each other. Communal places (and the inherent social structure) have to attract new members to let them place their identities. We can recognise that the appropriation of communal places does not only depend on gender but also on age and generation (Herzig 2007).

## Changing identities and shifting communal networks

One reason for the changing role of communal networks is that most Kenyan Asians have lost the 'myth of return'. In the earlier days communities provided places of home and belonging as well as places of networking. According to the interviewees (interviews 1998) elderly men met the other retired men at the community hall. The family was not involved in community issues, except when functions were taking place. Elderly men appropriated the physical space in order to place their identities. The former coincidence between community and class (and caste occupation) is vanishing, since education and occupation is not defined along community lines anymore. These results in dissolution of communal occupations and therefore the communal networks lose their importance. Since the younger men and women choose the subject of their professional training more or less independently, i.e. not referring to the traditional community occupation, they do not necessarily need communal places for business connections anymore. In this sense, parents contribute to the loss of significance of the communities as a social network for business issues by fostering a higher level of education of their children (Herzig 2006). In addition, since the Africans have increased their level of education during the last decade as well, the competition in the Kenyan labour marked has become so high that, according to one informant (personal communication 2004), some parents encourage their children to stay abroad after completing their education. Since these young professionals will mostly work as employees instead of founding their own enterprises, they cannot continue the business related networks. As a result of these developments the family businesses will decline (personal communication 2004 and 2007).

Among the middle-aged and elderly men the communal networks are also slowly replaced by social networks which induces that the boundary of community has started to lose its importance in favour of social groups which follow common ideals or life-styles. As a result of the increasing social contacts outside the community, communal intermarriages are increasing (according to the interviewees but not necessarily according to the respondents in the survey 2000), however preferably within the same religion. An increasing number of young intermarried women state that they neither had to change the community nor their religion anymore, which implies a more open handling of communal and religious boundaries.

The social networks with relatives abroad constitute an important characteristic of the Asian communities in Kenya. However, ties with South Asia, which were very important at the beginning of the 20th century, started to lose their importance after the Second World War. After independence, the focus of communal networks started to shift to the UK and North America. The vast majority of the respondents (survey 2000) have relatives in Britain, whereas slightly fewer state they have relatives in India and/or Pakistan. In addition, there is a community specific pattern of the different countries with relatives, which in fact shows that migration functions along social networks.

Communal networks are not necessarily based on positive commitment as the example of the recent immigrants from South Asia shows. They are considered as outsiders by the 'established' Kenyan Asians, and called 'rockets' pejoratively which again shows that the social networks are not always considered as a positive source (cf. Portes and Sensenbrenner 1993). Although there is an increasing number of love marriages, the (remaining) marriage alliances are preferred to be established within Kenya or between Kenyan Asians and East African Asians abroad, i.e. UK and North America but not from the 'homeland'. The 'rockets' are positioned as inferior by the 'established' Kenyan Asians because they do not possess that kind of social, cultural and economic capital that is highly esteemed by the Kenyan Asians (Herzig 2006).

Communal organisations do not fulfil the same tasks anymore as they had during colonial times or after independence. The majority of the Kenyan Asians has created places of belonging that are not limited to communal places anymore. They are 'established' enough to socialise with relatives, or friends who do not necessarily belong to the same community. Nonetheless, religion as well as community is still an important pillar in the conception of the majority of the Kenyan Asians' lives, however, in a rather individualised manner.

## Conclusion

This paper shows the role of communal networks as keys for the successful social mobility of both, the Kenyan Asian individuals and the communities. Although the reason for migration was mainly economic, the establishment of community organisations and religious institutions helped the people to feel more at home in Kenya. The identities with regard to religion and community have been changed although the religious and communal attachment is still important. Communities might not be assigned to a specific community occupation anymore since class boundaries cross-cut and overlap in various ways. The boundaries of caste or sect have generally lost their significance in the Kenyan Asian context, except for endogamy and worship. However, marriage between different communities but within the same religion is increasingly common. The vast majority of the Kenyan Asians are members of a community, but there are differences between the gendered age groups and the generations in this respect.

The social networks constitute an important characteristic of the Asian communities. However, the ties with South Asia, that were most important in the first phase of

Asian settlement in East Africa, have started to decline after the Second World War. After independence, the focus of communal networks shifted more and more to the UK and North America. Since the 1980s, migration to Kenya has started again from both, South Asia and the West. While the latter are considered as 'home comers' by the 'established' Kenyan Asians, the former are ascribed as outsiders.

Further, the paper illustrates the constructions and appropriations of communal places by taking intra-communal boundaries of the Asian minority in Kenya into account. The paper shows, that first, the appropriation of communal places is gendered and divided by age and migratory generation and second, the mutually interlinked relation of place and identity is important for the comfort and the sense of belonging of the migrants. As the example of the Kenyan Asians shows, it is particularly important for migrants that they are allowed to place their identities in order to feel more at home or in place. The semi-public communal places play a major role in constructing and sustaining a sense of belonging.

## Notes on contributor

Dr Pascale Herzig is a human geographer. Her main areas of interest are migration and gender studies, children and youth studies, social differences and identities (intersectionality). Her regional focus is South Asia, East Africa and Switzerland. She is the author of *South Asians in Kenya: gender, generation and changing identities in diaspora* (2006).

## References

Anthias, F., 1998a. Evaluating 'diaspora': beyond ethnicity? *Sociology,* 32, 557–580.

Anthias, F., 1998b. Rethinking social divisions: some notes towards a theoretical framework. *Sociological Review,* 46, 505–535.

Anthias, F. and Yuval-Davis, N., 1983. Contextualizing feminism – gender, ethnic and class divisions. *Feminist Review,* 15, 62–75.

Anthias, F. and Yuval-Davis, N., 1989. Introduction. *In:* N. Yuval-Davis and F. Anthias, eds. *Woman – nation – state,* 1st ed. Basingstoke: Macmillan.

Appadurai, A., 1991. Global ethnoscapes: notes and queries for a transnational anthropology. *In:* R.G. Fox, ed. *Recapturing anthropology: working in the present.* Santa Fe: School of American Research Press.

Barth, F., ed., 1969. *Ethnic groups and boundaries: the social organization of culture differ- ence.* Bergen: Universitets Forlaget.

Bhachu, P., 1985. *Twice migrants: East African Sikh settlers in Britain.* London: Tavistock.

Bhachu, P., 1990. Twice versus direct migrants: East African Sikh settlers in Britain. *In:* I.F.S.S. Research, ed. *California immigrants in world perspective: the conference papers.* 1st ed. Los Angeles: University of California.

Bharati, A., 1964. Political pressures and reactions in the Asian Minority in East Africa. *African Studies Bulletin,* 7 (4): 25–26. Report of the Seventh Annual Meeting of the African Studies Association.

Bhopal, K., 1997. *Gender, 'race' and patriarchy: a study of South Asian women.* Aldershot: Ashgate.

Bourdieu, P., 1985. The forms of capital. *In:* J.G. Richardson, ed. *Handbook of theory and research for the sociology of education.* New York: Greenwood.

Brah, A., 1996. *Cartographies of diaspora: contesting identities.* London: Routledge.

Clarke, C., Peach, C., and Vertovec, S., 1990. Introduction: themes in the study of the South Asian diaspora. *In:* C. Clarke, C. Peach and S. Vertovec, eds. *South Asians overseas: migration and ethnicity.* 1st ed. Cambridge: Cambridge University Press.

Cohen, R., 1997. *Global diasporas: an introduction.* Seattle: Universitiy of Washington Press.

Cresswell, T., 1996. *In place/out of place: geography, ideology and transgression.* Minneapolis: University of Minnesota press.

*Daily Nation,* 1998. Foreigners taking jobs in Kenya. *Daily Nation,* 18 November 1998. Available at: http://www.nationaudio.com/news/dailynation/1998/181198/letters/letters3. html (accessed 15 February 2001).

Denis, A.B., 2001. Multiple identities … multiple marginalities: Franco-Ontarian feminism. *Gender & Society,* 15, 453–467.

Ehrkamp, P., 2005. Placing identities: transnational practices and local attachments of Turkish immigrants in Germany. *Journal of Ethnic & Migration Studies,* 31, 345–364.

Fredrich, B., Herzig, P., and Richter, M., 2007. Geschlecht räumlich betrachtet: ein Beitrag aus der Geografie. *In:* D. Grisard, J. Häberlein, A. Kaiser and S. Saxer, eds. *Gender in Motion: Die Konstrucktion von Geschlecht in Raum und Erzählung,* 56–80. Frankfurt: Campus.

Ghai, Y. and Ghai, D., 1971. The Asian minorities of East and Central Africa (up to 1971). London: Minority Rights Group.

Glick Schiller, N., Basch, L., and Blanc-Szanton, C., eds, 1992. *Towards a transnational perspective on migration: race, class, ethnicity, and nationalism reconsidered.* New York: The New York Academy of Sciences.

Gregory, R.G., 1971. *India and East Africa: a history of race relations within the British Empire 1890–1939.* Oxford: Clarendon Press.

Herzig, P. 2006. *South Asians in Kenya – gender, generation and changing identities in diaspora.* Münster: Lit.

Herzig, P. 2007. Communal places and gender – appropriating public spaces and placing identities among South Asians in Kenya. *In: International Symposium 'Sustainable Public Spaces', The International Geographical Union (Igu), Commission on Gender and Geography, 1–3 June 2007,* Zurich, Unpublished manuscript.

Herzig, P. and Richter, M., 2004. Von den 'Achsen der Differenz' zu den 'differenzraü-men': Ein Beitrag zur theoretischen Diskussion in der geografischen Geschlechter-forschung. *In:* E. Buehler and V. Meier, eds, *Geschlechterforschung. Neue Impulse für die Geographie.* Zurich: Wirtschaftsgeographie und Raumplanung 33, 43–64.

Herzig, P. and Thieme, S., 2007. How geography matters: neglected dimensions in contemporary migration research. *Asiatische Studien/Études Asiatiques,* 61, 1077–1112.

Hugo, G., 1996. Migration and the family. *In:* United Nations Iyf Secretariat, ed. *Family: challenges for the future.* 1st ed. Geneva: United Nations.

Jacobs, J.M. and Fincher, R., 1998. Introduction. *In:* R. Fincher and J.M. Jacobs, eds. *Cities of difference.* 1st ed. New York: The Guilford Press, 1–25.

Kiem, C.G., 1993. *Die Indische Minorität in Ostafrika: Ursachen Und Verlauf Eines Ungelösten Konflikts.* Bielefeld: Universität Bielefeld.

Kuper, J., 1979. 'Goan' and 'Asian' in Uganda: an analysis of racial identity and cultural categories. *In:* W.A. Shack and E.P. Skinner, eds. *Strangers in African societies.* Berkeley: University of California Press.

Lie, J., 2001. Diasporic nationalism. *Cultural Studies – Critical Methodologies,* 1, 355–362.

Mangat, J.S., 1969. *A history of the Asians in East Africa 1886–1945.* Oxford: Oxford University Press.

Massey, D., 1993. Raum, Ort Und Geschlecht: Feministische Kritik Geographischer Konzepte. *In:* E. Bühler, H. Meyer, D. Reichert and A. Scheller, eds. *Ortssuche: Zur Geographie Der Geschlechterdifferenz.* Zürich/Dortmund: Efef-Verlag, 109–122.

Mirzoeff, N., 2000. Introduction – the multiple viewpoint: diasporic visual culture. *In:* N. Mirzoeff, ed. *Diaspora and visual culture: representing Africans and Jews.* 1st ed. London: Routledge.

Nagar, R., 1995. Making and breaking boundaries: identity politics among South Asians in postcolonial Dar Es Salaam. PhD thesis, University of Minnesota.

Nagar, R., 1998. Communal discourses, marriage, and the politics of gendered social boundaries among South Asian immigrants in Tanzania. *Gender, Place & Culture,* 5, 117–139.

Nagar, R. and Leitner, H., 1998. Contesting social relations in communal places: identity politics among Asian Communities in Dar Es Salaam. *In:* R. Fincher and J.M. Jacobs, eds. *Cities of Difference.* 1st ed. New York: The Guilford Press, 226–251.

Okalany, D.H., 1996. Ethnicity and 'culture of eating' in Uganda. *In:* B.A. Ogot, ed. *Ethnicity, nationalism and democracy in Africa.* 1st ed. Maseno: Institute of Research and Postgraduate Studies, Maseno University College.

Portes, A. and Sensenbrenner, J., 1993. Embeddedness and immigration: notes on the social determinants of economic action. *American Journal of Sociology,* 98, 1320–1350.

Pratt, G., 1999. Geographies of identity and difference: marking boundaries. *In:* D. Massey, J. Allen, and P. Sarre, eds. *Human geography today.* Cambridge: Polity Press, 151–167.

Preston, P.W., 1997. *Political/cultural identity: citizens and nations in a global era.* London: Sage.

Ranja, T., 2003. Success under duress: a comparison of indigenous Africans and East African Asian entrepreneurs. Economic and Social Research Foundation. Globalisation and East Africa Working Paper Series No. 7. Available at: http://www.esrftz.org/global/output/wps07_ranja_asians%20vs%20africans.pdf

Rothchild, D., 1973. *Racial bargaining in independent Kenya: a study of minorities and decolonization.* London: Oxford University Press.

Safran, W., 1991. Diasporas in modern societies: myths of homeland and return. *Diaspora: A Journal of Transnational Studies,* 1, 83–99.

Safran, W., Sahoo, A.K., and Lal, B.V., 2008. Indian diaspora in transnational contexts: introduction. *Journal of Intercultural Studies,* 29 (1), 1–5.

Salvadori, C., 1989. *Through open doors: a view of Asian cultures in Kenya.* Nairobi: Kenway.

Seidenberg, D.A., 1996. *Mercantile adventurers: the world of east African Asians 1750–1985.* New Delhi: New Age International.

Sheffer, G., 1986. A new field of study: modern diasporas in international politics. *In:* G. Sheffer, ed. *Modern Diasporas in International Politics.* London: Croom Helm, 1–15.

Silvey, R. and Lawson, V., 1999. Placing the migrant. *Annals of the Association of American Geographers,* 89, 121–132.

Tandon, Y. and Raphael, A., 1978. The new position of East Africa's Asians: problems of a displaced minority. Minority Rights Group, London.

Tatla, D.S., 1999. *The Sikh diaspora: the search for statehood.* London: UCL Press.

Thieme, S., 2006. *Social networks and migration: far west Nepalese labour migrants in Delhi.* Münster: Lit.

Twaddle, M., 1990. East African Asians through a hundred years. *In:* C. Clarke, C. Peach and S. Vertovec, eds. *South Asians overseas: migration and ethnicity.* 1st ed. Cambridge: Cambridge University Press, 149–163.

Van Hear, N., 1998. *New diasporas. the mass exodus, dispersal and regrouping of migrant communities.* London: UCL Press.

Verdery, K., 1994. Ethnicity, nationalism, and state-making – *ethnic groups and boundaries*: past and future. *In:* H. Vermeulen and C. Govers, eds. *The anthropology of ethnicity: beyond 'ethnic groups and boundaries'.* 1st ed. Amsterdam: Het Spinhuis, 33–58.

Vertovec, S., 1997. Three meanings of 'diaspora', exemplified among South Asian religions. *Diaspora: A Journal of Transnational Studies,* 6, 277–299.

Vertovec, S., 1999. Conceiving and researching transnationalism. *Ethnic & Racial Studies,* 22, 447–462.

Voigt-Graf, C., 1998. *Asian communities in Tanzania: a journey through past and present times.* Hamburg: Institut Für Afrika-Kunde.

Wahlbeck, Ö., 2002. The concept of diaspora as an analytical tool in the study of refugee communities. *Journal of Ethnic & Migration Studies,* 28, 221–238.

Warah, R., 1998. *Triple heritage: a journey to self-discovery.* Nairobi: Colour Print.

Werbner, P., 2002. The place which is diaspora: citizenship, religion and gender in the making of Chaordic transnationalism. *Journal of Ethnic & Migration Studies,* 28, 119–133.

Zarwan, J., 1974. Social evolution of the Jains in Kenya. *In:* B.A. Ogot, ed. *History and social change in East Africa: Proceedings of the 1974 conference of the Historical Association of Kenya.* Nairobi: East African Literature Bureau.

# Trajectory of social mobility:
# Asian Indian children coming of age in New York City

Rupam Saran

*Medgar Evers College, City University of New York, New York*

Contextualized within constructivist paradigm and the phenomenological hermeneutic framework, this minority performance ethnographic study on social mobility and second-generation Asian Indian immigrants examines the intergenerational and intragenerational social mobility of children post-1965 Indian immigrants in the metropolis of New York. This study explores two issues: first, to what extent the current challenges in the US economy hinder upward social mobility of the children of Indian immigrants. Second, how parental messages of taking advantages of both worlds contributes to second-generation Asian Indians' success or failure in American society. While economic and financial globalization facilitated mobilization across national borders the recent economic crisis poses tough challenges for Indian immigrants and their children. Findings indicate that positive ethnic structure, social mobility and the cultural capital provide the younger generation with an adaptive advantage to meet the challenges of mainstream society. The study concludes that despite recent constraints of US economy, in general, there is significant economic gain from the first to the second generation. In the case of second-generation Asian Indians economic and non-economic forms of social mobility compliment each other.

## Introduction

This cross-generational ethnography examines the intergenerational and intragenerational social mobility of children of post-1965 Indian immigrants in the metropolis of New York. The study focuses on upwardly mobile second-generation (US born) and 1.5 youth (foreign born) Asian Indians who are members of a large second-generation group that is entering the labor market in New York City. Foner introduces this new second generation, 'Newcomers who arrived in the 1970s and 1980s are by now old-timers and a large second generation is growing up and entering the job market' (2001, p. 24). The study is motivated by concerns that the impact of the current economic crisis, which began in December 2007 (Papademetriou and Terrazas 2009, Leonhard 2009, Sacchett 2009, Lawless *et al.* 2008), is unfavorable to the future of children of Asian Indian immigrants, and it might lead second-generation Asian Indians on a downward spiral. The overall objective of this study is to examine the trajectory of social mobility of children of Asian Indian immigrants who have experienced upward mobility and face challenges and constraints because of the recent recession in the USA. Although many of my respondents were recent college graduates, young professionals, or still pursuing their education, their future job options might bear consequences of the economic recession.

The key motivating questions of this study are: (1) how the recent economic crisis in the US economy impacts social mobility of second-generation and 1.5 youth, (2) how parental cultural, social and human capitals contribute to second-generation Asian Indians' social mobility, (3) what is the relationship between intragenerational and intergenerational mobility within Asian Indian context, (4) how second-generation and 1.5 generation youth are situated in the web of realities and how they navigate their positionality at the time of recession.

In the times of economic uncertainties, while the US economy worsens, anti-immigrant sentiments become more prevalent and immigrant minorities are subjected to racism and prejudice (Olsen 1997, Kessler 2001, Sandhu 1995, Suarez-Orozoco and Suarez-Orozoco 2000). The USA has a long history of anti-immigrant sentiments. Public attitude towards immigrants in the USA is directly related to economic concerns and often minorities are blamed for the decline of the US economy and the downfall of living standards (Kessler 2001, Simon 1993, Simon and Alexander 1993). Kessler (2001) claims that aggrieved individuals who feel that they face a greater threat or competition from outsiders (immigrants) have oppositional attitude towards immigrants (Borjas 2006). Olsen (1997) states that the original white settler population 'express anxiety and resentment at the increasing number of immigrants and Asians they perceive as pushing them out in academic hierarchy' and in the labor market. Olsen provides an example of a widespread sentiment and the way immigrants are talked about, 'They come to take our jobs, and they are willing to break their backs for shit pay, and we can't compete'. In such a context, the study intends to provide insight into the struggles of high-skilled second-generation and 1.5 Asian Indian in professional, high technology and engineering sectors of the US labor market.

The US economy is experiencing a great recession. The Migration Policy Institute report prepared by Papademetriou and Terrazas (2009) states, 'On December 1, 2008 the National Bureau of Economic Research (NBER) officially declared the United States in recession, and estimated that it began in December 2007' (p. 1). A report from the Organization for Economic Co-Operation and Development (OCED) in 2008 described the economic crisis in the USA, 'The US economy is going through an exceptionally difficult period after having been hit by converging adverse development some in reaction to previous excesses during the upswing, others more exogenous' (p. 1). Recessions are not 'unique' to New York City, in the past 38 years it has occurred many times. In the study of new immigrants and employment trend in New York City, Foner (2001) provides analysis of three recessions that occurred between 1969 and 1997. According to Foner, 'during the 1973–1975 recession the city endured is the renowned period of near fiscal collapse ... starting 1977, the city's economy began to revive' (p. 87). Again because of the stock market crash of October 1987, economy in the city declined from 1987 to 1990 (Foner 2001, Brauer and Flaherty 1992). The mid 1990s and onward was a period of overall job growth and major employment gains in many sectors.

Foner (2001) stresses that some of the restructuring forces and globalization of production generated 'many "high-end" jobs in business services, law, investment-banking, advertising, and consulting'. At the same time there was growth in 'low-end' jobs also. This job-growth was beneficial to Asian Indian immigrants and their children. However, this job growth and expansion of employment is experiencing a period of severe fiscal collapse.

The current US recession is longer and deeper than the great depression (Papademetriou and Terrazas 2009) and its impact on the labor market is unfavorable to the immigrant population. The immigrants, either high-earning or low-earning are not faring well during the economic crisis (Sachett 2009).The growing unemployment and shrinking economic opportunities have a negative effect on social mobility of immigrant population. The report by Ratha *et al.* (2009) reports that economic crisis in the US is forcing many immigrants (high-skilled or low-skilled) to face unemployment and 'dip into their savings' and assets and rely on their families and friends for help.

While economic and financial globalization facilitated mobilization across national borders, the recent recession poses tough challenges for immigrants and their children (Sacchett 2009).The current instability of the US economy has begun to affect the upward mobility of the first and second-generation Asian Indians as a group. The following examples/evidences provide insights into how this is playing itself out.

Amir, 31, is out of a job and is busy job hunting. Amir was born in India, and arrived in New York with his parents and his sister at the age of six. His father worked with a bank as a Vice President. He and his sister graduated from Columbia University and attended Harvard University for their graduate studies. He earned his MBA from Harvard. Amir's wife, a corporate lawyer, is born and brought up in New York. Amir with his business partner and friend, Adam ventured and opened the first 'Sports Museum of New York' in June 2006 at 'Ground Zero' (the former World Trade Center site). This was a multi million project in which The City of New York invested and matched the fund that was raised by Amir and his business partner. At the opening of the 'The Sports Museum' 150 sports dignitaries and players along with Mayor of New York attended the opening ceremonies. Amir and his friend's dream came true. They started their business venture from a one room office at the World Trade Center. They worked long hours and made their way through the tough business world. The Sports Museum started in a grand way at the wake of economic recession in May 2008 and had to file bankruptcy in March 2009.

I graduated from Columbia Law School in 2008 and I am unable to get a job in New York law firms. For the time being I am working in a bank as a loan officer till I secure a job in a law firm. (Lalima, 2009)

I did my schooling in New York. For my undergraduate study I went to Emory University. I graduated with a degree in Business Administration in 2009, with a grade point average of 3.9; however, I and many of my classmates could not secure a job through early placement programs. Previously it was the norm to get early job placements before graduation ... for graduate school admission I need a few years of work experience in the business world ... there are no jobs. (Swapnil, 2009)

I do have a job at a competitive law firm but the law firm has deferred my appointment for a year. I am graduating from New York University Law School in Spring of 2009. I have to wait for one year ... I am skeptical it might be for more than a year. (Rima, 2009)

My respondents confided that for many low-paying jobs they are over-qualified and employers will not hire them on the assumption that they will have to pay them more compared with a less-qualified worker. Aditya, one of the respondents of this study stated:

My father lost his job ... he is unable to find a job ... he is over-qualified for jobs that are available. He is a computer scientist. He was one of the vice presidents of his company. His company went out of business. My mother is a medical technologist but she is not working for a few years. I am preparing for Medical License exam. I finished my study of medicine last year. My father has good savings but none of us in my family is working .... (Aditya)

Careful analysis of the data of this study provides a nuanced understanding of the implications of the economic crisis. These upwardly mobile respondents of this study have high educational attainment and an impressive track record but are facing challenges largely because of tough economic conditions. Many of my second-generation participants and their parents expressed fear of losing their jobs and by the time this study was completed many lost employment. The data/life stories of my participants reveal that these young people made it in mainstream society. However, despite their academic success they have fallen into a vulnerable situation.

> I worked for one of the most challenging corporate law firms after my graduation from Columbia University Law School. I had a senior position at the firm and I earned a reputation of as being a diligent worker. I was let go by the firm when I came back from the maternity leave. The rationale for my firing was that the firm is experiencing heavy loss and they had to cut down. In my department I was the first one to be fired. I could have filed a law suit but I did not . . . I do not want get into legal mess . . . similar thing happened to my one of my friends . . . . She has Latina roots. She is not like me – she has filed the lawsuit against her firm. (Karinma, 2010)

The social, political and economic structure of the USA is built by people who migrated from different parts of the world. Historically, the USA has promised upward mobility to immigrants and their families. Immigrants from different parts of world migrated to America to fulfill their dream of a prosperous life and upward mobility (Glazer 1980, Glazer and Moynihan 1963, Foner 2001, Kasinitz *et al.* 2008). The recent study by Philip Kasinitz *et al.* (2008) illuminates social, economic, cultural and political lives of second-generation youth of five immigrant-origin groups (excluding Asian Indians) living in metropolitan New York. According to this study, although there is variability in social mobility within various immigrant groups, in general, most of the immigrant population in New York area has been successful in establishing themselves financially and socially and their children's mobility has been upward (Kasinitz *et al.* 2008). Similar to many new immigrants' children, the children of post-1965 Indian immigrants have grown up and are significantly visible in metropolitan New York. The educational institutions, business firms and information technology fields have a heavy presence of the second-generation Asian Indians.

## Profile of Asian Indians in Metro New York

The context of this study is the New York area that has been a promising land and a place to 'rise' for immigrants since the creation of this nation (Foner 2001, Glazer and Moynihan 1963, Mayo and Parella 1989, Osajima 1988). New York is an immigrant city. Kasinitz *et al.* (2008) assert:

> In New York City the second generation inherits an environment where the second generation advantages work to particularly good effect. While these young people feel the sting of disadvantages and discrimination, they move in a world where being from somewhere else has long been the norm. For them, being a New Yorker means both ethnic and American, being different both from native whites and from their immigrant parents. In this feeling they are reaping the benefits of New York's long history of absorbing new immigrants. (p. 360)

Although Indian immigrants are branching out to smaller and many remote cities of the USA, the magnet city of New York is the most popular city for documented and undocumented Indian immigrants because of its historical tolerance to immigrants (Foner

2001) and its dense Asian Indian ethnic enclaves. Diversity and cosmopolitism of New York City has welcoming connotations for newer immigrants. Like many newer immigrants from Asia, the West Indies, Russia, Mexico, the Dominican Republic, West Africa and many more; Asian Indian immigrants feel comfortable in the social, educational and economic spheres of the city.

Data from this study reveals that the Asian Indian experiences are similar to experiences of many newer immigrants in the city. Documented and skilled Asian Indian immigrants come to New York for the vast opportunities the city provides them and undocumented immigrants come to New York because they can easily blend into the mass immigrant population of the city and earn a living by getting low paying jobs in various ethnic establishments found through a strong social network. In New York the four largest Asian groups are Chinese (39% of all Asians), Indians (27%), Koreans (10%) and Filipinos (8%). In 2007 the Asian Indian population grew by almost 21% (Census Bureau Population 2005–2007). According to the 2005–2007 Community Survey Public Use Data Microdata Sample, 232,417 Indians are living in New York City. In the adjoining suburb of Long Island 55,506 Indians are residing. In Putnam, Rockland and Westchester counties the Indian population is about 25,661. The Asian Indian population is growing rapidly in New York City.

According to research literature, Asian Indians are a recent immigrant group marked by significant upward social mobility. Indian immigrants are one of the newer immigrants who migrated to the USA for a better life and opportunities for themselves and their children (Feigelman and Saran 2002, Schafer 2002). In general, Asian Indians believe in the American dream and share a common belief that the USA promises considerable upward social mobility. Asian Indians and their children are positively stereotyped as hardworking, industrious 'successful minorities' because their educational and economic profile competes with the profile of whites (Kitano and Danield 2001, Glazer 1980, Sandhu 1995, Saran 1985, 2009, Winnick 1990). Glazer (1980) describes the Asian Indian population as 'Marked off by a high level of education, by concentration in the profession' (pp. vi–viii). Research shows that, in general, post-1965 Indian immigrants have been successful in ensuring their children's success in school and stay on the path of upward mobility (Gibson 1988, Saran 1985, 2009a, Walker-Moffat 1995, Winnick 1990). They are a privileged middle-class marginalized minority who are ascribed model minority status in mainstream society (Bhatia 2007, Lessinger 1996, Saran 1985). Asian Indian students hold a 'disproportionate representation' in American academia. Recent research shows that Asian Indians have high rates of school enrollment in comparison with the total population (Ogbu 1991, Rong and Grant 1992, Feigelman and Saran 2002). In 1999, the percentage of Asian Americans 25 years or older with bachelor's degrees was 42% higher than the White American population. Among all Asian groups, Asian-Indians, Chinese Americans and Japanese Americans, Asian Indians have the highest level of educational achievement (Schafer 2002).

## Intergeneration and intragenerational mobility in Asian community in New York

The study of the social mobility trajectory (upward or downward) of migrant population is an innate phenomenon in immigrant studies. Social mobility is related to a multitude of multidisciplinary migration issues of new immigrants and the economic conditions of the USA. Since the nineteenth century the USA has been regarded as a fluid society with higher levels of social mobility in which its people had the opportunity to rise to economic and political power. Social mobility is defined as the social movement of people from one class to another; social mobility as upward or downward movement across higher or lower social class (Barber and Barber 1965). Obtaining a college degree, a decent to high paying job and securing higher status in society are markers of *upward social mobility*; failing in school, dropping out of school or college, losing a job or obtaining a job with lower salary than one's parents contributes to *downward social mobility*.

Barber and Barber (1965) view upward and downward social mobility as a process and a movement across social position and social roles. The term *intragenerational social mobility* implies changes in social position in one's lifetime. *Intergenerational social mobility* refers to relational upward or downward social mobility of individuals' that occurs in relation to their parents. Studies of intergenerational mobility indicate that about 80% of the second-generation shows at least some type of social mobility in relation to their parents (Blau and Duncan 1967). The literature on new immigrants and their children suggests a strong relationship between parents' economic status and intergenerational mobility. Intragenerational social mobility is a good predictor of intergenerational upward and downward social mobility (Borjas 2006, Chiswick 1977, Carliner 1980, Wilson and Portes 1980, Portes and Rumbaut 2001).

In the context of social mobility of Asian Indian immigrants and their children Borja's (2006) assertion is significant. Many participants in this study, Asian Indian parents with low levels of human capital and limited means work hard to provide their children better opportunities. The intragenerational mobility of Indian immigrants plays a major role in their children's upward mobility. As an example, consider the case of Ram, a participant in this study, born to parents who started their immigrant life in New York living in a relative's house. Ram's father worked in an Indian business as an accountant and his mother started working in an Indian beauty salon seven days a week. Within six years they saved enough money to buy a small house in Queens, New York. They sold their house in two years and moved to one of the wealthy suburbs of Long Island to provide good schools for children. Ram witnessed his parents' hard work and experienced improvement in their lifestyle. Ram is completing Manhasset High School and has been admitted to the Baruch College, City University of New York, Business Management Program, which is very competitive.

According to Borjas (2006), not all children of highly successful immigrant parents earn more than parents but in general their social mobility is upward, and on average, children of immigrants earn 5–10% more than their parents. Borjas observes:

> The second-generation Americans earn more than both their parents .... A common explanation is that the children of immigrants are 'hungry' and have the drive and ambition to ensure economic success in US labor market ... and this hunger is lost once the immigrant household becomes fully Americanized .... (2006, p. 933)

Borjas' observation is very true in the context of social mobility of second-generation Asian Indians. Overall, most of my respondents who were employed earned more than their parents and the ones who were finishing up at high school or college aimed for a high salary career. The participants in this study confirmed that their parents emphasized upward social mobility and shaped their selection of academic choices that would lead to a profession that yields greater economic returns. Borjas explains that in general, there is a significant economic 'catching up' from the first- to second-generation immigrant groups and the socioeconomic status of the first generation immigrants and their children are 'strongly correlated'. Further, in examining economic perspective of social mobility Borjas refers to the phenomenon of regression towards the mean. This phenomenon suggests that children of very successful parents are not as successful as their parents and their economic performance may 'revert downward'. Similarly, children of low-skilled immigrants are likely to be better skilled than their parents and 'there is a reversion upward toward the population average' (Borjas 2006, p. 58). The concept of regression toward the mean plays a vital role in understanding social mobility of second-generation and 1.5 children of Asian immigrants in mainstream society. Asian Indians are skilled immigrants and they have done very well in the labor market. Their average earning is more than many other ethnic groups. According to the 2000 census 38% of Asian Indian households have an income of more than US$55,000 compared with 22% among white non-Hispanic groups among all other minority households.

## Social mobility and assimilation of second generation

In order to gain insight into social mobility of the second-generation and 1.5 Asian Indians it is vital to have an understanding of various theoretical lances of assimilation and social mobility. The discussion of upward or downward mobility of any ethnic group revolves around the volume of group members' assimilation in mainstream society and how successfully they access resources available to them for economic gains. The 'straight line' assimilation model of Warner and Srole (1945) describes full assimilation in mainstream society or higher degree of Americanization as a trajectory of upward mobility. This model asserts that second-generation ethnic groups move to the upward trajectory by abandoning their ethnic identity and becoming American by embracing American values and culture.

According to 'straight line' theory assimilation is intertwined with upward mobility and future success of second-generation immigrants. The 'straight line' provided an explanation for the success of European immigrants but this theory is not relevant to the success of newer immigrants who have been successful but have not fully assimilated into American culture. The weakness of this theory is that it overlooked the cultural and ethnic diversity within the immigrant groups, and diverse ways of assimilation (Portes and Zhou 1993, Portes and Sensenbrenner 1993, Portes and Rumbaut 2001). Many successful immigrants and their children have adapted to American ways but they have not fully assimilated into American society, and have retained their ethnic culture and values.

The theory of 'segmented assimilation' (Portes and Zhou 1993) provide an explanation of the non-white second generation's assimilation and social mobility in mainstream society. According to Portes and Zhou the socioeconomic status and the mode of incorporation of the first generation provides cultural, social and economic resources to the second generation. The second generation who belong to an ethnic group with a higher degree of social, cultural and human capital develop a positive identity and have better chances of upward mobility. On the contrary, youths from adverse conditions demonstrate oppositional behavior and take a path of downward mobility. Portes and Rumbaut (2001) introduced the concept of 'selective assimilation' that leads immigrant children to the path of upward mobility. They describe that selective acculturation occurs when the second generation adapts American ways but retains certain ethnic values, and uses their cultural and social resources/capital for upward mobility.

In his theory of 'second-generation decline', Gans (1992) predicts that the post-1965 second generation of color will face more discrimination and economic hardship than their parents and will be on trajectory of downward mobility. According to Gans many children of working class immigrants will be more Americanized than their parents, and they will refuse to take low paying long hour jobs and consequently will earn less than their poor parents. These Americanized youths would cultivate oppositional identity, negative attitude towards their ethnic culture, their parents' work ethics and education. Gans (1992) predicts these second-generation youths will experience downward mobility. The debate concerning second-generation experiences and social mobility and various theories such as 'second-generation decline', 'segmented assimilation' and 'selective acculturation', suggest that full assimilation and complete Americanization of a given ethnic group often has negative consequences (Waldinger and Feliciano 2004). All these theories have been successful in explaining the social mobilization of children of Indian immigrants.

## Methodology

This critical ethnography is contextualized within the critical constructivist paradigm and follows the phenomenological hermeneutic framework. This study is in the form of a classic ethnography in which the researcher does not stay with participants for a long period of time. I have used the critical ethnography research method because I am investigating a marginalized immigrant population in the web of social and economic realities.

Kincheloe (2001) argues that critical ethnography enables researchers to examine social complexities, understand the nature of contradictions, discontinuities and inconsistencies in the social structure of a given society, and allows ethnographers to develop a holistic approach and interpretations of social phenomenon. Criticality also allows researchers to understand the complexities of political structures and the impact of agencies on individual and collective experiences. In addition, critical ethnographers are equipped to gain understanding of the way people evaluate their position in the dominant society and to examine the world through the lenses of race, class and gender.

In this study I examine children of non-white racial minority and their problems and conflicts. I conceived the critical ethnographic methodological framework to be best suited for my study because it enabled me to record and analyze the trajectory of social mobility of the second-generation Asian Indian critically (in an urban setting) within the context of the *immigrant advantages* (Kasinitz *et al.* 2008) that 'stem from their parents' positive selection, their embeddedness in ethnic networks and economics, and their cultural orientation' (p. 20).

*Phenomenological methodology and lived experiences*

In this study I applied phenomenology to study lived-experiences of my respondents and their parents. An individual's experiences are his or her awareness of their lived-world (Fujita 1987). Pinar writes about this research method saying, 'The phenomenological investigator questions how phenomena – "the things themselves" – present themselves in the lived experience of the individual, especially as they present themselves in lived time' (Pinar *et al.* 2000, p. 405). Phenomenology studies how an experience relates to the occurrence or prevalence of other conditions or events that influence a chain of experiences. For example, the study investigates how Asian Indian parents' educational and economic successes lead their children to upward mobility, and how economic conditions affect academic and professional opportunities of their life world. Because I am investigating Asian Indian students' lived experiences of their lifeworld, this study is phenomenological.

Van Manen (1990) asserts that phenomenological study investigates lived-experiences and studies lifeworld as it is immediately experienced; it cannot be reduced to 'results' because phenomenology is interested in analysis, description and interpretation of a situation. For example, I am not concerned with how Indian youth perform on tests. Rather I focus on what it means to an Indian youth to be upwardly mobile and face challenges. Phenomenological research does not solve problems; my research study is not capable of solving the problems that emerged as a result of the economic crisis, but it is interested in exploring the significance of the limited job market and gaining insights into the experiences of my participants.

In this study I used the *narrative inquiry* technique to interpret meanings of *powerful realty stories* and analyzing responses of second-generation and 1.5 Asian Indian and their parents. The study applies the *participant observation* method that is, 'simultaneous emotional involvement and objective detachment', and at the same time provides opportunities to be an engaged participant and to be a 'dispassionate observer' (Tedlock 2000, p. 465).

### A researcher in a critical constructivist paradigm: insider and outsider status

Critical ethnography assumes the equal involvement of researcher and participants in a research process. As a participant observer and as an 'inquirer' I am a part of this study and as a researcher I have a position of 'outsider'. However, I cannot position myself outside the research process completely because a constructivist belief asserts that an 'inquirer and the inquired-into are interlocked in such a way that the findings of an investigation are the literal creation of the inquiry process' (Guba and Lincoln 1989, p. 84). As a critical researcher and as an insider I am in an advantaged position. I have applied my insider knowledge and the insights of the Asian Indian community in this study, and have explored the dialectical relationship of academic achievement, upward mobility and parents' educational and socioeconomic backgrounds.

Regarding issues of 'authenticity' and 'authority of experiences' in ethnography and reduction of 'otherness' that very often prevails with insiders, experiences of an insider has a natural authority over outsider's perception and experiences. It would be unfair of me to claim that my identity was neutral in the research process and that it had no influence on participants' attitudes or their responses. My identity as an insider was a very important factor in winning participants' trust and that is one of the vital elements of ethnography. The success of an ethnographic study is often contingent upon the trust developed between the ethnographer and the participants. My identity was an equal catalyst in winning the participants' and the schools' trust. School and College officials perceived my insider status to be beneficial to the research process.

### Data collection

The participants in this study are second-generation and 1.5 Asian Indians and their parents. Since this study concentrates on upwardly mobile youth and because the data are used to examine the relationship between upward mobility and economic crisis, the study does not include lowest-achievers and working class Indian immigrants. The participants in this study are 100 second-generation and 1.5 Asian Indians, aged 18–34. I interviewed 55 parents. I define second generation as Indian children born in the USA, and 1.5 generation as children who migrated to the USA with their parents at five years of age or after. The second-generation and 1.5 youth were selected on the basis of their high academic performance, career choices, career trajectory and upwardly mobility. I recruited participants for interviews through ethnic, cultural and professional networks, and through schools and colleges I observed, through community events and through community organizations.

I used the multi-method of data collection for this study: ethnographic observation of participants, informal and in-depth interviews of participants and their parents, audio-taping of interviews and field notes. Since this is an ethnographic study and in the ethnographic tradition researchers are not required to follow a standard questionnaire protocol, I did not use structured questionnaires in this study. Informal interviews were guided by questions focused on participants' educational and work experiences, nature of jobs, economic status, their social network and their positionality in the economic crisis of the USA.

All informal interviews lasted 40–90 minutes in the form of conversations that unfolded in natural pace and were audiotaped to capture participants' experiences and their life stories in informal settings of school, colleges, community centers, cultural events and participants' homes. First generation participants preferred informal settings for interview. All audio-tapes were subsequently transcribed and analyzed. In order to investigate lives of participants in academic context I spend four months in a magnet high school, four months in a CUNY college and four months in a private college with a dense Indian population. I wrote in-depth field notes and took a role of observer.

In order to collect data, I regularly attended many community events, social gatherings of young Indian professionals, community centers and cultural clubs of many colleges. As an ethnographer I spend time with participants in this study in social gatherings, visited their homes frequently, and observed their cultural and social lives. I participated in events of Indian Clubs of many City University of New York (CUNY) Colleges with a dense Indian population. I attended cultural events at the Club Zamana (India Club) of Columbia University, India Club of New York University, Stony Brook College India Club, India Club of Stuyvesant High School in Manhattan and Asia Club of Great Neck High School, Long Island.

The member-checking process provided me opportunities to verify lived world experiences (data) with participants who provided them (Guba and Lincoln 1989). During the collection and analysis period I constantly asked participants to verify their narratives, their responses and their life stories for accuracy and consistency between what was recorded and 'what was intended to communicate'. The member checking provided me with chances to correct errors and it allowed participants to confirm data and judge the adequacy of the interview.

This study follows the City University of New York Human Research Internal Review Guidelines (IRB) to protect human research participants. Pseudonyms are used to protect participants' identity. Consent forms were signed before interviews.

## Socioeconomic status, human capital, mode of incorporation and social mobility

Participants of this study shared their academic and professional experiences, their ambitions and future employment opportunities. Their life stories revealed how their parents' economic status, human capital and educational background served as a physical and symbolic resource for them:

If I do not get a job in a good law firm of my choice I have the option to work at my father's law firm. The job market in almost all fields is very bad . . . . This is my last year of my MBA at the London School of Economics. I do not need an MBA degree to be in law school but it might be an asset to my law career. Next semester I start my study at New York University Law School. My father is a lawyer and he taught at New York University Law School for many years. I come from a family of lawyers. My mother has a Law degree from India and she completed her second BA from City University of New York. A career in law is natural for me. (Nidhi)

I am chief of surgery at a University hospital in Manhattan, New York. My wife is a gynecologist. My father is a heart specialist at a New York hospital. My undergraduate degree is in Computer Science. I think unconsciously I was motivated by my father's profession and I decided to go into the medical profession. I come from a family of doctors . . . my grandfather was a surgeon. In my wife's family her mother, father, and grandfather are doctors. All of my brothers and sisters are very well settled and have high paying jobs in high tech fields. My two sisters are married to doctors and my brother's wife is in the medical technology field. (Anurag)

Nidhi, Anurag and many respondents like them earn more than their parents, or have option of earning as much as of their parents, belonged to middle class homes where at least one parent is a successful professional. Although many factors contribute to upward social mobility of the second-generation Asian Indians, one of the most important elements is the human capital that the first generation brought with them. The literature on educational and social stratification demonstrates that parental human capital and their socioeconomic status significantly influences their children's educational and economic achievement and social mobility (Blau and Duncan 1967, Featherman and Hauser 1978, Sewell and Hauser 1975).

Portes and Rumbaut (2001) define human capital as 'the skills immigrants bring along in the form of education, job experience and language are referred to as their *human capital* and play a decisive role in their economic adaptation' (p. 47, original emphasis). Asian Indians migrated to the USA with higher human capital and the asset of English language proficiency. Because changes in immigration law in 1965 gave preference to skills over nationality, US immigration opened doors to doctors, engineers and other educated people from India. Most of these professionals earned higher degrees in American institutions and added to their human capital. They establish themselves professionally and occupationally in competitive economic American society in a shorter period of time. The first generation Indians' higher socioeconomic status and their human capital are material and emotional resources for their children. Rima, one of the participants said:

I knew I had to do better . . . . My mom always said go for law school you will make good money. After three years of law school I started working with one of the nation's top corporate law firms in New York, with a salary that I asked for. I have worked with this firm before my graduation as a paralegal. I do earn a handsome salary but work is very hard and demanding. I am a New Yorker. I am born and brought up in New York. My father came to New York as a graduate student to do his PhD at the Graduate Center of the City University of New York. My mother earned her second BA, Masters, and Doctorate at City University. (Rima)

This is my final year at Columbia University Master in Public Health program. Growing up, our home was filled with books on history and politics, and my parents are both professors. This influenced me a lot when I was in school from a young age through college. I enjoyed school, and I was motivated to do well. Even though my parents never forced me with my schoolwork and studying, I knew that doing well was the right thing to do and would help me later in life. They did not lecture me, but the natural environment at home made me appreciate school, learning, and the importance of doing the best I could possibly do. (Suman)

The upward social mobility of second-generation and 1.5 Asian Indians is influenced by their parents' higher socioeconomic status in American society. Data of this study reveal that Indian immigrants with a lower level of human capital also have been on trajectory of upward mobility with hard work and use of social capital. They provide resources to their children. Intragenerational mobility among first generation Indians has been a strong force of intergeneration upward social mobility. Although there is an insignificant sign of downward mobility within the community (Saran 2010, 2009b, 2007), second-generation success stories are overwhelming. A majority of my respondents (70%) belong to middle and upper-middle class families. Their families live in large suburban homes in good neighborhoods (predominantly white) with good schools.

A smaller number of the participants (20%) are children of nonprofessional, less educated Indian immigrants who migrated to the USA during 1980 and onward on the basis of kinship. Although these immigrants were less educated and did not hold a professional degree from India and many of them hold semi-professional jobs or have started their own business, the intragenerational mobility among them is upward.

> At the age of six I came to New York with my family. My uncle, has a catering business. He was instrumental in bringing my family to New York. My father was a plant manager in a factory in India but in New York he worked as a mechanic at a car repair shop and my mother works as a cashier at a drug store. My father has a Masters in history and my mother holds a Masters degree in psychology but they could not find jobs in their field. Me and my two brothers also worked at neighborhood stores after school throughout schooling years. My family saved enough money to buy a house in a good neighborhood. I and my brothers have decent jobs in computer field. My sister works for New York transit as a supervisor and earns a decent living.

With higher economic resources and human capital participants' parents have been able to provide resources needed for academic success, such as affordability of good schools, expenses of a private college, to their children. Research in the area of educational achievement and future success reveals that Asian American students' academic success and their performance are influenced by parental social status (Kao and Tienda 1995, Schmid 2001). According to Kao and Tienda (1995) Asian families' higher socioeconomic status (SES) contributes to their children's educational attainment and upward mobility. Kao and Tienda's assertion is very true in the case of Asian Indians and their children.

Although SES and human capital are one of the predictors of second-generation success upward social mobility is not fully dependent only on these factors. The first generation immigrants' social status (voluntary or involuntary), the mode of incorporation and the context of reception in mainstream society have a significant effect on the second generation's trajectory of social mobility (Alba and Nee 2003, Fejgin 1995, Ogbu 1991, Portes and Rumbaut 2001, Schmid 2001, Zhou and Bankston 1994). Ogbu's study of Asian American immigrants (1988, 1991) concluded that Asian children had higher level of educational achievement regardless of their lower SES, cultural and linguistic differences. Ogbu's theory of 'voluntary minority' (1991) explains higher educational achievement and economic success of children of Indian immigrants. Ogbu (1991) stresses that Asian immigrants behave like voluntary minorities. Asian Indians are skilled immigrants and because of their higher level of human capital, their higher social status back home, they had a better context of reception in the USA. Ogbu notes that voluntary immigrant minorities do better in school and attain higher academic achievement because they interpret their struggle in their host country as an obstacle to overcome not a permanent impediment blocking their way. As a group Indian immigrants view discrimination, racism, prejudice and their marginalized status as realities of immigrant life and as obstacle that can be overcome by hard work and economic success. The qualitative data of this study demonstrates that in spite of low SES of their parents and lower level of human and educational capital many members of the second generation experience upward mobility.

## Cultural capital: a resource of academic and economic success

> I am a writer and a real New Yorker. My books have been best sellers. I graduated from Columbia University with a BA and MA in creative writing. My parents wanted me to get a degree in Business Administration or become a doctor. My mother and father have a master's degree in Business Administration and they are running a very successful jewelry business. They thought creative writing was not a secure field and I was taking a chance. However, they supported my decision. They assured me that if things did not work out for me I can always join the family business . . . . (Aniket)

According to Ogbu (1991) voluntary immigrants' cultural capital promotes upward mobility. Cultural capital is all cultural practices, dispositions, all skills, attitudes and way of life. The concept of capital can be understood as the pool of all resources (physical and symbolic) and power. Immigrants bring their cultural capital with them and their cultural capital contributes to their advancement or disadvantage in a foreign land. Increase or decline in the volume of different kinds of capital educational, economic, cultural, human and social capital mediates one's movement across social class. Often cultural capital serves as a resource and mediates one's success in mainstream society.

> I and my brother are doctors. My wife is a doctor also. At a very early age I realized that I had to compete with my parents and me and my brothers had to do better or equally good as our parents. My father is an engineer and my mother is a computer scientist. My mom has a great track record. She was a top student throughout school and college. I am impressed by her awards and gold medal she won for her academic achievements in India and in USA. In my family lower grades were not allowed. My parents very closely monitored our homework . . . . (Trilok)

> I am always on the honor roll and I always want to be on it. My parents never pressure me to get good grades but when I get 95 my mom says, what happened to the other 5? I do not mind this. You know this is good for me. She keeps me on track. If she is happy with 85, I guess I will not work hard to get more than 80 or 85 that is not a good grade for me. (Anil, 10th grade)

Asian upward mobility is credited to their cultural values and belief that views education as a means to achieve economic prosperity and social status. Portes and Rumbaut (2001) concluded that Asians cultural values and structure is the vital force of their children's success in dominant culture. Research in the area of voluntary minority performance (Gibson 1988, Ogbu 1991, Ogbu and Simons 1998, Portes and Rumbaut 2001, Zhou 1997, Kim and Zhou 2006) suggest that voluntary immigrants value education and for them high educational achievement is a road to economic success and access to middle and upper class. Similar to children of many voluntary immigrant groups, Indian children are constantly told by their parents that academic success is the weapon to fight discrimination and only way to upward mobility (Bhatia 2007, Gibson 1988).

Bourdieu (1979) describes a strong relationship between investment of scholastic and cultural capital and class mobility, and states that in society cultural capital is measured by the volume of educational qualification. According to Bourdieu academic success mainly depends on inherited cultural capital and on the inclination and ability to invest in the educational system. Bourdieu's theory (1979) provides explanation for the high concentration of Asian Indian students in elite schools and high-ranking colleges. In general, my first generation respondents believed education as an asset and a commodity to get economic capital and secure their position in hierarchy of American class structure. The path to *upclassing* or *downclassing* is determined by volume of academic achievement and qualification. Asian Indian immigrants know that as a minority group they do not have much political and social power in America. However, they realize that by using their educational capital and acquiring professional status they can make social connections, earn social capital and gain power in the dominant society.

## Upward mobility and social capital

Like many post-1965 non-European immigrants of color, Indian immigrants have mediated their children's social mobility through their social capital. In this study social capital is defined in terms of second-generation and 1.5 generation Asian Indians' social relationships in educational and professional fields, and within their ethnic community. Second-generation upward mobility is related with their affordance of social capital available to them. Their ethnicity, ethnic network and cultural capital have served as resources of social capital for their children. Through reconversion of inherited educational and economic capital Asian Indian children produce social capital. Second-generation social capital varies according to inherited familial and ethnic capital. Banshal, one of the respondent shared benefits of ethnic network:

> After graduating from Yale University and before starting New York University Dental Program I wanted to take a break, and wanted to work with a good dentist to wet my feet in the dental profession. I worked in one of my father's close dentist friend's clinic for six months. I learned a lot from dentist uncle ... after finishing up the dental program at NYU dental school while I was looking for jobs another family friend offered an internship at his dental office ... it was great ... I have my own dental practice now.

Suruchi's experiences are similar:

> I always wanted to work in New York. After completing the dental program at Boston University I came back to New York and worked at a hospital in Brooklyn. I did not like working at the hospital and joined my father's Dental Practice as a partner. I did not have to worry about establishing a practice ... to build a clientele.

Although Sukiran did not benefit from the ethnic network her mother's social network of medical doctors was a resource for her:

> I am a doctor ... my mother is a gynecologist and my father is a general physician. After graduating from high school I worked on a research project at the hospital where my mom works, with a very well known doctor. Although I graduated as a valedictorian and

I would have the internship on my own it was my mom who suggested to apply for this internship. Growing up with two doctors is tough but it is helpful also.

Recent studies on newer immigrants of color reveal that immigrant children benefit from their parents' individual and collective social capital, ethnic network and social solidarity of their ethnic community. Bourdieu (1979) states that the degree of social capital is a volume of social relation, and social energy/resources that are produced and reproduced through mediation of cultural capital. According to Bourdieu individual produce social capital at the social space of family and school by reconserving resources of both sites and guided by norms of that site. Social capital is defined as closed social network of support, trust, collective values and solidarity, and reciprocity (Coleman 1990, Portes and Sensenbrenner 1993, Zhou and Bankston 1994). Zhou and Bankston (1994) define social capital as closed system of social networks. A close observation of the social interaction of the first-generation respondents of this study revealed that parents created a close social structure and network to keep their children within their ethnic enclave and pass their ethnic values to them. In Indian parties a common theme of conversation among parents was to enable their children to become good students and enter prestigious colleges and professional trajectories.

Coleman (1988) analyzes the influence of social capital on children's academic performance, schooling experiences and future options. According to Coleman, a community's collective strength and strong structure enables families to develop social capital, establish norms and reinforce expectations. Parental and community's social capital provides guidance and support to second-generation individuals. Coleman observed that Asian families teach their children conformity, obedience and respect for hard work and education. Like majority of Asian immigrants, Indian parents teach their children to adapt meritocratic values of their families and mainstream society, to retain their cultural values and stay away from 'Americanized' Indian youths and native peers (Gibson 1988, Saran 2009b).

My participants reported that with their good conduct and their hard work they were successful at school and work place. For example, 25 year-old Nita has been working at one of the New York's top public relation firms for two years after receiving a BA in Political Science from Emory University. She is earning a good salary and she received a proposal to work on a special project as a senior program manager. She shared her experiences in her school and at her work place:

Everybody at my work likes me. I have to work really hard ... I am always working. At work they all praise me. They say I do wonderful job. You know my boss said my parents did excellent job with me they raised me right way. I have to give credit to my parents. My mom says one's best friend is one's hard work. At my high school I was the president of School Government Club. I participated in debates and won award for my services to school .... My teachers liked me a lot ....

Many participants like Nita used their social capital to earn symbolic capital (respect, admiration and friendship) in school and at the work place, and with higher level of symbolic capital they produced/reproduced a higher volume of social capital.

A distinct form of social capital is parental expectations and aspirations (Coleman 1988, Portes and Rumbaut 2001, Zhou and Bankston 1994). Participants in this study expressed that parental expectations and aspirations guided them towards upward mobility. Educated and professional parents of my participants had the know-how of American education they monitored their children's schooling vigilantly. They guided their children's academic work, their college choices and their selection of careers. These Asian Indian parents with an insights of American Education served as information channel to other members of their social network who lacked know how of American Education system. The social network enables immigrants to guard their children from downward mobility (Portes and Rumbaut 2001).

Overall, microsocial and macrosocial structure and norms of the positively stereo-typed Indian community is advantageous to the second-generation Asian Indians. The structural norms of Indian community expect community members to adapt positive values of American society and move to upward mobility. The Indian community has set high standards for second-generation youth, and those who meet those standards are constantly celebrated by social, political and economic local Indian associations and organizations. For example, the community's oldest newspaper, *India Abroad*, has a youth section in which accomplishments of high achieving youths are celebrated. Every year the India Abroad Foundation holds an award ceremony for outstanding Indian students and professionals. In general, the structural constraints of the Indian community impose model minority standards for second-generation individuals. Utilization of available familial and community resources afforded participants in this study upward mobility.

### Negotiation of advantages of two worlds: affordance of best of two worlds

> I tell my children they have best of both worlds available to them, it is in their favor to make a smart use of it. Just before I left India at age of 18 with my husband, then a PhD candidate and a lecturer at the City University of New York, my grandfather cautioned me, 'You are going to a country that has a lot to offer to you – good and bad both. I have lived there for 15 years so I know America very well. It is your respon-sibility to be mature and pick only good things of American life. You are very lucky you have a choice to pick from two cultures … be careful do not let America ruin you.' I have followed his advice, and have made best of opportunities available to me. I always remember my grandfather's advice and have tried my best to instill this message in my children. (An Indian mother)

Parental messages of utilizing best of two cultures have afforded many youths to negotiate challenges successfully and take advantage of opportunities available to them. I am not generalizing because there are always exceptions to generalization, not all second-generation Asian Indians are successful. An insignificant number of them are on a path of downward assimilation and have adapted street culture (Saran 2010). However, the data of this study speaks for an evident trajectory of upward mobility.

Although it is very hard to live between two worlds and maintain a healthy balance, in general my participants have done it successfully by taking advantage of the best of both worlds. In the process of taking advantage of two worlds they have created some-thing that is very unique – that is neither fully Indian nor fully American. It is like mixing two types of soil and carving a shape that has the essence of both soils but has a very distinct character of its own. One of my respondents expressed:

> Throughout my nursery to elementary school my mom visited my class and talked about India. It made me feel very special and made me aware that I had access to two very special worlds. I knew at a very early age that I was an American and at the same time I was an Indian … I am a mix … .

Garrod and Kilkenny (2007) describe this process of 'becoming their own personalities' and 'process of becoming' as a struggle with the contradictions of race, generation, economics, class, work, religion, gender and sexuality within all spheres of their life-world. Second-generation Asian Indians, participants in this study, have experienced complexities of school as children of immigrants, they have faced challenges of growing up in two cultures, experienced silent racism of American society and the burden of high expectations in schools and home yet they have been able to compete in mainstream. Kasinitz *et al.* (2008) assert that although there is variation among children of immigrants, compared with their parents they have achieved success and they are 'remaking the mainstream with truly remarkable speed'. In their study of children of immigrants coming of age in New York, they conclude, 'On the whole, second and 1.5 generation New Yorkers are already doing better than their parents. The Chinese and Russian Jews have demonstrated particular rapid upward mobility' (Kasinitz *et al.* 2008, p. 342). Kasinitz *et al.* (2008) explain that members of the immigrant second-generation community share the *immigrant advantage* that allows them to benefit from positive parental positions in American society.Through assimilation in mainstream society and taking advantage of their familial and cultural resources they sometime become 'wholly new'. On the contrary, some immigrant youth experience *immigrant disadvantages:* the lack of symbolic resources, such as lack of English Language Proficiency, lack of human capital and negative family structure. For some second-generation youth *immigrant disadvantages* create road blocks.

The second-generation Asian-Indians perceive themselves as American. At the same time, they are aware of the fact that they are not 'full Americans' and are perceived by the mainstream as foreigners because of their color of skin. Rima, a lawyer in one of the top corporate law firms of the nation confided:

> I am born and brought-up in New York ... I attended a very good law school, and I am considered a hard working very competent lawyer at work but often I get very frustrated. I am always taken as 'different/other' you know they are so ignorant of India. They even do not want to identify me with India. At work I am always mistaken as an Iranian woman ... is it not too hard to remember my ancestry? May be they do not want to acknowledge the fact that an Indian woman can be as competitive as a male white lawyer. It is very tough to survive in law profession as a woman of color specifically of Indian ancestry. My Indianness has no value in a competitive professional world. However, I have made it. I am working for this law firm for eight years and now I am ready to move on for a higher position in another law firm. (Rima)

My respondents constantly talked about their hardship in balancing in two worlds and their experiences of growing up in America in a culture that is very different than their parents' culture. At the same time, they acknowledged advantages that their family afforded them and how they were successful or unsuccessful in adapting or rejecting the best or worst of both worlds. Kasinitz *et al.* (2008) explain the scenarios of adaptation and elimination:

> Members of second generation sometimes negotiate among the different combination of immigrant and native advantage to choose the best combination for themselves .... Members of the second generation neither simply continue their parents' ways of doing things nor simply adopt native ways .... Sometimes they chose one, sometimes other, and sometime they try to combine the best of both worlds. They also sometimes create something wholly new. (pp. 20–21)

Second-generation youths in this study expressed that 'the best of both worlds' was a normal thing for them and 'it was the way of their life'. Maira (2002) discussing Asian Indian youths in New York City and Hall (2002) exploring second-generation youth in

Southall, London talk about 'the best of both worlds' notion and note that the sense of living in two worlds and creating a 'third world' is a way of life for second-generation Asian Indian youth. My assertion is that second-generation youth living in 'two worlds', have an advantageous position to access resources of both worlds. The positionality of second-generation and 1.5 Asian Indian between tow culture; and location between intersections of two cultures affords them advantages of both cultures. Kasinitz *et al.* (2008) describe second-generation advantage, 'We often attribute drive and creativity to the self-selection of immigrants or to ethnicity itself, but the real second-generation advantages come from being located between two cultures' (Kasinitz *et al.*, p. 356). The life stories of a majority of my respondents suggest that they moved ahead with the symbolic and physical assets they received from home and by selecting the best that American society offered to them.

## Coda

My research was initially motivated by concerns about the futures of second-generation Asian Indian youth who are upwardly mobile. The current recession is not only exclusive to New York; it has occurred nationally and internationally. In this context, the declining employment opportunities for immigrants and their children in New York mirrors that of the nation. Reflecting on the future of immigrants and their children in the labor market in times of recession Foner (2001) asserts that factors such as 'worker skills and education, employer preferences, discrimination, racism, union exclusion of minorities, and job networks will become much stronger determinants of ethnic group employment' (p. 23). In this scenario, my analysis centers on the impact of recession on second-generation Asian Indians in New York. It is hard to tell how second-generation and 1.5 Asian Indians will fare in New York's economy of the future because so much depends on economic conditions. However, the study provides some speculations as to what lies ahead in the years to come. Although the data reveals little evidence of second-generation decline, the study is concerned that in future upwardly mobile second-generation and 1.5 Asian Indians would be in accord with the predictions of second-generation decline theory (Gans 1992). The economic crisis raises many questions about how they will fare in the labor market and how they will respond to the already severe downturn. I argue that upwardly mobile Asian Indian youth are more vulnerable to unemployment than their native-white peer with a similar level of human capital as theirs and they might face more obstacles to economic gains.

This study worries about skewed upward mobility and fears that children of Asian Indians might experience downward mobility. As argued earlier, the study is concerned that the aftermath of the economic crisis in the USA would have negative consequences for upwardly mobile second-generation youth and they will experience *native disadvantages* (discrimination and racial segregation). Social scientists such as Gans, Kasinitz, Portes and Zhou, and Rumbaut hypothesize that second-generation youth of color will experience *native disadvantages* (prejudice, racial discrimination), would truncate their educational and professional opportunities, and it will be harder for them to get and retain decent jobs. Their color of skin and ethnicity might be more prominent than their educational and professional attainment, and they might earn less than their immigrant parents. Gans' (1992) theory of intergenerational socio-economic decline is relevant in the context of economic slowdown. The continuing economic disadvantages generated by the recession might produce a higher level of discrimination and prejudice. Perhaps some second-generation Asian youth would manage to avoid the impact of economic recession. On the contrary, many second-generation Asian Indian youth will be lumped with native and immigrant minorities and will be treated as 'people of color'. Despite their high educational accomplishments and professional preparation they will face problems in getting high-paying, high-skilled employment.

The data in this study show that the job situation has deteriorated because of the recession and for many participants it is hard to find even entry-level jobs in their field of expertise. This situation has increased 'the pressure of competition' for respondents who are pressured to excel. Some respondents felt more pressure owing to their parents' high level of economic/financial success, because they were expected to do better than their parents. While others felt pressure because their parents did not experience a high level of economic/professional success and they were expected to fulfill their parents' American dream. Many respondents indicated that they felt pressured to compete against their parents in terms of economic and professional success. They had to earn more than their parents and had to climb to a higher social position than their parents. At the same time, it was also harder for the children of upwardly mobile Indian immigrants because their parents expected them to do better financially. Raman's (a participant in this study) father is chief executive officer of a very successful fashion design company. Raman is expected to do better than his father. Raman was interested in a fine arts career but he opted to become a doctor because that is a secure field. My participants felt intense pressure; the financial crisis and parental class-coded expectations are a source of anxiety. Many participants in this study experience career-threat and anxieties related to upward mobility.

Participants in this study are young and are trying to do their best by reworking two worlds. Their success comes from their location between two cultures and their profound creativity to bridge the differences of two cultures. As I have asserted earlier, the participants in this study, second-generation and 1.5 Asian Indians, are on the path of upward mobility and their relative success conforms to the *segmented assimilation* and *selected acculturation* model (Kasinitz *et al.* 2008, Portes and Rumbaut 2001). These models assert that children of immigrants experience economic upward mobility with parental support, strong parental human capital, community support, holding onto ethnic values and adapting positive American norms and values. My respondents are from two-parent families and households that relentlessly pursue children to gain economic success by doing well academically. Although the respondents of this study showed ease with living in two worlds and benefiting from the best of the two worlds, they are not reaping the benefits of their hard work in the labor market.

Highly skilled youth like Amir and Lalima who are experiencing the constrains of the US economy look at recession as a temporary phenomenon that will get better soon. Although my participants showed optimism and hope I could see a faint sense of despair. Amir, one of the participants stated:

> I am sure I will find a job ... sometimes I think why this happened to me? There were days when I did not sleep for two days in a row and worked to make the Sports Museum a success ... it did not work out. Maybe I will start another venture ... I am exploring, but first I have to get a job. (Amir)

Frustration and disappointment are evident in Amir's narrative. One needs to explore psychological effects of the recession on members of the second generation who 'did everything right' to become successful but are not doing well in the labor market and suffering from a sense of failure. Anusha, a lawyer and a participant in this study, working in a medical insurance company, is skeptical that in the near future she will be able to get a job in a law firm. Participants of this study are flexible and are willing to take jobs that are underpaid and are not in their field of expertise. Their attitude and willingness to get employment is commendable, however, the pressure to obtain employment and job insecurity might bear negative psychological consequences for them.

Somesh, one of the respondents, who graduated from New York University Business School, confided that he is constantly under the stress of losing his high-paid job at an investment banking firm. He stated:

> I cannot ask my parents for financial help . . . . They have no money. My mother has a masters in economics and my father was an engineer in India. But here (USA) my mother is a cashier in a department store and my father works in his friend's computer business that can shut down any day. (Somesh)

In a household where parents have faced limited social mobility Somesh has found his way up through the educational route into a highly paid profession. However, like many of my respondents, Somesh is under job-security pressure. I observed that my respondents' confidence and their ability to 'work their way up' are shaken by the economic crisis that is not unique to young Asian Indians but to all immigrants and native groups.

Recent setbacks in the economy have impacted all, but it is more severe for the children of immigrants in the context of growing anti-immigrant sentiment and insensitivity. In the environment of anti-immigrant sentiments that is on the rise because of the recent fiscal crisis in American society, Asian Indian youth are vulnerable to job-related insensitivity. They tend to suffer job losses and experience economic constraints. Evidence from recent recessions confirms that second-generation Asian Indians, who are especially susceptible, move down the skill chain and are willing to take underemployment rather than unemployment. By being willing to settle for low salaries, high-skilled Asian Indian youth are likely to affect the wages of native workers of high skill and are susceptible to overt and covert anti-immigrant sentiments. The qualitative data from this study suggest that there is a significant economic up-grading from the first generation to the second generation and, in general, the second-generation Asian Indians have achieved striking upward mobility despite their marginalized status in mainstream society. Overall, second-generation and 1.5 Asian Indian youth are already doing better than their immigrant parents. Many respondents who are attending high school or ones who are enrolled in college expressed optimism and thought that economic conditions would improve by the time they entered the labor market. Some respondents mentioned the *immigrant disadvantages*, that is, their parents' lower level of human capital, lack of English language proficiency and dissonant cultural orientation (Kasinitz *et al.* 2008); however, they negotiated these *immigrant disadvantages* and have tried to overcome them. These Indian youth have done better than their immigrant parents in terms of education and earnings and they are showing upward mobility. While it is true that in this economy an insignificant number of Asian Indian youth are experiencing hardship, data from this study suggest that highly quali-fied youth have a positive attitude toward the economic crisis and they are hopeful for their future employment opportunities. Only time will answer how they will adjust to the labor market shock and how they will compete with native-born white high-skilled youth with shrinking employment opportunities as people of color.

## Notes on contributor

Dr Rupam Saran is Associate Professor of Education at Medgar Evers College, City University of New York. Dr Saran's research focuses on learning and achievement of the second-generation Indian students and math education of children of immigrants in urban schools. She is the author of *Beyond Stereotype: Minority Children of Immigrants in Urban Schools* (Rotterdam: Sense Publishers, 2010).

## References

Alba, R.D. and Nee, V., 2003. *Remaking in the American mainstream: assimilation and contemporary immigration*. Cambridge, MA: Harvard University Press.

Barber, J.A. and Barber, E.G., 1965. *European social class: stability and changes*. New York: Macmillan.

Bhatia, S., 2007. *American Karma: race, culture and identity in the Indian diaspora*. New York: New York University Press.

Blau, P. and Duncan, O.D., 1967. *The American occupational structure*. New York: John Wiley & Sons.

Borjas, J.G., 2006. Making it in America: social mobility in the immigrant population. *Future of Children*, 16 (2), 55–71.

Bourdieu, P., 1979. *Distinction: a social critique of the judgment of taste*. New York: Routledge.

Brauer, D. and Flaherty, M., 1992. The New York City recession. *Federal Reserve Bank of New York Quarterly Review*, 17, 66–71.

Carliner, G., 1980. Wages, earnings, and hours of first, second, and third generation American males. *Economic Inquiry*, 18 (1), 87–102.

Chiswick, B.R., 1977. Sons of immigrants: are they at an earning disadvantage? *American Economic Review*, 67 (1), 376–380.

Coleman, J.S., 1988. Social capital in the creation of human capital. *American Journal of Sociology*, 94, S95–S120.

Coleman, J.S., 1990. *Foundations of social theory*. Cambridge, MA: The Belknap Press of Harvard University Press.

Featherman, D.L. and Hauser, R.M., 1978. *Opportunity and changes*. New York: Academic Press.

Feigelman, W. and Saran, P., 2002. Asian Indians: a census based portrait of advantaged American minorities. *72nd annual meeting of the Eastern Sociological Society*, March 15, 2002, Boston, MA.

Fejgin, N., 1995. Factors contributing to the academic excellence of American Jewish and Asian students. *Sociology of education*, 68 (1), 18–30.

Foner, N., 2001. *New Immigrants in New York*. New York: Columbia University Press.

Fujita, M., 1987. Dialogical approach to lived meaning. *Bergamo conference on curriculum theory and classroom practice*, Dayton, Ohio.

Gans, H.J., 1992. Second-generation decline: scenarios of the economic and ethnic futures of the post-1965 American immigrants. *Ethnic and Racial Studies*, 15 (2), 173–192.

Garrod, A. and Kilkenny, R., 2007. *Balancing two worlds: Asian American college students tell their stories*. Ithaca, NY: Cornell University Press.

Gibson, A.M., 1988. *Accommodation without assimilation: Sikh immigrants in an American high school*. Ithaca, NY: Cornell University Press.

Glazer, N., 1980. Forward. *In*: P. Saran and A. Eames, eds. *The Asian Indian experience in the United States*. New York: Praeger, vi–viii.

Glazer, N. and Moynihan, D.P., 1963. *Beyond the melting pot: the Negroes, Puerto Ricans, Jews, Italians, and Irish of New York City*. Cambridge, MA: Harvard University Press.

Guba, E.G. and Lincoln, Y.S., 1989. *Fourth generation evaluation*. Thousand Oaks, CA: Sage.

Hall, K.D., 2002. *Lives in translation: Sikh youth as British citizens*. Philadelphia, PA: University of Pennsylvania Press.

Kao, G. and Tienda, M., 1995. Optimism and achievement: the educational performance of immigrant youth. *Social Science Quarterly*, 76 (1), 1–19.

Kasinitz, P., Mollenkopf, J.H., Waters, M.C., and Holdaway, J., 2008. *Inheriting the city: the children of immigrants come of age*. New York: Russell Sage Foundation.

Kessler, A., 2001. Immigration, economic insecurity and the ambivalent American public. Working paper 41. University of Texas, Austin. Available from: http://www.escholarship.org/uc/item/6k5531rt.

Kim, S.S. and Zhou, M., 2006. Community forces, social capital, and educational achievement: the case of supplementary education in the Chinese and Korean immigrant communities. *Harvard Educational Review*, 76 (1), 1–29.

Kincheloe, J.L., 2001. *Getting beyond the facts: teaching social studies/social sciences in the twenty-first century*. New York: Peter Lang.

Kitano, H.H.L. and Danield, R., 2001. *Asian Americans: emerging minorities*. Upper Saddle River, NJ: Prentice Hall.

Lawless, R.M., Littwin, A.K., Porter, K.M., Pottow, J.A.E., Thorne, D.K., and Warren, E., 2008. Did bankruptcy reform fail? An empirical study of consumer debtors. *American Bankruptcy Law Journal*, 82, 349–406.

Leonhard, D., 2009. United States economy. *New York Times*, 13 August 2009, 10.

Lessinger, J., 1996. *From Ganges to the Hudson: Indian immigrants in New York City*. Needham Heights, MA: Allyn & Bacon.

Maira, S.M., 2002. *Desis in the house: Indian American youth culture in New York City*. Philadelphia, PA: Temple University Press.

Mayo, L. and Parella, M., 1998. *History of minorities in the United States*. New York: Whittier Publications.

Ogbu, J.U., 1991. Immigrant and involuntary minorities in comparative perspective. *In*: M. Gibson and J.U. Ogbu, eds. *Minority status and schooling: a comparative study of immigrant vs. involuntary minorities*. New York: Garland, 3–33.

Ogbu, J.U. and Simons, H.D., 1998. Voluntary and involuntary minorities: a cultural-ecological theory of school performance with some implications for education. *Anthropology & Education Quarterly*, 29 (2), 155–188.

Olsen, L., 1997. *Made in America: immigrant students in our public school*. New York: The New Press.

Osajima, K., 1988. Asian American as the model minority: an analysis of the popular press image in the 1960s and 1980s. *In*: G.Y. Okihiro, S. Hune, A.A. Hansen and J.M. Liu, eds. *Reflection on shattered windows: promises and prospects of Asian American studies*. Pullman, WA: Washington State University Press, 165–174.

Papademetriou, D.G. and Terrazas, A., 2009. Immigrants in the United States and the current economic crisis. *Migration Information*, Migration Policy Institute, Washington DC. Available from: www.migrationinformation.org/Feature/print.cfm?ID=723 [Accessed 15 March 2010].

Pinar, W.F., Reynolds, W.M., Slattery, P., and Taubman, P.M., 2000. *Understanding curriculum*. New York: Peter Lang.

Portes, A. and Rumbaut, R.G., 2001. *Legacies: the story of the immigrant second generation*. Berkeley, CA: University of California Press.

Portes, A. and Sensenbrenner, J., 1993. Embeddendness and immigration: notes on social determinants economic action. *American Journal of Sociology*, 98 (6), 1320–1350.

Portes, A. and Zhou, M., 1993. The new second generation: segmented assimilation and its variants. *Annals of the American Academy of Political Sciences*, 530 (1), 74–96.

Ratha, D., Mahapatra, S., and Silwal, A., 2009. Outlook for remittance flows 2009–2011: remittances expected to fall by 7–10 percent in 2009. *Migration and Development Brief 10*, World Bank, Washington, DC. Available from: http://siteresources.worldbank.org/INTPROSPECTS/Resources/334934-1110315015165/Migration&DevelopmentBrief10.pdf.

Rong, X.L. and Grant, L., 1992. Ethnicity generation and school attainment of Asians, Hispanics, and non-Hispanic Whites. *Sociological Quarterly*, 33, 625–636.

Sacchett, M., 2009. American dreams deferred: recession batters immigrants at all economic levels. *The Boston Globe*, 24 March 2009, 3.

Sandhu, G.S., 1995. Indian-Americans are industrious, resourceful, and prudent. *India Worldwide*, 31 January 1995, 1.

Saran, P., 1985. *The Asian Indian experience in the United States*. Rochester, VT: Schenkman.

Saran, R., 2007. Model minority imaging in New York: the situation with second generation Asian Indian learners in middle and secondary school. *The Anthropologist*, (Special volume), 2, 67–79.

Saran, P., 2009a. Asian Indian experience in the United States: then and now. *The Anthropologist*, (Special volume), 4, 65–69.

Saran, R., 2009b. *Anthropologist*, (Special volume), 4, 51–64.

Saran, R., 2010. Beyond stereotype: second generation Asian Indian students in urban schools. *In*: R. Saran and R. Diaz, eds. *Beyond stereotypes: minority children of immigrants in urban schools*. Rotterdam: Sense Publishers.

Schafer, T.R., 2002. *Racial and ethnic groups: census 2000 update*. Upper Saddle Reiver, NJ: Prentice Hall.

Schmid, C.L., 2001. Educational achievement, language-minority students, and the new second generation. *Sociology of Education*, (Extra Issue: Current of Thought: Sociology of Education at the Dawn of the 21st Century), 74, 71–87.

Sewell, W. and Hauser, R., 1975. *Education, occupation, and earnings: achievement in the early career*. New York: Academic Press.

Simon, R., 1993. Old minorities, new immigrants: aspirations, hopes, and fears. *The Annals of the Political and Social Science*, 530, 61–73.

Simon, R. and Alexander, S.H., 1993. *The ambivalent welcome: print media, public opinion, and immigrants*. Westport, CT: Praeger.

Suarez-Orozco, C. and Suarez-Orozco, M.M., 2001. *Children of immigration*. Cambridge, MA: Harvard University Press.

Tedlock, B., 2000. The observation of participation and the emergence of public ethnography. *In*: N.K. Denzin and Y.S. Lincoln, eds. *The Sage handbook of qualitative research*. Thousand Oaks, CA: Sage, 467–482.

Van Manen, M., 1990. *Researching lived experience*. Albany, NY: State University of New York Press.

Waldinger, R. and Feliciano, C., 2004. Will the new second generation experience 'Downward assimilation'? Segmented assimilation re-assessed. *Ethnic and Racial Studies*, 27 (3), 376–402.

Walker-Moffat, W., 1995. *The other side of the Asian American success story*. San Francisco, CA: Jossey-Bass.

Warner, W.L. and Srole, L., 1945. *The social system of American ethnic groups*. New Haven, CT: Yale University Press.

Wilson, K.L. and Portes, A., 1980. Immigrant enclaves: an analysis of the labor market experience of Cubans in Miami. *American Journal of Sociology*, 86 (2), 295–319.

Winnick, L., 1990. America's model minorities. *Commentary*, 90 (2), 22–29.

Zhou, M., 1997. Growing up American: the challenges confronting immigrant children and children of immigrants. *Annals of Review of Sociology*, 23, 69–95.

Zhou, M. and Bankston, C.L., 1994. Social capital and the adaptation of the second generation: the case of the Vietnamese youths in New Orleans. *International Migration Review*, 28 (4), 821–825.

# The power of technology: a qualitative analysis of how South Asian youth use technology to maintain cross-gender relationships

Arshia U. Zaidi[a], Amanda Couture[a] and Eleanor Maticka-Tyndale[b]

[a]Faculty of Social Science and Humanities, University of Ontario Institute of Technology, Oshawa, Canada; [b]Department of Sociology, Anthropology and Criminology, University of Windsor, Windsor, Canada

This research explores how South Asian youth in Canada use computer-mediated communication (CMC) such as social networking sites, cell phones and instant messaging in their cross-gender intimate relationships. Using 42 qualitative interviews conducted with second-generation South Asian Canadians living in the Greater Toronto Area and Durham region, this article sheds light on the motives for using CMC as well as negative consequences that can emerge. The data reveal that South Asian youth are using CMC to initiate and build relationships, remain connected with partners, engage in discreet communication, to ease uncomfortable and intimate discussions, and to communicate when face-to-face interaction is not available. Gender, religion and country of origin differences were rare, but did appear in a few motives. Negative consequences of CMC use volunteered by participants include parental–child conflict over restriction and questioning CMC use and its use leading to parents' discovery of a 'secret' relationship. Overall, CMC provided a means for second-generation South Asian youth in Canada to overtly adhere to norms of gender-separation while covertly engaging in cross-gender relationships. If not discovered, this helped to maintain family honour within the South Asian community while fulfilling their perceived need for cross-gender friendships and romantic involvements.

## Introduction

This is the age of the technological revolution. These days the power of technology is felt and seen in most aspects of social life today. For most individuals, its use has become second nature (Bargh and McKenna 2004) and somewhat habit forming. Individuals today use technology, specifically computer-mediated communication (CMC), in their personal lives for the purposes of communication, information, formation and maintenance of relationships, and solely entertainment. Historically, prior to the telephone, connecting to loved ones was a daunting task that entailed written cards or letters that eventually required paying a visit to the nearest post office (Ramirez and Broneck 2009). Today, however, CMC has facilitated the social exchange process for relational partners and interpersonal communication in more ways than one (McKenna and Bargh 1999). A variety of Internet, email and instant messaging (IM) tools have allowed for relational social exchange to occur in 'real' time or at a much faster pace. The rapid advancement of CMC has changed the way the social world and interpersonal relationships operate. Regardless of distance, such technologies not only allow people the opportunity to communicate with loved ones, but also let individuals maintain relationships in a convenient and inexpensive manner (Rabby and Walther 2003, Johnson *et al.* 2008). This is further supported by many scholars who have suggested that one of the manifest functions of the Internet, email and IM is development, expansion, formation, as well as maintenance of social networks and interpersonal relationships (Zakin 1996, Wolak and Mitchell 2002, Kindred and Roper 2004, Johnson *et al.* 2008, Ramirez and Broneck 2009).

It is important to note that much of the existing scholarship on CMC has focused on the 'hows' and the 'whys' of various CMC use by individuals in relationships from a western and individualistic perspective/culture (Ye 2006). Moreover, most research reports results from quantitative data about how many people report using various forms of CMC and how many report using it for specific reasons. There are few studies which examine qualitative differences in individual use or that more specifically explore the motives and negative consequences of such use. There are also few that consider use by youth who belong to collectivistic cultures (for example, South Asian culture) with respect to interpersonal relationships or who analyse their results from an ethno cultural standpoint. Current literature does indicate that there are differences in CMC use by gender, race and age; however, there appears to be an absence of scholarship exploring the individual experiences of specific cultural and religious groups with CMC. While scholars like Jackson (2007, p. 154) suggest 'social and cultural norms may reinforce usage', as well as perceptions of such technologies, there remains a dearth of scholarship on individual experiences of those from collectivist cultures with CMC (Yum and Hara 2005). Other scholars have also reported that culture plays a pivotal role in communication and communication styles and may influence, govern and regulate CMC usage (Ting-Toomey 1991, Amant 2002, Hanna and Nooy 2004). To begin to address this gap, this article explores how one racialized group, South Asian youth, make use of CMC in their cross-gender relationships, their motives for doing so, and potential negative consequences of such use.

## Why South Asian youth: the rationale

Given the increasing diversification of Canadian society, understanding CMC usage from an ethno-cultural perspective becomes relevant and important. For example, most recent statistics suggest that increasing numbers of immigrants come from non-European countries and that South Asians form the largest portion of the immigrant community in Canada. By 2031, South Asians are expected to represent almost 30% of the visible minority population in Canada (Statistics Canada 2010).

The traditional South Asian family is a collectivistic entity, which embraces cohesiveness, loyalty and compliance from immediate and extended family members. At the heart of the socialization process, elements of family honour and shame are taught, especially to young women (Hickey 2004). In this culture, cross-gender relationships (i.e. male–female associations) are ideally contained and expected to occur only within marriage. This is necessary to maintain the honour of the family (Haddad *et al.* 2006). Any deviation from this norm, especially by women, is frowned upon by family and community members[1] (Dodd 1973, Abu-Laban 1974, Wakil *et al.* 1981, Ghosh 1984, Naidoo 1984, Shapurian and Hojat 1985, Das Gupta 1997,

Akpinar 2003, Handa 2003, Dion and Dion 2004, Kallivayalil 2004). Face-saving strategies, to preserve family honour, are an integral part of collectivistic cultures.

Based on the above family structure and core value-system, it becomes difficult for young South Asians to have an open and expressive relationship with the opposite sex. Social interactions as well as communication may be policed and guarded by the family and community. Within the context of such limitations and/or restrictions, CMC technologies can ease the process of communication with an opposite-gender friend or relationship partner. CMC can make relationship development, formation and maintenance convenient for South Asian youth as well as provide them with the necessary privacy and confidentiality. It becomes an effective solution for these racialized youth where face-to-face interactions with members of the opposite sex may not always be feasible.

While there is considerable literature that suggests traditional physical or face-to-face interaction is more desirable for relationship development and maintenance than CMC (Baym 2002, Ramirez and Zhang 2007), the scholarship supporting the benefits of CMC usage by individuals in relationships is fast growing. Studies on CMC and relationship initiation, development and maintenance suggests CMC has become a socially acceptable form of communication with relational partners (Bargh and McKenna 2004) with a primary reason for using CMC the maintenance of relationships (Nardi *et al.* 2000, Dainton and Aylor 2002). Much of the most recent literature discusses the positive outcomes and/or contributions that CMC makes to the social world and to interpersonal relationships. For example, Long (2010) found that digital communication technologies serve as a means of communication when no other forms are available (e.g. across large geographical distances); thus, she suggests that digital communication is not being used as a substitute for face-to-face communication, but rather as a complement. This is further supported by Nachbaur (2003) whose results show that IM acts as a supplement for traditional forms of communication rather than a replacement. As a result, he argues that it allows for more frequent communication that can assist in relationship-building (Nachbaur 2003). Additional research has explored how CMC is used to maintain relationships by allowing individuals to have 'more freedom and comfort in their interpersonal interactions' (Sidelinger *et al.* 2008, p. 342). Walther (1992, p. 4) refers to this as 'hyperpersonal communication'. He suggests that CMC conversations, compared to face-to-face conversations, ease the process of communication because conversational discomforts, which may be present in face-to-face interactions, are minimized (Walther 1992). There is also literature that examines individual differences in media usage with use varying by how sociable individuals are and whether or not they like face-to-face communication (Utz 2000). Surprisingly, cultural differences or variations are not mentioned.

It has been reported that in the USA and Canada 78.6 million individuals over the age of 16 use the Internet (Merkle and Richardson 2000). However, studies on CMC have consistently reported that younger people are more heavily engaged in CMC technology usage than older people (Leung 2001, Blais *et al.* 2008, Sidelinger *et al.* 2008). More specifically, Lenhart *et al.* (2010) found that in the USA 14% of individuals between the ages of 18 and 29 blog, 72% use social networking sites and 93% own a cell phone. According to the Pew Internet & American Life Project (2002), 26% of college Internet users indicated that on average they communicate daily through IM. This is almost twice as likely as non-college student Internet users.

With respect to gender differences in CMC usage, research produces mixed results. While some studies suggest that the so-called 'gender divide' of men using these technologies more than women is narrowing (Odell *et al.* 2000), others suggest that men continue to have greater experience with interactive technologies than women and use it for very different reasons. For example, women use it more to talk to family and friends and men more to pursue recreational goals (Morahan-Martin and Schumacher 1999, Schumacher and Morahan-Martin 2001, Boneva and Kraut 2002, Ledbetter 2008). Research by Punyanunt-Carter and Hemby (2006) suggests that women in particular use CMC, specifically Internet and email, to maintain relationships.

While there has been a recent push towards incorporating culture into understanding CMC, the work is limited in its scope. Conducted primarily in the USA and Europe, it focuses on comparing the number of individuals from various racial/ethnic groups engaging in CMC use, their access to computers, and the relative influence of ethnicity or race, socio-economic status and past experience on CMC use (Hoffman and Novak 1998, Eastin and LaRose 2000). There are few studies that elaborate on the social, cultural and religious reasons for variation in CMC use. Leung (2001) and Flanagin (2010) examine diverse motives for CMC use, including relaxation, entertainment, 'fashion', affection, sociability, ease of communication, to stay in touch, convenience, to pass time, to get to know others, to learn things, to meet people. However, as in other research on CMC, this work also does not look at the unique experiences and/or social context of membership in various racialized groups for shaping reasons and negative consequences of using CMC or for preferring CMC to face-to-face interactions in particular types of relationships such as those that are cross-gender.

Several scholars have suggested that the psychological theory, *Uses and Gratification* (U&G), is a relevant approach to explaining the use of new media technologies, in this case CMC (Morris and Ogan 1996, Newhagen and Rafaeli 1996, Wright 2002). U&G theory is the theoretical perspective that guides this research and helps explain how and why people use CMC. U&G theory views people as agents who actively pursue specific goals. It focuses on motives for use, how people use CMC to fulfil their needs, and the outcomes and/or consequences of media use (Katz *et al.* 1974). Rubin (2002) recently specified the four components of U&G theory. First, individuals are active and motivated in choosing their media. Second, communication methods are chosen to fulfil certain needs and desires. Third, psychosocial factors play a role in communication behaviour. Fourth, social and psychological contexts may influence how well media can serve and satisfy an individual's desires. Depending on the social context, functional alternatives may be sought to satisfy the needs of social interaction. Traditionally, U&G has been used to explain mass media (i.e. TV, radio and newspaper) use. Using U&G to analyse CMC use helps us understand the 'hows' and 'whys' by focusing our attention on the motives, consequences and gratification of CMC use by South Asian youth.

## Methodology

### Sample and sampling technique

Non-probability purposive sampling was used to gather a sample of unmarried second-generation South Asian youth (which includes: Bangladesh, Bhutan, India, Nepal, Pakistan and Sri Lanka). For the purpose of this study, second generation is defined as individuals who were born in Canada or moved here before the age of eight. The three main religious communities targeted for participation in this study were

Muslims, Hindus and Christians. A sample of individuals between the ages of 18 and 34 years was sought. This was done to maximize the probability that participants will have had some experience of cross-gender interactions and/or relationships. Furthermore, at this age, most are completing or just out of high school and parental control is likely to be more relaxed. Beyond 34 years most are married.

### Data collection and recruitment

According to Statistics Canada (2001), Toronto has one of the largest and diverse South Asian populations in Ontario. As a result, the Greater Toronto Area (GTA) was targeted for recruitment. Recruitment focused primarily on university and college campuses across the GTA. Recruitment strategies included: posters, campus-wide e-mails, movie theatre advertisements and flyers given out at locations frequented by South Asians. Interested participants were instructed to email the research team and arrangements were made for face-to-face semi-structured interviews. In addition, an honorarium was offered to participants to cover transportation and thank them for their time.

The interview schedule addressed, but was not limited to the following themes: participant's background, parent's socio-economic status, race/ethnic relations within the host country, family, school and community characteristics, personal accounts of cultural scripts of cross-gender relationships of host and heritage country, participants' interpersonal scripts and experiences of cross-gender relationships, primary/secondary socialization agents and intergenerational conflicts. Of note is that the use of CMC was not the specific focus of the interview, but emerged as a theme in the analysis of early interviews and was consequently added as an area to explore in all later interviews. All interviews were audio recorded, upon informed consent by participants, such that verbatim transcription could take place and confirmability of data determined. Each transcription was checked by members of the research team to ensure accuracy.

### Data analysis

Data analysis was done using an interpretive methodology assisted by QSR N6 software. Each transcription was uploaded to QSR N6 software. Members of the research team immersed themselves in the data by going through an iterative process of reading, re-reading and reviewing all transcripts to create an individual profile of each participant's reports of cultural and interpersonal scripts. Profiles created by different members of the team were compared and inconsistencies discussed, with transcripts returned for clarification.

The goal of this research was not to produce estimates of the prevalence of different motives for use or the different forms of CMC that were used, but rather to more fully understand how and why CMC was used. In the terminology of U&G theory, this research sought to elicit motives for use, the needs that CMC fulfilled and the outcomes or consequences of use. With this goal in mind, and consistent with qualitative interviewing methodology, participants were not questioned specifically about each motive, but instead asked a general question that encouraged them to speak about their CMC use. Consequently, the preponderance of use of specific CMCs or specific motives reported in results cannot be taken as a valid estimation of frequency or importance, but are merely an indication of the motives or consequences about which participants most often spoke during the interview.

## Results

### Sample profile

57 participants were interviewed. Of these, 42 spoke of CMC. It is these participants who provided data for this paper. The sample of 42 consists of slightly more males (23) than females (19) with an average age of 20 years. It is religiously diverse with participants adhering to Islam, Hinduism and Christianity. Participants and/or their families migrated from a range of countries including: Sri Lanka Pakistan, India, Nepal and Bangladesh. Participants perceived themselves to be relatively economically advantaged with the majority reporting that their families are middle- or middle to upper-class. Table 1 presents the sample profile details.

### Use of technology – analysis of motives and negative consequences

During discussions of intimate relationships in early interviews, some participants mentioned using various communication technologies. As a result, the interview guide was adjusted to probe for the use of communication technologies, the role they had in intimate relationships or participants' motives for using them, and the effect they had on relationships. 41 of the 42 participants who discussed CMC reported using it in cross-gender relationships. Regardless of sex, religion and country, the majority of participants used MSN and texting. Facebook was the least discussed form of CMC. In most cases, MSN, texting and Facebook were used in combination, especially MSN and texting. Email and speaking on the phone were also mentioned.

The analysis below examines the six motives for using communication technologies that participants volunteered during the interviews. In order of most to least popular, these include: building relationships, keeping connected with partners, discreet communication, initiating relationships, easing potentially uncomfortable discussions (i.e. it is easier to say some things online) and, a motive that overlapped with several of the other five, communicating when face-to-face interaction is not possible (i.e. it is the next best thing). The majority of the sample who used CMC reported multiple motives for using communication technologies. Gender, religion and country of origin differences were rare, but did appear in a few motives. The motives spoken of by the largest number of male participants were building relationships, discreet communication and relationship initiation. Although a majority of females also spoke of building relationships, keeping connected was the motive spoken of by the largest number, with these two followed by discreet communication. Discreet communication also evidenced religious, as well as country differences, with it offered as a motive primarily by Muslim participants and exclusively by participants from Pakistan and Sri Lanka. While less often spoken of and no direct questions were asked to elicit this information, nine participants also spoke of negative consequences to using communication technologies which included conflict with parents about their use of CMC and their parents' discovery of their secret relationship resulting from their CMC use.

### Motives

#### Building relationships

Building relationships was the most commonly volunteered reason for CMC use. Participants discussed how online communication allowed their relationship to evolve by providing them with a means of becoming increasingly familiar with one another.

Table 1.   Sample profile.

| | |
|---|---|
| *Sex* | |
| Male | 55% ($n = 23$) |
| Female | 45% ($n = 19$) |
| *Religion* | |
| Muslim | |
|    Female | 47% ($n = 7$) |
|    Male | 53% ($n = 8$) |
|    Total[a] | 36% ($n = 15$) |
| Hindu | |
|    Female | 53% ($n = 8$) |
|    Male | 57% ($n = 7$) |
|    Total[a] | 36% ($n = 15$) |
| Christian | |
|    Female | 67% ($n = 8$) |
|    Male | 33% ($n = 4$) |
|    Total[a] | 29% ($n = 12$) |
| *Country of origin* | |
| India | |
|    Female | 67% ($n = 6$) |
|    Male | 33% ($n = 3$) |
|    Total[a] | 21.4% ($n = 9$) |
| Pakistan | |
|    Female | 44% ($n = 7$) |
|    Male | 56% ($n = 9$) |
|    Total | 38% ($n = 16$) |
| Sri Lanka | |
|    Female | 50% ($n = 7$) |
|    Male | 50% ($n = 7$) |
|    Total | 33.3% ($n = 14$) |
| Nepal | |
|    Female | 100% ($n = 1$) |
|    Total | 2.3% ($n = 1$) |
| Bangladesh | |
|    Female | 100% ($n = 1$) |
|    Total | 2.3% ($n = 1$) |
| Sri Lanka/India | |
|    Female | 100% ($n = 1$) |
|    Total | 2.3% ($n = 1$) |
| *Socio-economic status* | |
| Lower | 2.4% ($n = 1$) |
| Lower-middle | 2.4% ($n = 1$) |
| Middle | 63.4% ($n = 26$) |
| Middle-upper | 24.4% ($n = 10$) |
| Upper | 7.3% ($n = 3$) |
| Total | 41[b] |

[a]Percent of those who discussed communication technology (42).
[b]One missing case.

Asad, a 20-year-old Muslim male whose family is from India, explained the role technology played in his relationship. He said:

> It was more of a tool that we used to build it I guess ... And, you know, small things like that maybe don't have, you know, you don't see a sudden impact. But, you know that, you talk and you become more comfortable ... And so that advances the relationship for sure ... Yeah, well it helped us, um, become more comfortable with each other.

Rizwan, an 18-year-old Muslim male whose family is from Pakistan, also commented on how his relationship benefited from communication technologies. He stated:

> I don't know, built it [is] stronger 'cause we got to know each other better.

Another example of this was provided by Abid, a 21-year-old Muslim male whose family is also from Pakistan. He said:

> If you talk more, learn more about each other. The more we talk the more we learn, right? I didn't really know much about her in the beginning. The more I get to know her the more I like her.

Sonia, a 22-year-old female Hindu whose family is from Sri Lanka. She said:

> Through MSN like it created a better communication level, right?

During the interviews, it also became evident that certain modes of communication are more intimate and personal than others. Some participants described a progression from impersonal to increasingly more intimate forms of communication as comfort increased. Facebook was the most impersonal, followed by MSN, texting and then speaking on the phone. This is evident in the statement below by Govinda, a 22-year-old male Hindu whose family is from India.

> (How did the relationship begin?) Facebook ... it was just talking and one thing led to another. Two weeks later talking, we just ... decided to start dating .... Either she added me or I added her then we were just talking. Just being friends ... It was through messages and it progressed from Facebook to MSN, then texting ...

Having online conversations with their partner appears to have made some participants feel more comfortable at the beginning stages of their relationship. Once a particular comfort level was reached, they felt more relaxed in sharing their telephone numbers and meeting face-to-face. A quote from Vanessa, an 18-year-old female Christian whose family is from Sri Lanka, provides an example of this.

> It (technology) did (play an important role in the development of the relationship) because it was the starting point. It was where we basically first started talking. Like you kind of find it easier to talk when you don't see the person's face and then when you finally meet them it's easier. Right? ... So it played a big role in, like, how our relationship started ... Once I met him in person I gave him my cell phone number and then we started texting and he'd call every so often.

The above examples illustrate how communication technologies allow for the relationship to progress. The quotes are also suggestive of how modes of CMC become increasingly intimate as the relationship evolves and comfort is achieved.

*Keeping connected*

The next most common motive for using CMC was keeping connected with their partners throughout the day and also over long distances. Nicole, a 19-year-old female
Christian whose family is from Sri Lanka, explained how she used communication
technologies to stay connected with her boyfriend who lived in another city. She said:

> He lived in Markham and I lived in Etobicoke and, like, I didn't really see him much. So
> pretty much we'd either talk on the phone or we'd talk on MSN.

Aliya, a 20-year-old female Muslim whose family is from Pakistan, also discussed this.
She said:

> Like MSN and the phone play a huge role in our relationship and now he's done univer-
> sity. He finished, he graduated in April, so he lives in Hamilton. So that plays a huge role
> now 'cause we can't really see each other as much. And even now, he's currently in Paki-
> stan so ... we still talk on MSN.

Another example of this can be seen in the quote below from Dolly, a 19-year-old
female Christian whose family is from Sri Lanka.

> Only once in the summer when we were both travelling I just used Facebook to message
> him. So just with those 'cause we weren't always on at the same time and since we were in
> different countries couldn't really text a lot so we would do Facebook. And then when he
> came back from England to Canada I was still in New York so we would just message,
> message each other on ah Facebook or just email.

With regard to keeping connected with each other throughout the day, Sarah, a 20-year-
old Christian female whose family is from India, discussed this. She said:

> In class. When we're in class, on breaks, that kind of thing. Ah texting would be for like a
> quick update like um meet me here at this time or like I'm gonna be late. That kind of
> thing. We don't really use texting as a main form of communication, it's just a quick
> update.

Overall, the respondents identified the practicality of Facebook, MSN, texting and email
for staying connected with their partners during the day and even over long distances.
The participants pointed out CMCs were particularly advantageous when individuals
are geographically distant or lead busy lives that prevent them from meeting in person.

*Discreet communication*

CMC was discussed by some participants as a useful means of hiding communication
with partners, especially from parents. Soha, a 21-year-old Muslim female whose
family is from Pakistan discussed how MSN helped her hide her relationship from
her father. She said:

> (She says she hides her relationship using MSN) I'm trying to be good now, I'm trying to
> get in his good books so that's how we communicate (phone when dad is not around) or
> MSN because we have our laptops now. So MSN.

The quote below by Ajay, a 20-year-old male Hindu whose family is from Sri Lanka,
also provides an example of this. He said:

It (MSN and texting) was only when I was around my parents. I can't really pick up the phone and say 'hi honey' kind of thing.

Not only was CMC used to hide relationships when parents were unaware of them, but it was also used when parents did know about the relationship to hide the amount of time they were spending communicating. Melvin, a 25-year-old Christian male whose family is from Pakistan, said:

Using MSN, you know Facebook, it just, it makes it easier and I guess you can maybe talk for more . . . more amount of time.

Another example is provided by Rohan, a 19-year-old Hindu male whose family is from Sri Lanka, who discussed how he used MSN so his relationship would not be 'in the face of' his parents. He stated:

'Cause . . . my parents don't really like us talking on the phone. They don't like to see our relationship out in the open . . . MSN now still plays a big role.

Dolly said:

At times it was (a big part of the relationship) because my parents would be a little bit more strict. They wouldn't let (me) see him sometimes; so . . . we would have to rely on texting or MSN to communicate a lot . . . Yeah, it helps, especially if I'm in trouble. I can just say I'm studying and talk to him on MSN without having them know. Especially going to a laptop school is useful.

Overall, numerous participants noted CMC as an effective method of hiding either their relationships or the quantity of interactions with their partner.

*Relationship initiation*

Some respondents reported using MSN and Facebook to initiate intimate relationships. Participants explained how their relationships began because of MSN, Facebook and the like. Rizwan said:

Our relationship started on MSN . . . I asked her out on MSN . . . yeah that's how it started.

Below are two additional examples. The first quote is from Rohan and the second is from Vanessa.

Um, so then I talked to her before she could talk to me. Then I talked to her the first couple times then it started from . . . Then it stemmed from MSN. Um MSN, phone calls and texting. Those are the three.

We met here at school. It's kind of like the people that you see often and you want to, you know, you want to talk to. But you never really got the chance. And then I think he saw me at school and then he added me on Facebook and, you know, we started talking. We started meeting, you know, and then we liked each other kind of thing. So we started dating.

Sonia described how a man used MSN conversations to get her attention. She stated:

His brother's in my class. Like one day he came on MSN and then like, 'oh I like you or something' but he didn't know me. The next day he's like, 'oh you're [name]'. Like he

147

didn't even know me and he just tried to get to talk to me in a different way. Like to grab my attention.

Dolly described a similar experience. She said:

I didn't really talk to him. I ignored him. He asked me for study notes and then ah he wanted my email so I gave to him after he asked me like three times.

These quotations illustrate how South Asian youth use CMC to initiate relationships with intimate partners.

### Easier to say things online

A less common theme, but one that did emerge in some discussions of CMC was its ability to make the participants feel comfortable enough to engage in awkward or difficult conversations. These uncomfortable conversation topics ranged from individuals just telling the other person how they felt, to more explicit conversations about sexual activities. Many participants specifically stated that, 'it's easier to talk about things over MSN than it is in person'. This was evident in an interview with Asad:

Like I said, there's things you can say through text that you can't say or that . . . you don't feel comfortable saying in person . . . You talk late at night and there's things you say on the computer that you, doesn't sound right if you say it out loud.

Ali, a 24-year-old Muslim male whose family is from Pakistan, also conveyed the ease of awkward conversations when he said:

'Cause one thing she told me that night . . . that first night that I talked to her she's like, 'you know I I don't know why I'm talking to you so much. I don't usually talk so much. It's just easy to talk to you' is what she said. So I mean . . . It probably wouldn't have flown that well if it wasn't online . . . I personally find it easier to carry a lot of conversations like, of that type, online than I do in person . . . you kinda more develop your questions and that, just a little more so . . . Um the first time that I talked to her online was that first night, or whatever, was for like 4 or 5 hours and that whole thing of sex did come up that first night.

Sadiq, a 19-year-old Muslim male whose family is from Pakistan, provided another example. He said:

On MSN I feel more relaxed, like she's not here with me so I can say what I want to, but like you know.

### The next best thing to face-to-face interaction

When face-to-face interactions were not possible, participants indicated that CMC was the next best thing. Some participants reported that they would rely on MSN or texting when they were at school, family members' houses, when their parents were nearby or when they were just unable to meet in person. What is evident is that this motive overlaps with or is a subcategory of at least three of the previous five motives. When face-to-face interaction was not possible, a relationship could be initiated or built and partners could stay connected using CMC. This was especially the case when face-to-face interaction was not possible because the relationship or communicated had to be kept hidden or discreet.

Ajay discussed how communication technologies were useful when he and his girl-friends could not interact in person or on the phone. He said:

> At points where I couldn't talk on the phone, they'd text me 'cause they know I wouldn't receive or I'd hang up on them and they'd text me and they'd do the same ... so it kind of mediated for rather than speaking to her you'd the message would still be conveyed on they feel or what they want to talk about ... It [texting] wouldn't kind of compensate for it [face-to-face] but it it's a start.

Another male, Akshay, a 23-year-old Hindu whose family is from Sri Lanka, also explained what he thought about the use of communication technologies. He said:

> Um, it, I guess it would help just talking to somebody. 'Cause like if, if you can't talk, like if you're not there in person I guess the only thing you can do is [use MSN].

### Negative consequences: the double-edged sword

While participants primarily discussed positive experiences with CMC, there were also instances when discovery of their use by parents caused problems. These might be stricter monitoring or restriction of use or open conflict with parents.

For some participants, even before their cross-gender communications were discovered, CMCs, especially online activities, were a point of contention between them and their parents. In some cases, parents restricted and/or monitored such use. Soha's father, for example, restricted her use of the Internet and telephone specifically for the purpose of preventing their use to form cross-gender relationships or any relationships with non-Muslims. She said:

> My dad would try to control it by, like he, he never wanted me to have a cell phone ... like he's done a lot to like try to control that; try to make me, like, a really good Muslim girl. Wouldn't let me go on MSN. He didn't want me to have a phone. I'm not allowed to, like, he just, like, you know, how you're allowed to have guy friends over to study or whatever, he's like 'no you're not allowed to do that'. If he finds out I had a friend who's not Muslim, he'd be angry about it and he'll talk it down all the time to the point where I just don't want to have any non-Muslim friends and I don't really have any close non-Muslim friends. So that's what he's done physically.

Rekha, a 20-year-old Hindu female whose family is from Sri Lanka, also described how her parents prevented her from using the computer, she said:

> I never had a computer until I got to university. Like my dad is a computer whiz so he knows everything, like, all the sites you can go on and ... like MSN, yahoo and all those other things. So, like, it was his computer if we needed it. We can use it for school related stuff, but no computer, no MSN, and no friends.

In addition, some said when parents would see them on MSN, they would frequently question whom they were talking to and why. For example, Ajay stated:

> You can't ah stand next to another girl. You can't actually talk to her even on MSN ... Which they're kind of strict on 'cause at one point I was talking to a girl and my

parents would look at my MSN and, like, 'Who's that?' I'd be like, 'a friend' and [they'd] be like, 'Are you sure?' 'Yes'. And one of those kind of situations.

Parents monitoring CMC by looking through cell phones or email accounts was also reported. This is evident in the following quote by Manisha, a 19-year-old female Hindu whose family is from India.

On my dad's computer he just opened my MSN messenger and then he, he clicked on the email button like I don't know what drove him to do that, but he figured he should and he went through my email.

Difficulties were reported by several participants whose parents discovered their cross-gender relationships because of their use of CMC. Soha described how her neighbour found pictures of her with her boyfriend when she was added to the neighbour's Facebook contacts. She said:

When he saw those, he showed his mom and his mom showed it to my parents and my parents freaked out.

For Karishma, a 21-year-old Hindu female whose family is from India, it was her brother who discovered her relationship on Facebook. He 'ratted' her out by telling their parents about her relationship. Sunil, an 18-year-old Hindu male whose family is from Sri Lanka, reported that his mom realized he had a relationship because of the time he was spending on the computer. He said:

She knew after a while like, just 'cause me on, me on the computer, on MSN and stuff.

Rohan discussed similar experiences. He said:

My mom sort of caught on her own. Um phone calls and texting and things like that.

Sometimes 'getting caught' because of CMC caused difficulties between parents and participants that might not have existed had their parents been informed of the relationship or had it not been discovered at all. The situation discussed by Manisha is one example of this. Had her parents not found out in the manner they did, she thinks they may have actually liked her partner. She said:

He was the one that actually could have been okay because he fit the requirement, right?

Soha described a particularly negative experience resulting from getting caught, one that progressed to violence. She said:

I was never allowed to go on MSN until I had my own computer in University. So he [her father] would tell me not to do it. But I would still do it behind his back. But my dad's a computer analyst, so he would always find like I would always leave tracks that he would find. Then he would read my conversations, and stuff that I would be having with guys. So he would really freak out. So one time this is what happened. He saw my chat logs ... So that kind of got really gross and we started yelling at each other and I'm like 'you're a horrible person', and he's like 'you're a horrible daughter', and so I was trying to get him away from the computer and trying to shut down the computer and he wouldn't like let me do it and that kind of got physical cause I was trying to push him away and he was trying to push me away so that got, and then that led him to hit me and then I would hit him back and stuff like that.

From these illustrations, it is clear that CMC can be a double-edged sword. While it can play a key role in the development and maintenance of intimate relationships, it can cause family conflict and have a negative impact on the users' lives.

## Discussion and conclusions

This exploratory research provides insight into how South Asian youth use CMC technologies in their cross-gender relationships. Consistent with other research, ours demonstrates that South Asian youth, like other youth, are using CMC to initiate, build and maintain relationships (Kindred and Roper 2004, Pauley and Emmers-Sommer 2007, Sidelinger *et al.* 2008). While CMC may be more impersonal than face-to-face interaction, it is a liberating experience with respect to cross-gender relationships for this ethnic group. It provides these youth with a tool to build relationships that would otherwise be difficult or impossible to build (Rheingold 1993, Turkle 1995). Our findings also illustrate the salience of the four key components of U&G theory specified by Rubin (2002) to understanding CMC use in this population.

Rubin's first component addresses CMC as an active, conscious choice. South Asian youth actively choose CMC and the specific form of CMC they will use. Of the 57 participants in our original sample, 42 either introduced CMC into the discussion of cross-gender relationships or responded positively when they were asked whether CMC played a part in these relationships. In terms of Rubin's second component, 41 of our participants used CMC to fulfil communication needs in their relationships. The specific CMC that was used related to the specific needs that they had at different phases of a relationship. For example, Facebook was used primarily to initiate relationships. The fact that Facebook messages may be left on a site whether or not the owner of a page is online meant that it could be used asynchronously and that some participants also used it when several time zones separated them from their partners. MSN and texting were the most commonly used CMC and were used as relationships were developing and partners were drawing closer to each other. Both of these modes of communication are closer to being one-on-one and more private.

Rubin's third component was that CMC meets psycho-social needs. This was true for our participants; in particular, the need for communication to build and maintain a relationship, the need for cross-gender relationships and even communication to remain hidden and discreet, and potentially the need to gradually build such communication. In cultures where cross-gender communication is restricted and supervised, opportunities to develop the skills for face-to-face communication across gender lines during the process of maturation and socialization are limited. CMC makes it possible to 'try out' and gradually develop such skills, as an adult, in a way that can be under the control of the individual. With CMC, participants are not physically present in the same space, affording them considerable protection and the ability to easily shut-down communication if they wish. CMC – unless it includes 'chat', verbal interaction or a webcam – involves only words, not tone of voice, body language or facial expression. There is no eye-to-eye contact and it is even possible to take time to think about a response. Progress to verbal (as compared to typed/keyed) communication or to visual contact can be introduced as participants become more comfortable, self assured and skilled at communicating. The greater use of CMC by women than men for the purpose of staying connected (also the most frequently reported use by women) that was found in this study, as well as in prior research (Morahan-Martin and Schumacher 1999, Schumacher and Morahan-Martin 2001, Boneva and Kraut 2002, Ledbetter 2008), suggests that women may have a stronger psycho-social need for frequent contact and connection than men have. Alternatively or supplementally, it may indicate that women are using CMC to fulfil an ascribed gender role and responsibility for maintaining the close ties and connections that hold relationships together. On the other hand, men in our study most often, and more often than women, reported CMC use to initiate a relationship, a gender role that is often assigned to them.

The single religious variation that we found in CMC use may also reflect psycho-social needs. It is not surprising that participants who identified as Muslim more often identified 'discreet communication' as a motive for CMC use. Their socialization, from the onset, was likely influenced by religious and cultural parameters that are based on the code of family honour, especially for women. This prohibits or strictly limits and controls cross-gender communication outside the family. While Christian and Hindu South Asians also maintain such ethics with respect to their behaviours, their socialization is more relaxed. McGoldrick *et al.* (2005, p. 384), for example, observed that 'Asian Christians tend to be more flexible', compared to Hindus and Muslims, even allowing their children to date. Keeping cross-gender communication hidden or discreet is not always necessary for Christians and Hindus. Thus, the psycho-social need for combining communication with discretion may be more pronounced for our Muslim participants.

The fourth component of U&G theory specified by Rubin (2002) is that social contexts influence how well CMC can serve one's needs. The social context for our participants included ready access to laptop computers. All were university or college students and many required or had laptop computers for their schoolwork. This made several forms of CMC readily available to them. Several offered that this was not the case before they were in university, with parents – particularly fathers – controlling or prohibiting computer use before this time. Cell phones were available to almost all of our participants, although some also mentioned that this had been prohibited in the recent past and that this curtailed CMC. Some were still subject to surveillance of their computer and cell phone with email, MSN and texting monitored. The social context also involved a need for discreet, non-face-to-face communication. Many participants who used CMC spoke of parents who did not approve of cross-gender relationships and/or communication. How well CMC served their need for cross-gender communication depended on how access, parental prohibitions and monitoring combined. Most did not speak of parental discovery of their CMC. In this social context, CMC met their need for secrecy and discretion in their cross-gender relationships. However, nine of our participants reported parent–child conflict resulting from their use of CMC (e.g. parents restricting and questioning their use) and discovery of their cross-gender communication because of their CMC use, and the difficulties that ensued. For some, the discovery was because they were unable to maintain full secrecy either because a parent (typically a father) regularly checked their CMC use or the extent of their use raised suspicion, or, in two cases, someone else disclosed knowledge of their cross-gender relationship because of access to their CMC. For these participants, CMC use did not serve their need for cross-gender communication specifically because it could not be kept secret within their social and familial environment.

The results of this research are evidence of the relevance of the U&G theory to this specific ethnic group as it contributes to our understanding of the whys and hows of CMC use in cross-gender relationships by second-generation South Asian youth. Overall, the results of this study suggest that the rapid advancement of technology has changed how interpersonal relationships are initiated and maintained within the South Asian community. These youth have greater opportunity to connect in real time with a significant other in a very subtle and discreet manner both from inside and outside the home and without directly threatening the honour of the family. It provides them with alternatives to face-to-face or telephone communication with their boyfriend or girlfriend. CMC not only provided greater convenience but also gave youth more freedom as well as comfort in communicating and expressing themselves romantically and/or sexually. Thus, Walther's notion of 'hyperpersonal' communication is seen in this research. While technically family honour is still being compromized, and our participants demonstrated awareness of this, it is being done in an indirect and hidden manner, especially if parents are unaware of it. CMC technology does not afford total secrecy and privacy, however, and when our participants were caught by their parents, conflict was a real possibility with the affect of cross-gender communication on family honour held out as the reason.

This study makes a unique contribution in this subject area. It goes beyond the existing literature that focuses on CMC use in general and for primarily 'western' populations. In applying U&G theory, it more fully elaborates motives for use, how different forms of CMC are used to meet specific relationship and psycho-social needs, and how the social context combines with these needs to influence use and lead to negative consequences that inhibit the ability of CMC to meet needs. This research illustrates the importance of considering CMC from within a multicultural context.

This research does not come without limitations. The major limitation is that the sample comprised largely of South Asian youth enrolled in university/college in the GTA and Durham region, thus they all had access to technology. This leaves unanswered the question of whether CMC would be used in a similar manner among those without such access and/or with less education. Also, while our sample targeted individuals 18–35 years of age, most fell on the younger end of the spectrum (i.e. average age of the sample was 20 years) and thus they are not representative of our targeted population, especially older individuals. Broadening the scope of the study so one can make comparisons may help establish a better understanding of the role ethnicity plays in technological usage, something that is lacking in the literature. Finally, this was a qualitative study with a small sample. This provided in-depth information about the hows and whys of CMC use in cross-gender relationships but not valid population estimates of how many or how much.

The strength of this research is that it provides insight into how cross-gender relationships are technologically evolving and changing for South Asian youth and highlights some of the tensions and conflicts associated with such advancement. It also provides suggestions for future research and creates awareness for researchers, teachers, parents and counsellors and social service providers about how South Asian youth are managing their social relationships through CMC. We suggest that future research focus in more detail on the individual differences between online communication and face-to-face communication for couples in relationships. Research could explore how, or if, CMC and face-to-face interactions differ in progressing towards (or perhaps inhibiting progress towards) a goal of marriage. Moreover, South Asian parents' perspectives should be targeted to explore their perceptions of CMC and the relationship they see between CMC and cultural norms.

## Note

1. It is important to note that policing and guarding of cross-gender relationships by parents and elders varies by their religious views, education and social class; not every parent places these restrictions on their children; but this is the widely accepted and idealized norm; women in South Asian cultures are under far greater pressure to maintain family honour (Zaidi and Shuraydi 2002).

## Notes on contributors

Dr Arshia U. Zaidi examines intersectionalities of immigration, family, culture and gender. Dr Zaidi received her BA (honours) and Masters Degree in Sociology from the University of Windsor and a PhD in Sociology from Wayne State University. This research is based on this SSHRC funded study. Email: arshia.zaidi@uoit.ca

Amanda Couture has a BA (honours) and MA in Criminology from the Faculty of Social Science and Humanities at UOIT. Amanda will continue to pursue her academic career by starting a PhD program at the University of Toronto in Fall 2012. Her research interests include: South Asian women and dating abuse, women abuse and gender. Email: amanda.couture@uoit.ca

Dr Eleanor Maticka-Tyndale holds a Canada Research Chair in Social Justice and Sexual Health. Her research focuses on how sexuality and sexual behaviours are embedded within social and cultural contexts. This has included research on ethnic variations in sexual behaviours and HIV risk. Current projects include: the influence of policies and programmes on health and safety when engaging in sex work, research and evaluation of a school-based HIV prevention programme in Kenya, and analysis of Canadian sexual behaviours and sexual health. Email: maticka@uwindsor.ca

## References

Abu-Laban, S.M., 1974. Arab-Canadian family life. *Arab studies quarterly*, 1, 135–156.

Akpinar, A., 2003. The honour/shame complex revisited: violence against women in the migration context. *Women's studies international forum*, 26 (5), 425–442.

Amant, K., 2002. When cultures and computers collide. *Journal of business and technical communication*, 16 (2), 196–214.

Bargh, J. and McKenna, K., 2004. The internet and social life. *Annual review of psychology*, 55 (1), 573–590.

Baym, N.K., 2002. Interpersonal life online. *In*: L. Lievrouw and S. Livingstone, eds. *The hand book of new media: social shaping and consequences of ICTs*. London: Sage, 62–76.

Blais, J.J., Craig, W.M., Pepler, D., and Connolly, J., 2008. Adolescents online: the importance of internet activity choices to salient relationships. *Journal of youth and adolescence*, 37 (5), 522–536.

Boneva, B. and Kraut, R., 2002. Email, gender and personal relationships. *In*: B. Wellman and C. Haythornthwaite, eds. *The internet in everyday life: the information age*. Oxford: Blackwell, 372–403.

Dainton, M. and Aylor, B., 2002. Patterns of communication channel use in the maintenance of long-distance relationships. *Communication research reports*, 19 (2), 118–129.

Das Gupta, M., 1997. 'What is Indian about you?': a gendered transnational approach to ethnicity. *Gender and society*, 11 (5), 572–596.

Dion, K.K. and Dion, K.L., 2004. Gender, immigrant generation, and ethnocultural identity. *Sex roles*, 50 (5), 347–355.

Dodd, P.C., 1973. Family honor and the forces of change in Arab society. *International journal of middle east studies*, 4 (1), 40–54.

Eastin, M.S. and LaRose, R., 2000. Internet self-efficacy and the psychology of the digital divide. *Journal of computer-mediated communication*, 6 (1).

Flanagin, A.J., 2010. IM online: instant messaging use among college students. *Communication research reports*, 22 (3), 175–187.

Ghosh, R., 1984. South Asian women in Canada: adaptation. *In*: R. Kanungo, ed. *South Asians in the Canadian mosaic*. Montreal: Kala Bharati, 145–155.

Haddad, Y.Y., Smith, J.I., and Moore, K.M., 2006. *Muslim women in America the challenge of Islamic identity today*. New York: Oxford University Press.

Handa, A., 2003. *Of silk saris and mini-skirts: South-Asian girls walk the tight-rope of culture*. Toronto: Women's Press.

Hanna, B.E. and Nooy, J., 2004. Negotiating cross-cultural difference in electronic discussion. *Multilingua: journal of cross-cultural and interlanguage communication*, 23 (3), 257–281.

Hickey, M.G., 2004. Identity negotiation in narratives of Muslim women immigrants in the United States: 'so things are different...doesn't mean they're wrong'. *Asian women*, 19, 1–18.

Hoffman, D.L. and Novak, T.P., 1998. *Bridging the digital divide: the impact of race on computer access and internet use* [online]. Available from: http://elab.vanderbilt.edu [Accessed 24 January 2011].

Jackson, M., 2007. Exploring gender, feminism and technology from a communication perspective: an introduction and commentary. *Women's studies in communication*, 30 (2), 149–156.

Johnson, A.J., Haigh, M.M., Becker, J.A.H., Craig, E.A., and Wigley, S., 2008. College students' use of relational management strategies in email in long-distance and geographically close relationships. *Journal of computer-mediated communication*, 13 (2), 381–404.

Kallivayalil, D., 2004. Gender and cultural socialization in Indian immigrant families in the United States. *Feminism psychological*, 4 (4), 535–559.

Katz, E., Blumler, J.G., and Gurevitch, M., 1974. Utilization of mass communication by the individual. *In*: J.G. Blumler and E. Katz, eds. *The uses of mass communications: current perspectives on gratifications research*. Beverly Hills: Sage, 19–32.

Kindred, J. and Roper, S.L., 2004. Making connections via instant messenger (IM): student use of IM to maintain personal relationships. *Qualitative research reports in communication*, 5, 48–54.

Ledbetter, A.M., 2008. Chronemic cues and sex differences in relational e-mail: perceiving immediacy and supportive message quality. *Social science computer review*, 26 (4), 466–482.

Lenhart, A., Purcell, K., Smith, A., and Zickuhr, K., 2010. *Social media & mobile internet use among teens and young adults* [online]. Pew internet & American life project. Available from: http://pewresearch.org/pubs/1484/social-media-mobile-internet-use-teens-millennials-fewer-blog [Accessed 2 May 2010].

Leung, L., 2001. College student motives for chatting on ICQ. *New media society*, 3 (4), 483–500.

Long, S.M., 2010. *Exploring web 2.0: the impact of digital communications technologies on youth relationships and sociability*. Thesis (BA). Occidental College.

McGoldrick, M., Giordano, J., and Garcia-Preto, N., 2005. *Ethnicity & family therapy*. New York: Guildford.

McKenna, K.Y.A. and Bargh, J.A., 1999. Causes and consequences of social interaction on the internet: a conceptual framework. *Media psychology*, 1 (3), 249–269.

Merkle, E.R. and Richardson, R.A., 2000. Digital dating and virtual relating: conceptualizing computer mediated romantic relationships. *Family relations*, 49 (2), 187–192.

Morahan-Martin, J. and Schumacher, P., 1999. Comparison of computer and internet competency, experience, and skills by gender. *Proceeding of the annual meeting of the society for computers in psychology*. Los Angeles, CA.

Morris, M. and Ogan, C., 1996. The internet as mass medium. *Journal of communication*, 46 (1), 39–50.

Nachbaur, A., 2003. *College students and instant messaging: an analysis of chatting, flirting, & using away messages* [online]. The mercury project for instant messaging studies. Available from: http://www.stanford.edu/class/pwr3–25/group2/pdfs/IM_Flirting.pdf [Accessed 28 February 2010].

Naidoo, J.C., 1984. South Asian women in Canada: self-perceptions, socialization, achievement aspirations. *In*: R. Kanungo, ed. *South Asians in the Canadian mosaic*. Montreal: Kala Bharati, 123–142.

Nardi, B., Whittaker, S., and Bradner, E., 2000. Interaction and outeraction: instant messaging in action. *Proceedings of the CSCW 2000 conference on computer-supported cooperative work*. New York: ACM Press, 79–88.

Newhagen, J.E. and Rafaeli, S., 1996. Why communication researchers should study the internet: a dialogue. *Journal of communication*, 46 (1), 4–13.

Odell, P.M., Korgen, K.O., Schumacher, P., and Delucchi, M., 2000. Internet use among female and male college students. *Cyber psychology & behavior*, 3 (5), 855–862.

Pauley, P.M. and Emmers-Sommer, T.M., 2007. The impact of internet technologies on primary and secondary romantic relationship development. *Communication studies*, 58 (4), 411–427.

Punyanunt-Carter, N.M. and Hemby, C.O., 2006. College students' gender differences regarding e-mail. *College student journal*, 40 (3), 651–653.

Rabby, M.K. and Walther, J.B., 2003. Computer-mediated communication effects on relationship formation and maintenance. *In*: D.J. Canary and M. Dainton, eds. *Maintaining relationships through communication*. Mahwah, NJ: Lawrence Erlbaum Associates, 141–162.

Ramirez, A. and Broneck, K., 2009. 'IM me': instant messaging as relational maintenance and everyday communication. *Journal of social and personal relationships*, 26 (2–3), 291–314.

Ramirez, A., Jr. and Zhang, S., 2007. When online meets offline: the effect of modality switching on relational communication. *Communication monographs*, 74 (3), 287–310.

Rheingold, H., 1993. *The virtual community: homesteading on the electronic frontier*. Reading, MA: Addison-Wesley.

Rubin, A.M., 2002. The uses-and-gratifications perspective of media effects. *In*: J. Bryant and D. Zillmann, eds. *Media effects: advances in theory and research*. 2nd ed. Mahwah, NJ: Lawrence Erlbaum Associates, 525–548.

Schumacher, P. and Morahan-Martin, J., 2001. Gender, internet and computer attitudes and experiences. *Computers in human behavior*, 17 (1), 95–110.

Shapurian, R. and Hojat, M., 1985. Sexual and premarital attitudes of Iranian college students. *Psychological reports*, 57 (1), 67–74.

Sidelinger, R.J., Ayash, G., and Tibbles, D., 2008. Couples go online: relational maintenance behaviors and relational characteristics use in dating relationships. *Human communication*, 11 (3), 341–356.

Statistics Canada, 2001. *Ethnocultural portrait of Canada, 2001 Census Data* [online]. Available from: http://www.statcan.gc.ca/bsolc/olc-cel/olc-cel?catno= 95F0363X&chropg=1&lang=eng [Accessed 28 September 2005].

Statistics Canada, 2010. Study: projections of the diversity of the Canadian population. *The daily* [online]. Available from: http://www.statcan.gc.ca/daily-quotidien/100309/ dq100309a-eng.htm [Access 13 December 2010].

Ting-Toomey, S., 1991. Intimacy expressions in three cultures: France, Japan, and the United States. *International journal of intercultural communication*, 15 (1), 29–46.

Turkle, S., 1995. *Life on the screen: identity in the age of the internet*. New York: Simon & Schuster.

Utz, S., 2000. Social information processing in MUDs: the development of friendships in virtual worlds. *Journal of online behavior*, 1 (1) [online]. Available from: http://www.behavior.net/ job/v1n1/utz.html [Accessed 23 February 2011].

Wakil, P., Siddique, C.M., and Wakil, F.A., 1981. Between two cultures: a study in socialization of children of immigrants. *Journal of marriage and the family*, 43 (4), 931–940.

Walther, J.B., 1992. Interpersonal effects in computer-mediated interaction: a relational perspective. *Communication research*, 19 (1), 52–90.

Wolak, J. and Mitchell, K., 2002. Close online relationships in a national sample of adolescents. *Adolescence*, 37 (147), 441–455.

Wright, K., 2002. Motives for communication within on-line support groups and antecedents for interpersonal use. *Communication research reports*, 19 (1), 89–98.

Ye, J., 2006. *Maintaining online friendship: cross-cultural analyses of links among relational maintenance strategies, relational factor, and channel-related factors*. Thesis (PhD). Georgia State University.

Yum, Y.-O. and Hara, K., 2005. Computer-mediated relationship development: a cross-cultural comparison. *Journal of computer-mediated communication*, 11 (1), article 7 [online]. Available from: http://jcmc.indiana.edu/vol11/issue1/yum.html [Accessed 2 April 2012].

Zaidi, A. and Shuraydi, M., 2002. Perceptions of arranged marriages by young Pakistani Muslim women living in a western society. *Journal of comparative family studies*, 33 (4), 495–514.

Zakin, R.H., 1996. *Hobbes' Internet timeline* [online]. Available from: http://www.pbs.org/opb/nerds2.0.1/timeline [Accessed 15 January 2010].

# Place of subcaste (*jati*) identity in the discourse on caste: examination of caste in the diaspora

P. Pratap Kumar

*Discipline of Religion, School of Religion, Philosophy & Classics, University of KwaZulu Natal, Durban, South Africa*

Caste as a social phenomenon has undergone many changes. The most important operative unit that has exemplified caste in its discourse is subcaste (*jati*) identity. Both within India and certainly in the diaspora, there is now increasing evidence of the dissolution of subcaste (*jati*) identities giving rise to various other formations of groups replacing the endogamous relationships with other arbitrary group formations. In this article, I examine some evidence from South Africa, the West Indies and the UK to analyse how caste has transformed in these places and what it means for a discourse on caste that is historically rooted in subcaste identity.

## Introduction

In India, several scholars have identified changes in the system of caste for some time. M.N. Srinivas characterized the possibility of a lower order caste group moving upward through his concept of Sanskritization. Srinivas contested the previous notions of caste that they are fixed and their relations are bound by purity and pollution (Dumont 1970). Contrary to the idea of the social boundaries of castes being fixed, he introduced the idea of segmentation. He pointed out:

> This segmentation is probably the result of a long historical process in which groups continually fissioned off. As a result of this long process of development there has come into existence several cognate groups .... each of which retains a sense of its identity as well as its linkage with other similar groups .... All the members of this group pursued a common occupation or a few common occupations, and this group was the unit of social and ritual life. ... During the last sixty years or more, however, the linkages between groups have become more and more significant, and the strong walls erected between subcastes have begun to crumble. The endogamous circle is widening, especially under the impact of the dowry system which is especially characteristic of the high castes. (Srinivas 1962, pp. 3–4)

I find this to be still one of the most coherent descriptions of caste and its sub-groups. But as early as the 1950s, Srinivas noted the increasing changes in caste based on economic ties and forming cognate castes, Okkaligas, Reddis *inter alia* (Srinivas 1962). Béteille (1965) identified changes in caste in alliance with class in his classic study of

Tanjore village (also see Béteille 1969, 1974). However, focusing on the joint family system in India, Madan (1962, p. 14) argued in favour of kinship bonds being 'immutable'. In a comparative study of caste and race, Dipankar Gupta highlighted two important points – in dissonance from Dumontian theory, he points out that, castes do not display a uniform hierarchy based on purity and pollution simply because there is no agreement among castes on this point and therefore operate on multiple hierarchies. Even though Sanskritization might offer upward mobility, the castes that do move upward rarely give up their earlier beliefs and practices (Gupta 2000).

In other words, the idea of caste as a system that is cast in stone has been challenged by a number of scholars for a long while now. Nevertheless, Srinivas (1955, 1987) might still stand out as an example of scholars who profiled *jati*. Scholars generally look at *jati* as the most important place for the operation of caste as an endogamous unit that regulates exchange of food, marriage and other religious and customary beliefs in dealing with birth and death ceremonies. Notwithstanding the fact that Srinivas profiled *jati*, he also looked at it from the point of view of dominance in society (e.g. Srinivas 1955). In the context of increasing urbanization in India, and in particular Indians living abroad for generations, maintaining the endogamous units of caste has become difficult, thereby resulting in various other group formations for pragmatic purposes. Even as early as the eighteenth century, class consciousness was associated with caste. For instance, Sahai (2005, p. 549) argued that generally in eighteenth century India, artisanal groups displayed a mixture of caste and class consciousness. He pointed out, 'caste identities, with all their apparent solidity and cohesion, were not unitary but multiple' (Sahai 2005, p. 549). But during the same period, Sivakumar and Sivakumar (1979, p. 273) argued in the context of Tamilnadu, 'Considering the long term stability of dominant *jati* equations (to be broken up only through conquest or colonization), the social definition of the eighteenth century individual in Tondaimandalam appears to have consisted of his lineage, kinship, and *jati* origins'. Thus, despite scholarly views on caste as an institution in modern society undergoing changes, the notion of *jati* continues to be closely associated with caste. But in this context, scholarly studies paid most attention to the operations of caste in the Indian traditional setting, viz. the village, and to a certain extent, to the urban populations in the subcontinent. Not much attention has been given to the data in the context of the Indian diaspora.

In what follows, I shall offer examples of caste transformations in the diaspora and then raise the issue of how to rationalize the discourse on caste in the absence of the endogamous units of caste, viz. *jati*. As becomes clear, my presupposition here is that in the context of the complex nature of the Indian diasporic life, *jati* as an operational unit of caste has not survived. However, caste consciousness survived in the earlier generations perhaps upto fourth and fifth generations. The present younger generation holds the caste names as last names, but they do not seem to be too concerned about the status issues in relation to marriage in particular and in relation to the priesthood. In presenting the data, I first offer caste transformation in South Africa and then support the developments in South Africa with the example of Fiji and offer a contrasting situation in the UK.

## Indian community in South Africa

Before taking up the case of South Africa, it might be useful to offer some insight into how old the Indian contact with Africa generally is. The presence of Indians in Africa, especially East Africa, perhaps dates back to the ninth century when the then Omani

Sheikhs ruled much of East Africa and made Zanzibar the capital of their empire. They brought Indian merchants with them to trade in East Africa (Ingham 1965, p. 58). From the Cholas of South East India, the Bahamanis of the Deccan and all the way to the Gujaratis of what was then known as Cambay, Indian merchants had traded with the East African coastal territories. By the early nineteenth century, an Indian colony was established in East Africa under the rulership of the Omani Sultans. At the height of the slave trade, and the subsequent commercial treaty between the Sultan in Zanzibar and the British in 1839, there were already nearly 6000 Indians counted in East Africa (Beachey 1996, p. 365, Kumar 2008, p. 14). Although formally slave trade ended in British colonies since 1834, in reality many colonies still exported slaves to North America during that period. Under great international pressure, a new form of labour transfer between colonies was invented which gave rise to the system known as 'indenture system'. It was experimented in many colonies including Trinidad, Fiji, Malaysia and Mauritius by the mid- nineteenth century. In 1860, the formal introduction of the indenture system in South Africa took place under much controversy and uncertainty about its workings.

Between 1860 and 1870, several shiploads of Indian labourers were brought to Natal mainly from two ports in India – Madras and Calcutta (Brain 1989, p. 251, Henning 1993, p. 56). While the first four ships from Madras between 1860 and 1874 do not provide much detail on the social and religious backgrounds of Indian indenture labourers, the ships from the Calcutta port provided some important clues to the caste and religious backgrounds of Indians from North India (see also Bhana 1991, Kumar 2000, p. 7). They might have come from many different language backgrounds ranging from Tamil, Telugu, Kannada and Malayalam in the South; Hindi (largely Bhojpuri and Awadi dialects), Bihari, Bengali, Oriya, and Gujarati and other languages in the North. However, by the end of the first generation the Indian community became homogenized into four distinguishable linguistic groups – Tamil and Telugu in the case of South Indians, Hindi in the case of North Indians. The Gujarati linguistic community largely remained a homogenous group on the basis of language notwithstanding the many caste and subcaste divisions that are still noticeable among them (Kumar 2000, p. 70). In some general sense, it is safe to say that while both South Indians and North Indians mixed across caste lines but within North–South cultural boundaries, the Gujaratis have evidently practiced caste more systematically until recent times as pointed out above (see Bhana and Bhoola 2011). It should also be noted that although homogenization of groups into two cultural groups, and four linguistic groups occurred very early on, in the earlier period, that is, during the first and second generations, there has been also evidence of marriages even across the linguistic lines. Some of the family histories that were done at the University of KwaZulu Natal by students for their degree projects are replete with accounts of such marriages across linguistic lines, e.g., Telugu person marrying a Hindi speaking person.[1]

## Caste consciousness among Indians in South Africa

For purposes of this section, I focus mainly on the South Indian community of South Africa and the caste formations and transformations among them. Before proceeding further I need to make one point in regard to the South Indian community in South Africa. In the South Indian groups there are two categories that we are able to distinguish, viz. the Tamils and the Telugus. Although the Tamils and Telugus can be distinguished by their language and organizational identity, for all practical purposes they shared the Tamil culture and religious orientation and became closely integrated. This is to a certain extent attributable to the fact that some of the Telugus who came to South Africa were already immigrants to Tamilnadu in India by the sixteenth and seventeenth centuries. As such, in South Africa we can distinguish two kinds of Telugus – those who came from Tamilnadu and spoke Telugu at home and Tamil in public places; and those who came from the coastal regions of present Andhra Pradesh. One other important aspect that I need to clarify is the term caste consciousness. Presence of caste conscious behaviour is identified in various Indian diaspora locations, such as Malaysia and Fiji. I use the term here to refer to an awareness of social status in relation to other groups based on the memory of one's caste status in a traditional village system in India. Such consciousness is maintained by means of retaining caste names as last names for individuals, e.g. Naidoo.

Evidently caste as an institution could not be practiced by Indians in general and South Indians in particular due to a lack of both numbers of any given caste and the absence of caste-related institutions such as caste-led traditional councils (Panchayats) and rituals (see Kuper 1960, Kumar 2000, p. 32, chapter 15). However, by the end of the first generation, it becomes clear that the priesthood needs in the newly built shrines and temples on the one hand, and the need to find alliances for marriage on the other seem to have caused the South Indian community to engage in caste-conscious behaviour. That is, by the end of the first–generation, proliferation of the many caste names as last names becomes a practice. And today reference to the South African phone directory reveals at least several pages of, for instance, Naidoo as the last name.[2] This is strange given the fact that the various ship-lists between 1860 and 1874 do not mention caste names especially for most South Indian indentured Indians. The only generic name that was used to refer to Hindus in particular was the word 'Gentoo', obviously a corruption of the word Gentile (Bhana 1991, Henning 1993, pp. 72–74, 84–109; see Kumar 2000, p. 12).

We might explain this behaviour as a way of demonstrating the social status either for ritual purposes or for marriage purposes – that is either to become a priest or to find a marriage partner. It is perhaps worth noting here that by the early 1870s, temple building in Natal becomes evident (see Kumar 2000, p. 30). Also, Mikula et al. (1982) have not only extensively studied some of these early temples from an architectural point of view, but also shed interesting light on the sociological details of the early builders. Gradually it becomes clear that these two institutions, viz. marriage and priesthood (if we can identify them as such) seem to have forced people to become conscious of their caste status. One elderly lady that I interviewed in Pietermaritzburg narrated how her father never used to allow into his house a person who did not belong to one of the following castes – Naiker/Naicker, Naidoo, Padyachi for these were considered cognate castes with similar social status. In his life time, he made sure all the marriage alliances in his home were within the cognate caste group that he respected. In a sense, this interview illustrated for me the subtle nuances of caste influence in the South African Indian context, especially among those of South Indian background during the early phases. It is also noteworthy that some of the early theses conducted at the former Durban-Westville University focused on caste and its implications for South African Indians (Rambiritch and Berghe 1961; see Moodley 1981, Pillay 1991). Such caste consciousness seemingly existed in other places also where indenture system was introduced, e.g., Malaysia (see Rajakrishnan 1984).

In the South African context, in order to be a priest or to find a partner in marriage only cognate castes could exchange such relations in the past. In the case of Tamils and

Telugus for example, Pillays, Padayachies, Govenders, Naikers (alternative spelling – Naickers), Nayars (originally this caste name is from the Malayali background, but became assimilated into the Tamil group), Reddys, Naidoos (Naidus[3]) could exchange alliances in marriage and people holding such caste names generally acquired priestly responsibilities, there being no formal Brahmin-caste persons. If the Brahmins did come to South Africa, from the scant information on castes in the early records, it is difficult to confirm whether or not Brahmins were available for priestly responsibilities. The fact that most of the local priests were from one or the other castes cited above seems to indicate that there were no Brahmin-caste priests.[4] In fact, the title Brahman in South Africa simply refers to the one who deals with priestly duties and seems to have no caste signification.

The proliferation of caste names as last names in the first two generations seems also to indicate the possibility that some persons and families sought to raise their social status by acquiring the last name of a higher caste. Ship-lists do indicate contradictions between last names and caste names. This is evidenced by the inconsistencies in the recording of the names in the ship-lists. In an earlier study, I pointed out based on the examination of ship-lists that for instance a person listed as belonging to Vanniya/ Vaishya caste holds the last name as Iyer (Kumar 2000, p. 12). What is evident is that no one seems to have taken the caste name of a lower caste that we are aware of in South Africa. So, this acquisition of last names from the historically landed caste backgrounds seems so systematic and prolific (see the example in the appendix) that today we find virtually every South Indian in South Africa carries the last name from a predominantly landed caste background. Incidentally, such name changes or acqui-sition of last names of higher caste groups is not limited to the diaspora context. Ross Mallick reports of such practices in modern Indian urban locations. He point out, 'Upwardly mobile Untouchables usually change their surnames, hiding their traditional means of identification' (Mallick 1997, p. 346). Now the question is – how do we under-stand or explain such a voluminous presence of caste names as last names without caste-related institutions, such as *jati* panchayats, in the diaspora contexts such as South Africa? In the absence of caste-related institutions in the new society in which they began to live, why did caste consciousness survive at least in the earlier generations? What would have been the need for it in a society where there were other social factors that were perhaps more significant for displaying certain social behaviour?

The most obvious explanation would be to consider the fact that South Asian Hindu society is basically hierarchical in nature structured around caste and its institutions. So, it is obvious that the first-generation Indians in South Africa naturally tried to display the social behaviour that they were used to. The fact that in such large numbers they deployed caste names as last names and in particular the caste names they perhaps knew enjoyed a certain social status in the land of their origin demonstrates a conscious attempt to appropriate caste names. This social behaviour as far as I have surveyed seems limited to only purposes of two important social aspects as mentioned earlier – to gain prominence in ritual space, and to gain a suitable partner in marriage. Other than these two aspects, whether or not one is socially superior within a close group has no larger significance in the broader society given the nature of the apartheid society that applied discriminatory laws to control their life overall in which they were treated as inferior subjects. In other words, claiming higher social status within the Hindu society had no larger impact on the rest of society in South Africa. But it seemed important to demonstrate the caste status within the ethnic enclaves where matters of social relations are at stake.

However, this above explanation alone, it seems to me, insufficient as it fails to take into account how social behaviour is regulated in a caste society within South Asia. We know that caste behaviour in South Asia is regulated by two important factors – exchange of cooked food, and exchange of bodily fluids. While the former has significance for ritual status, the latter has significance for exchange of marriage alliances. Both these factors are regulated in an endogamous relationship within a *jati* system. For example, even though both are of Brahmanical caste the Iyers and Iyengars in Tamilnadu cannot exchange food let alone marriage partners. This behaviour is true of not only ritually superior castes, but also landed castes in South India. So, seen from this point of view, the South African Indians of the first two generations should have tried to stay within their respective *jati* systems if they wanted to display their respective social status. But in the case of the South African Indians of early generations (let alone the present) both rules of caste behaviour have been violated. In terms of ritual, non-Brahmins took over the ritual functions,[5] and in terms of marriages, they engaged in exogamous relations, viz. marriages between, for instance, Naidoo and Padyachi or Govender castes instead of Naidoos exchanging within the Naidoo caste.

This is contrary to how caste society in India generally maintained social homogeneity within a *jati* system of endogamy. The South African Indian Hindus of South Indian background exchanged marriage alliances primarily within the two cognate linguistic communities, viz. Tamil and Telugu, and within the various cognate social groups as cited earlier. The social groups that exchanged marriage alliances and gained access to priestly functions in shrines and temples were what we today identify as landed castes in South India. In other words, the South African Indian Hindus seem to have bypassed the *jati* rules in favour of the larger socio-political status that groups enjoyed in the land of their origin. Obviously this new situation became necessary in view of the paucity of requisite numbers of the same *jati* group to exchange marriage partners and perform ritual functions.

This then raises the interesting question whether it is possible to maintain caste consciousness without fulfilling the basic *jati* rules of social behaviour. For instance, in the context of marriage, families are generally guided by *jati* rules of exchanging alliances. But in the broader context of other matters such as economic and political affairs, *jati* rules and *jati* identities have been known to be violated. Acharya (1969, p. 1645) pointed out that

> [I]t cannot be denied that in the familial field, caste does remain a determining factor, especially in the choice of mate in marriage. Even in this matter, the hold of caste is weakening, while in the sphere of commensalism, its control is disappearing. What goes by the name of caste politics (Jati Model) is distinct and different from caste at the familial level. It has been observed that, within one caste, factions develop when the rich and the poor members of one caste have to share spoils unequally. The poor members feel cheated and join different political parties according to their interests and inclinations.

Nevertheless, in a society where *jati*-related institutions such as *jati panchayats* exist, it is easy to notice the operations and controls based on such institutions. But where such caste-related institutions are absent and rules of caste could not be maintained through appropriate rituals and ceremonies, it is difficult to maintain caste identity in its entirety. But caste consciousness seems to exist in the diasporic Indian community, such as the one in South Africa. Is this behaviour peculiar to South African Indians or is it common within the larger diaspora community of Indian origin? Or is it something that we are beginning to see in the urban society even in

India? On the latter two questions, my general understanding is that the changes in caste behaviour are becoming more common than we seem to acknowledge in the theory of caste. I have pointed out earlier about such prevalence of seeking higher caste status in Malaysia. But assuming that this behaviour is gaining more common ground across India and in the diaspora, then the first question that I raised becomes theoretically significant. If the answer to the first question is affirmative, that is to say that it is possible to maintain caste consciousness without fulfilling the basic *jati* rules under changed circumstances, then the significance of *jati* for our theoretical understanding of caste in modern times would be less than what traditional theories of caste had affirmed.

## Caste in other diasporas

### *Fiji*

South Africa is not an isolated case where caste transformed itself into other forms that influenced social relations to a certain extent. In Fiji, for example, Grieco (1998) demonstrates the existence of subcaste groups of Indian origin. She argues that network ties that the members of the migrant communities establish enable them to perpetuate caste group identity. She argues that when the migrants arrive as social units, they depend less on the 'host communities' and develop into 'ethnic communities' (Grieco 1998, p. 706). However, she recognizes that caste reformation does occur, although such reformation of caste is dependent on migration pattern. She also recognizes that caste as a total system does not migrate but only individuals within that system belonging to subcaste groups migrate. She therefore suggests that 'subcaste reformation would depend on whether or not the auspices of migration that established the community enabled enough members of a specific subcaste group to migrate and reorganize themselves overseas' (Grieco 1998, p. 712). She distinguishes three types of migration auspices, viz. indenture, *maistry* and *kangani* system. While the first two facilitated individual migrations with the exception of small family groups or negligible numbers, the *kangani* system of labour migration allowed subcaste group migrations.

In the case of Fiji she points out, it is mainly the indenture system of labour that facilitated migration which did not allow for survival of caste as a system. So, as in the case of South Africa, in Fiji caste has become what she calls 'a type of blurred status' (Grieco 1998, p. 720). As in South Africa, many have claimed higher caste status mainly as a status symbol. She points out

> Anyone can profess to be of high caste status, but because it is generally believed that many of the indentured labourers adopted higher castes after arriving in Fiji, all present-day claims are questionable. However, if a man maintains a good reputation within the community and possesses the qualities generally attributed to members of high castes, the claims he makes for himself and, by extension, for his family are more readily believed by the community at large. Conversely, if he is successful, his achievements may partially be attributed to his heritage, whether or not he is or has ever publicly claimed to be from a high caste. (Grieco 1998, pp. 721–722)

Social ties in Fiji are largely based on non-caste relations based on 'common experience, residential propinquity, and association at work' and formed sub-community memberships based on 'religion, linguistic group, and geographic area of origin in India' (Grieco 1998, p. 722).

This homogenization is significantly similar to the South African experience of the Indians of indenture system. Again as in the case of South Africa, among the Gujarati community of Fiji too subcaste identity was maintained by keeping links with their Indian counterparts by bringing wives from India or young men returning to India to marry. They also worked within their caste-related professions, such as goldsmiths. For example, as is the case in South Africa, Sonis became jewellers in Fiji (Grieco 1998, p. 726). Therefore, Gujarati groups maintain 'high levels of economic and social endogamy'. However, she points out that a caste system among the Gujaratis has not developed, for it would have needed intergroup social relations. She says, 'While ritual purity has maintained its group basis and is perpetuated by the Gujarati subcastes as overseas extensions of their caste groups in India, it has lost its intergroup basis and therefore much of its functional meaning in Fiji' (Grieco 1998, p. 728). Thus the Gujarati community, she says, can be considered an ethnic community in contradis-tinction from the Indians of indentured background. Nevertheless, it is unclear whether perpetuation of ethnic identity really meant maintenance of subcastes in terms of *jati* with its ritual rules. The difficulty in her thesis is that while pointing out that Gujaratis maintained subcaste identities, she towards the end conflates all of them as a hom-ogenous group when she refers to them (Gujaratis) as 'an ethnic community, socially distinct from the rest of the Indians in Fiji' (Grieco 1998, p. 731). Ethnic community is not the same as subcaste-(*jati*) based group.

In the case of South Africa, it was only in the late nineteenth century and up to the early twentieth century that the subcaste-based associations that they perpetuated could last. By the middle of the twentieth century, the subcaste-based associations such as the Pattini Soni association of Pietermaritzburg, and Kathiawadi Gujarati association, dis-appeared to make room for more universal affiliations flagging the generic name 'Gujarati' and not the individual subcaste names (Kumar 2000; see also Bhana and Bhoola 2011). This points to the gradual disappearance of *jati*-based identity in South Africa as well as in Fiji. This does not mean total disappearance of caste aware-ness in South Africa (Rambiritch and Berghe 1961; see Naidoo 1973, Ebr-Vally 2001).

## The UK

In the case of the UK, Waughray (2007, 2009) has shown some caste discrimination that is practiced among Indian communities. She points out

> Jati groupings are local or regional, not national; the local 'caste map' is a matter of local knowledge, especially in rural areas where seventy per cent of India's population lives, and this knowledge travels with migration. Markers for caste include place of origin and residence, name (although names can be changed), current or ancestral occupation, education, skin colour, appearance, body language and demeanour. In the UK, while such markers may not have the same cultural resonance, name, ancestral occupation, place of origin, residence and religious affiliation are used to identify caste background. (Waughray 2009, pp. 187–188)

Referring to the study of Ballard (1994), she further points out that caste loyalties are still strong in the UK, the reason being that the rules of endogamy are as strictly followed in the UK as in India, as in the case of Valmikis and the Jats (Waughray 2009, p. 196). Vivek Kumar also points out the caste discrimination meted out to the Dalit communities by the Jats in the UK. He refers to some classic cases of discrimi-nation based on pollution – in a case in Wolverhampton *jat* women working in the same factory as the Dalit women refused to share the same tap to drink water; in

Birmingham after an inter-temple tournament, the Langar food prepared by the Ravidasi (traditional Chamars) community was refused by the *jats* (Kumar 2004, p. 114).[6]

What neither Kumar (2004) nor Waughray (2009), however, clarify is that the Indian community in the UK, unlike that of either South Africa or Fiji, is still controlled by the first-generation families, and secondly that most Indians who came to the UK came in large family networks and not as isolated individuals (see Kalsi 1992, Rutten and Patel 2003). The nature of the indenture system prohibited large family networks in South Africa among the indentured Indians as it happened in the case of Fiji. The Gujarati community in South Africa may be considered an exception to this. And for this reason, the Gujarati community has been fairly successful in maintaining subcaste alliances, at least in the earlier phases of their life in South Africa. The many subcaste-based organizations that emerged in the earlier period such as Pattani Soni Samaj of Pietermaritzburg and so on are an evidence of their tendency to maintain sub-caste alliances (see Kumar 2000, p. 71). The presence of subcaste (*jati*) identity in the UK among Indians is directly related to the presence of the first generation and the traditional authority that they still hold in the family as well as the easily identifiable groups in sufficient numbers and their continued contact with their counterparts in India. Both in South Africa as well as in the Indian sub-continent, the name changes and appropriation of higher caste names occurred when individuals became anonymous after they moved away from their original locations. Mallick's (1997) point about name changes among Dalits in Indian urban places occurred only because such Dalit members could become anonymous in the urban mix of people. Thus, there is a close parallel between name changes in South Africa and the Indian urban places in the sense that both cases are individual based as well as such phenomena occurred when they become anonymous. On the contrary, in the UK, the visible number of a particular subcaste group coupled with the living memory of the first generation, the Dalit members could not have changed their caste identities through name changes. Instead, they chose to establish firmly their subcaste identities. One other important factor to be noted here is that maintenance of subcaste identities in the UK by the Dalits did not inhibit their economic progress as is the case in Indian rural sector.

In another study conducted in two cities of UK (Birmingham and Leamington Spa) Paramjit Judge confirms the caste practice among the Sikh community, although the younger generation seems to push for more liberal outlook on caste. In the specific case of Ad-Dharmis who are considered Dalits, Judge notes that in the UK 'over a period of five decades since independence the Ad-Dharmis have emerged as a sizeable and distinct social group within the Punjabi community' (Judge 2002, p. 3247). He notes that the Gurdwaras have played a role in the perpetuation of caste as each caste has its own Gurdwara.[7] This caste-based Gurdwaras in the diaspora is not unique in the sense that the Gurdwaras in Punjab are divided into two kinds – the historical ones that are associated with one or the other 10 Sikh Gurus, and the social Gurdwaras that are caste based and located in the particular villages around particular communities (Judge 2002, p. 3247). It is however significant that he notes the increasing number of intercaste marriages, especially among the non-Dalit Punjabis. While there seems to be some laxity of the endogamy rule within the non-Dalit groups, it remains still strictly rigid between non-Dalit and Dalit Punjabis. He, however, hopes that the younger generation would be able to eradicate caste practice in the UK (Judge 2002, pp. 3247–3249). This again makes my earlier argument that *jati*-based caste identities will gradually weaken with the succeeding generations although some semblance of caste consciousness might remain, as it happened in the case of

South Africa and Fiji. In the case of the UK, this view has been expressed by Patel and Rutten (1999)

> for the first generation migrants the ties with their relatives, villages, and country have romantic value and hence are quite powerful. They consider themselves British citizens and yet they think they are the self-appointed ambassadors of India to the UK. However, the same is not true with their children and grandchildren. They identify themselves relatively more with the British society and western culture. As a result, the biggest anxiety of the patels in the UK is how to reclaim the second and third generation. (p. 954)

## Caste without subcaste (*jati*) identity?

Based on the examples that we have looked at, the following changes of caste are identifiable that directly affected the practice of endogamous caste or subcaste (*jati*) identity in the diaspora. First, as Greico observed, the immigration of individuals through a system of indenture had more dire consequences for the practice of *jati* as opposed to the immigration that brought substantial number of people from a particular *jati*. Second, *jati* identity was exchanged for group identities based on religion and language affinity. That is, both in the case of South Africa and Fiji there is evidence of this transformation. In South Africa, the South Indian groups of Tamil and Telugu and (other minor South Indian languages that gradually disappeared in South Africa) became homogenized along South Indian group by appropriating rituals and ceremonies and by finding cognate castes to exchange marriage alliances. The food restrictions have virtually vanished in South African Indians. Third, by appropriating higher caste names, as happened in both South Africa and Fiji, the diaspora Indians sought to appropriate ritual duties as well as achieve higher social status. In other words, the caste and social status have not been radically de-linked from each other. The presence of caste consciousness in the diaspora albeit without the operative mechanisms of *jati*, meant that caste remains in some sense notionally significant. Fourth, economic and political interests of groups seem more significant than the maintenance of caste identity along *jati* lines. In other words, *jati* is no longer the significant factor for economic pursuits unlike the case in the context of rural India. In the case of India, for instance, Desai and Dubey (2011) have shown persistence of wage discrimination based on caste.

Even though such proliferation of caste names exists in the South African Indian diaspora, most of the present generation that I have been able to speak to seem either oblivious of what those last names mean to them or indifferent to those names as significant identity markers.[8] In other words, for the earlier generations, the caste consciousness might have meant social status, as I referred to in the narrative of the elderly person that I interviewed in Pietermaritzburg. But for the present generation of Indians, caste names do not necessarily represent caste consciousness, but simply a memory of the past. Here there seems to be a direct correlation between the emergence of class formation in Indian society since the 1950s in particular and the identity formation in the diaspora along class lines. Natrajan's (2005) study of the potter community in Chhattisgarh illuminates the class formation and its relationship to caste in the Indian context. In India the emergence of the Forward Class, Backward Class and the Dalits has obfuscated the internal distinctions between *jatis* and enabled the identity formation along economic and political interests of larger cognate groups. However, in the case of the Indian diaspora, it is the total disappearance of the *jati* system coupled with economic and political aspirations that seems to have enabled groups to form new identities. However, there is, for instance in South Africa, still a subtle presence of the exchange of marriage alliances between cognate castes such as Naidoos, Reddis, Padyachies and others on the basis of similarities of ritual practices.

## Conclusion

Let me conclude by suggesting that the dynamicity of caste and its function in modern society is more to entrench caste consciousness of a superior status even in the absence of its core elements, namely operations of *jati*. In that sense, caste can reinvent itself from a rigid hierarchical system into a more fluid structure that offers some sense of superiority of social status, however much it might be limited. More to the point, I would suggest that caste consciousness is more significant than actual caste mainten-ance in real society. Caste consciousness is deeply endemic in South Asian society and that is perhaps the only way they understand how social status is derived within that society. It is this consciousness that seems to tempt social groups and individuals to either display their caste name as part of their last name or discretely acquire caste names if they came from a lower order caste groups. It is in this sense the present gen-eration of South African Indian Hindus of South Indian background in particular might offer an example of how caste might transmute itself into modern forms without its tra-ditional core elements. Finally, I therefore wish to suggest that the Indian caste in modern society today is more to do with the symbolic consciousness of being superior than it is about maintaining strictly one's caste endogamy. As Jeffrey (2001, p. 231) put it

> Caste is changing in rural India. As it changes, it poses new and exciting questions for geographers interested in the reproduction of social inequality and resistance to this repro-duction. Caste as a religiously and culturally sanctioned system of resource transfer appears to be on the wane. The *jajmani* system and associated norms of authority described by Srinivas (1987) for rural south India in the 1950s have been eroded. But caste as an identity, form of social organization and basis for staking claims to resources remains significant.

In this sense, caste consciousness among South African Indians of South Indian background may have helped to access social capital in the form of religious functions and marriages. But as the present generation gradually becomes unaware of the signifi-cance of their last names as caste names, it would be interesting to see what relevance caste might hold for the diaspora Indian community.

## Acknowledgements

I wish to thank the two anonymous reviewers for their most helpful comments. I also wish to thank Dr Ajaya Sahoo for his unstinting support in the course of revising this paper and for his editorial support.

## Notes

1. These unedited papers are available in the School of Religion, Philosophy and Classics, Uni-versity of KwaZulu Natal, Durban, South Africa. They are in the process of being digitized to be put on the University website.
2. The 2011/2012 Telephone Book of Durban shows the list for Naidoo last name from pages 485–500 with four columns in each page. See the sample pages of 486 and 500 of the Tele-phone Directory in the appendix.
3. This alternative spelling reflected social origins of different Telugus – those who came from Tamilnadu region and those who came from coastal Andhra region. Those who came from coastal Andhra region spelled as Naidu and those from Tamil regions spelled as Naidoo.

4. Only since 1990s Brahmin priests from Sri Lanka began to arrive and take over priestly duties in some prominent temples. This was facilitated by some wealthy patrons who felt that their local temple priests did not have the requisite knowledge of rituals. However, this resulted in controversy about the rituals and procedures that the Sri Lankan priests followed (see Kumar 2000, p. 26).
5. This applies to shrines of non-vegetarian gods and goddesses, but also vegetarian gods and goddesses.
6. Jodhka (2009) notes that the 'Punjabi dalits did not expect to be reminded of their "low" status in the caste hierarchy. While they did not have any such problem at the workplace and in the urban public sphere in UK, they often experienced caste prejudice when they tried to be part of the local Punjabi community in the diaspora' (p. 84).
7. See Singh (2006) for a discussion on the growth of Gurdwaras in Britain and its role in the development of a 'Sikh community'.
8. My observation is based on the family histories project that some of my students for their undergraduate degree project conducted. These family histories offer an insight into how marriages took place across caste and linguistic boundaries. [Unedited family histories of student projects are available at the School of Religion, Philosophy and Classics, Howard College Campus, University of KwaZulu Natal, Durban, South Africa.]

## Notes on contributor

P. Pratap Kumar is a Professor of Hinduism and Comparative Religions. In addition to over 60 scholarly papers, his recent books include *The Goddess Lakshmi in South Indian Vaishnavism* (Scholars Press, 1997; Oxford University Press, 2000); *Hindus in South Africa* (University of Durban-Westville, 2000); *Methods and theories in the study of religions* (Sundeep Prakashan, 2004). His edited volumes include: *South Asians in the diaspora*, co-edited with Knut Jacobsen (Brill, 2004); *Study of religion in Southern Africa*, co-edited with Johannes A. Smit (Brill, 2005); and *Religious pluralism and the diaspora* (Brill, 2006).

## References

Acharya, H., 1969. Jati model: a few observations. *Economic and political weekly*, 4 (41), 1645–1646.
Ballard, R., ed., 1994. *Desh Pardesh: the South Asian presence in Britain*. London: Hurst & Co.
Beachey, R.W., 1996. *A history of East Africa 1592–1902*. London: I.B. Tauris.
Béteille, A., 1965. *Caste, class and power: changing patterns of stratification in a Tanjore village*. California: University of California Press.
Béteille, A., 1969. *Castes: old and new, essays in social structure and social stratification*. Bombay: Asia Publishing House.
Béteille, A., 1974. *Studies in agrarian social structure*. Delhi: Oxford University Press.
Bhana, S., 1991. *Indentured Indian emigrants to Natal 1860–1902: a study based on ships' lists*. New Delhi: Promila & Co.
Bhana, S. and Bhoola, K.K., 2011. The dynamics of preserving cultural heritage: the case of Durban's Kathiawad Hindu Seva Samaj, 1943–1960 and beyond. *South Asian diaspora*, 3 (1), 15–36.
Brain, J., 1989. Natal's Indians, 1860–1910: from co-operation, through competition to conflict. *In*: A. Duminy and B. Guest, eds. *Natal and Zululand, from earliest times to 1910: a new history*. Pietermaritzburg: University of Natal Press, 249–274.
Desai, S. and Dubey, A., 2011. Caste in 21st century India: competing narratives. *Economic and political weekly*, XLVI (11), 40–49.
Dumont, L., 1970. *Homo Hierarchicus: the caste system and its implications*. Chicago: University of Chicago Press.
Ebr-Vally, R., 2001. *Caste and colour in South Africa*. Cape Town: Kwela Publishers.
Grieco, E.M., 1998. The effects of migration on the establishment of networks: caste disintegration and reformation among the Indians of Fiji. *International migration review*, 32 (3), 704–736.
Gupta, D., 2000. *Interrogating caste: understanding hierarchy and difference in Indian society*. New Delhi: Penguin Books.

Henning, C.G., 1993. *The indentured Indian in Natal 1860–1917*. New Delhi: Promilla & Co.

Ingham, K., 1965. *A history of East Africa*. London: Longmans.

Jeffrey, C., 2001. 'A fist is stronger than five fingers': caste and dominance in rural North India. *Transactions of the institute of British geographers (N.S.)*, 26 (2), 217–236.

Jodhka, S.S., 2009. The Ravi Dasis of Punjab: global contours of caste and religious strife. *Economic and political weekly*, XLIV (24), 79–85.

Judge, P.S., 2002. Punjabis in England: the Ad-Dharmi experience. *Economic and political weekly*, 37 (31), 3244–3250.

Kalsi, S.S., 1992. *The evolution of a Sikh community in Britain: religious and social change among the Sikhs of Leeds and Bradford*. Leeds: Community Religions Project, Department of Theology and Religious Studies, University of Leeds.

Kumar, P.P., 2000. *Hindus in South Africa: their traditions and beliefs*. Durban: University of Durban-Westville.

Kumar, V., 2004. Understanding Dalit diaspora. *Economic and political weekly*, 39 (1), 114–116.

Kumar, P.P., 2008. Hindus in Africa. *In*: D. Cush, C. Robinson and M. York, eds. *Encyclopedia of Hinduism*. London: Routledge, 9–15.

Kuper, H., 1960. *Indian people in Natal*. Pietermaritzburg: Natal University Press.

Madan, T.N., 1962. The joint family: a terminological clarification. *International studies in sociology and social anthropology*, 3 (1), 7–16.

Mallick, R., 1997. Affirmative action and elite formation: an untouchable family history. *Ethnohistory*, 44 (2), 345–374.

Mikula, P., Kearney, B., and Harber, R., 1982. *Traditional Hindu temples in South Africa*. Durban: Hindu Temple Publications.

Moodley, P., 1981. *Indentured Indian immigration to Natal 1860–1870 with special reference to the Hindu caste system and its implications*. Unpublished BA thesis. Durban: University of Durban-Westville.

Naidoo, L.V., 1973. *Caste, class and social change in South Africa*. Cape Coast: L.V. Naidoo.

Natrajan, B., 2005. Caste, class, and community in India: an ethnographic approach. *Ethnology*, 44 (3), 227–241.

Patel, P.J. and Rutten, M., 1999. Patels of central Gujarat in greater London. *Economic and political weekly*, 34 (16/17), 952–954.

Pillay, G., 1991. *An investigation into the caste attitudes that prevail amongst Hindus in the Durban metropolitan area*. Unpublished MA thesis. Durban: University of Durban-Westville.

Rajakrishnan, R., 1984. *Caste consciousness among Indian Tamils in Malaysia*. Selangor: Pelanduk.

Rambiritch, B. and Berghe, P.L.V.D., 1961. Caste in a Natal Hindu community. *African studies*, 20 (4), 217–225.

Rutten, M. and Patel, P.J., 2003. Caste-based differences and contested family relations: social linkages between India and Britain. *Etnofoor*, 16 (1), 75–96.

Sahai, N.P., 2005. Crafts in eighteenth-century Jodhpur: questions of class, caste and community identities. *Journal of the economic and social history of the orient*, 48 (4), 524–551.

Singh, G., 2006. Gurdwaras and community-building among British Sikhs. *Contemporary South Asia*, 15 (2), 147–164.

Sivakumar, S.S. and Sivakumar, C., 1979. Class and Jati at Asthapuram and Kanthapuram: some comments towards a structure of interests. *Economic and political weekly*, 14 (7/8), 263–286.

Srinivas, M.N., 1955. The social system of a Mysore village in India. *In*: M. Marriot, ed. *Village India: studies in the little community*. Chicago: University of Chicago Press, 1–35.

Srinivas, M.N., 1962. *Caste in modern India and other essays*. New Delhi: Asia Publishing House.

Srinivas, M.N., 1987. *The dominant caste and other essays*. New Delhi: Oxford University Press.

Waughray, A., 2007. Caste-based discrimination is a reality in the UK. *New Law Journal* [online], 157 (7263). Available from: http://www.newlawjournal.co.uk/nlj/content/caste-invisible-discrimination [Accessed 29 February 2012].

Waughray, A., 2009. Caste discrimination: a twenty-first century challenge for UK discrimination law. *The modern law review*, 72 (2), 182–219.

# Appendix

NAICKER (CONTD)
S 2 PoonaPlce Mtbnk ... 031 468 9006
S 55 PrincsnPlce Rydvle ... 031 507 1435
S Magjcivd Prospct HaiRd PrspctHil ... 031 563 6773
S 1 ProteaRd ... 031 764 4380
S 9 RamayanSt Shlrcrs ... 031 409 6831
S 100 Richra CrteRd Xps ... 031 469 2522
S Whte Rign 215 RidgeRd Msgrve
Dbn ... 031 208 3838
S 25 RivghnCrcle FrstHvn Dbn ... 031 505 1231
S 47 ArikgmsWy Gmbry ... 031 539 1899
S 617 Road Mntfrd ... 031 404 4812
S 101 Road 701 Mhtfrd ... 031 404 6294
S 112 Road 729 Rsectf ... 031 404 1003
S 23 Road No 701Ru Montfrd ... 031 404 8278
S 489 Road No 701Rd Rsedf ... 031 404 6367
S 40 Road No 706Rd Montfrd ... 031 404 9564
S 84 Road No 707Dve Montfrd ... 031 404 9628
S 91 Road No 726St Montfrd ... 031 404 5123
S 99 Road No 728Rd Rsecdf Dbn ... 031 404 1002
S 35 Road No 733Rd Montfrd ... 031 404 7871
S 56 Road No 750Rd Rsecff Dbn ... 031 404 0239
S 76 Road729 Rsecff ... 031 404 8572
S 6 Robin Rd Smia ... 031 708 4882
S 67 Robinst Khrwstn ... 031 403 6279
S 23 RustonPlce Rckfrd ... 031 539 7147
S 23 Dunir Ct Crssmr Dbn ... 031 409 2372
S 6 ShefdiMws Rsvrrhls ... 031 262 1971
S 109 SilvrmntCrcle Rsecdf ... 031 404 6590
S 38 Skegness Av MrVinn ... 031 464 0611
S 298 Skyridge Crcle Moortn Dbn ... 031 404 3867
S Rrdne Soi HarsCres DbnCntrl ... 031 337 1373
S Dr Windsor SomersetDve SmrstPrk ... 031 572 4598
S 12 Sprinto Pl Moortn Dbn ... 031 404 0086
S 292 South CoastRd Rsdorgh ... 031 465 6362
S Spoorlyn Rd Wstcff Dbn ... 031 404 3974
S 1B Star St Woodhrst ... 031 401 2157
S 8 StatsmnDse Havnsde Dbn ... 031 400 9654
S 48 ShepfordRd Sunfrd ... 031 500 7506
S F169 StorkPlce Bayvw ... 031 400 7331
S 67 SummerfialRd Byvw ... 031 401 0944
S 80 SwaanRd Duffrkfo ... 031 505 1271
S 108 SweetWtrs Amnzmti ... 031 903 7512
S 10 Tbie MountnSt Shlrcrs ... 031 409 8623
S Kingtshi Court 16 Tngtne Grve OrnrPrk
Ispngo ... 031 902 5453
S 5 Tngrne Grve OrntPrk Ispngo ... 031 902 1495
S Block 639n 639H Taurus St Shlkcrs
Wstcff ... 031 409 9517
S 49 The Curl Rd GlnanI ... 031 572 6856
S 4 ThrntreeAv SavmnaPrcc ... 031 706 9109
S 32 Treadham Trce Wsthm ... 031 500 5118
S 5 TrustmorePlce GrveEnd ... 031 539 3838
S 33 UmarkotCres Mtbnk ... 031 468 6543
S 35 UmarkotCres Mrbnk ... 031 468 6543
S 128 Umgeni Rd OldFort ... 031 309 7228
S 106 UnderwoodRd FarninghmRdg ... 031 702 4494
S 31 UprCrftRd Lngcrft ... 031 500 5205
S 91 UprCrftRd Lngcrft ... 031 500 5205
S 15 MdnwiPrk Rdfn ... 031 564 7844
S 42 WatibrkCres Brkdle ... 031 505 5438
S 434 WestofDve Wstcff ... 031 401 5542
S 130 WesthamDve Wsthm ... 031 500 5121
S 20 Wilw Grve Mbniigts ... 031 400 2283
S 7 WintermnmPlce TrnndVnr ... 031 505 7394
S 33 WoodcrestAv Chtswrth ... 031 401 5078
S 10 WyvaiePlce Rydvle ... 031 507 5335
S 15 YelwdvCise Ctyld ... 031 500 2114
S 57 ZulwinGdns Amnzmti ... 031 903 3175
S Mntpno 2 Msgrve ... 031 208 7365
S 81 Road 701 Mntfrd ... 031 404 0685
S Mainldig Wstcff ... 031 401 7757
S 4 Road 703 Mntfrd ... 031 404 5363
S 9 Road 259 Chtswrth ... 031 400 5792
S 42 Road 726 Chtswrth ... 031 404 9626
S 30 Road 613 Amanzmy ... 031 207 6993
S Outldig Crkrhls ... 031 207 6753
S 22 Road 707 Mntfrd ... 031 404 5363
SA 20 OlympiaSt Shlrcrs ... 031 409 6290
SA 22 OlympiaSt Shlrcss ... 031 409 6610
NAICKER Sagie Cell ... 083 783 8217
NAICKER Samuellng Wstcff ... 072 216 4725
NAICKER Sarathkmmat 16 Kns-Nve Pl
Mvrn ... 031 464 4322
Saravathie S EarlicroftCse Lngcrft ... 031 500 4823
SE378 BrickhilRd Ovrort ... 031 208 7610
SC 34 Smith VlieRd twnHva Amnzmti ... 031 916 2973
SD 26 ColoradoCres Bayvw ... 031 400 5234
SD 27 CornelYce Mlvrn ... 031 463 2720
SD 125 LawnnawnAv FrstHvn ... 031 505 2140
SD 19 NaranPlce Hrnagr ... 031 409 6196
SI 3 Fremdeist Shlkcrs ... 031 409 7441
SG 2 Octabn Plce Phnx ... 031 500 5484
SG 20 Violet Rd GnPrk ... 031 708 6886
NAICKER Shireen Cell ... 031 502 0185
NAICKER Shunmugam 31 Road 217
Chtswrth ... 031 400 1558
Skalingum 667 MariannHil ... 031 706 2866
Sivapragasam 28 Road 224 Bayvw ... 031 400 1744
SK 6 24Av Umhlitzna ... 031 402 0748
SK 146 GreenburyAv Phnx ... 031 502 0442
SK 49 MainprkWy ShstrPrk ... 031 505 4922
SK 8 Maryland Av Virginia ... 031 564 2945
SU 25 ParvlghtSj Qnsbrgh ... 031 464 9272
SU 5 PantnianRd Mrbnk ... 031 468 2658
SM 4 ReyngRd Mrwnt ... 031 468 9062
SM 205 ElfPlce Crtd ... 031 269 2564
SM 18 FezprelRd Mrwnt ... 031 462 4676
SM 436 FrereRd Glnwd ... 031 205 1014
SM 5 PetrwoodCise Wdvw ... 031 505 2315
SM 20 Road No 740 Montfrd Dbn ... 031 406 1180
SM 103 StwrbrikRd Shrgin ... 031 401 3842
SM 307 SkyridgeCrcle Moortn ... 031 404 2932
SM SwalwCrt 13 OrntPrk ... 031 902 7241
SN 11 DuniverieCres Crtdne ... 031 401 1213
SN 6 EmkirgihRd Skrgin ... 031 401 8480
SN 58 Grve EndDve GrveEnd ... 031 539 6287
SN 53 Pomat Rd Rsvrrhls ... 031 262 3403
SN 15 TheOakt ... 031 404 3422
VCKER SN & KAMBARAN SR Ors
Gyncologst/Obsttrcn Medd Twrs Old Main
Rd Ispngo Box 23143 Ispngo ... 031 902 4321
Chatswrdt 17 ChatsmdMdCtr ... 031 403 6866
Kingsway Hospital ... 031 904 7202
Cel ... 082 449 7429
Res SB Saunders Av Ispngo ... 031 902 2979

NAICKER Sootbramoney 7 MagisbrgSt
Shlrcrs ... 031 409 7583
SP 13 DeltaRd Sdnhm ... 031 208 3457
SP 54 PenelopeSt Strwd ... 031 500 6418
SR 24 RobinSt Montrk ... 031 403 1159
SS 12 LibralRd Wshrst ... 031 403 9293
SS 293 Road No. 706Rd Montfrd ... 031 404 4401
SS 769 Sunset Av Woodhrst ... 031 401 6500
SS 39 UmarkotT Cres Mrewnt ... 031 461 1763
Stanley 2 TurfwoodPlce Hvnsde ... 031 400 3265
Sukunthalai 4 ShannonCrt Glnwd ... 031 201 9151
Sundrorubban 73 BradcroftCise Phnx ... 031 507 5060
SV 15 Ibody Grve Fosavi Dbn ... 031 577 1811
SV 76 Road No 789Rd Rsecdf ... 031 404 4489
SV Crest Edge Flats Silvr DaxAv
Essxwrd ... 031 208 6605
SV Sumsnds Sol HarsCres DbnCntrl ... 031 368 7643
SV 60 TurnstoneAv Byvw ... 031 400 0332
T 32 39Av Umhlitzna ... 031 403 9206
T 40 50 Av Umhlitzna ... 031 403 0908
T 90 AbervaIe Rd Rydvle ... 031 507 6664
T 3 BeryllfdFlce Skrgin ... 031 401 1708
T 46 BrayfordAv Phnx ... 031 500 4965
T 127 BurlrngronRd Rsvrrhls ... 031 262 3254
T 112 CamperDve Hvnsde ... 031 402 3374
T 94 CamphvnRd FrstHvn ... 031 505 8824
T 93 Cashew Av Crssmr ... 031 409 4787
T 167 Centre Rd HippoRd ... 031 577 4007
T 67 ChapeRd Sdnhm ... 031 209 1114
T 58 Chatswrth MainRd Umhlitzna ... 031 403 3798
T 143 Colorado Crde Bayvw ... 031 405 1263
T 67 Columbia Rd Kenvil ... 031 564 4634
Cmlia Gardns Glamis Av NwGrmny ... 031 502 3026
T 32 HeathburyPlce Eastbry ... 031 500 3846
T 53 HlmlvsRd Mrewnt ... 031 468 5442
T 127 Kennedy Rd CreHls ... 031 269 3383
NAICKER T 1688 Klaarwtrrd ... 031 409 9641
NAICKER T 47 Klaarwtrrd Shlrcrss ... 031 409 4033
T 15 MashaCres Moortn ... 031 404 3869
T 6 MontmoreRd Stnmre ... 031 539 7513
T 102 Mount EdgcmbeDve Edgevw ... 031 539 2064
T 166 Prksde Er Skrgin ... 031 401 6385
T 30 Pioneer Rd ... 031 764 1901
T 29 PfetrariaRd Chlrrnhls ... 031 262 6054
T 201 PowerlinSt Wstcff ... 031 401 4939
T 46 PrimroseRd Moortn ... 031 404 3011
T 4 RanaRd ... 031 902 7695
T 118 RoslynAv Sdnhm ... 031 208 5163
T 17 RudmoreRd FrstHvn ... 031 505 3156
T 22 Ruston Pl Rckfrd ... 031 502 5963
T 50 Sage Rd Jdps ... 031 468 9657
T D&D Heights Sparks Rd Sdnhm ... 031 207 3066
T 31 St ThomsRd Msgrve Dbn ... 031 202 4732
T 10 StanmoreDve Stnmre ... 031 539 7983
T 14 TamarindCise Snngdle ... 031 562 9941

NAICKER (CONTD)
T 101 Vctria EmbnknVictoria Embnknmnt
DbnCntrl ... 031 304 8911
TA 99 Road 726 Chtswrth ... 031 404 8531
TO 34 DaintreeAv Sdnhm ... 031 208 0515
TE 11 SucroseRd IspngoHts ... 031 902 4167
TS 782 MainRd Nrthdne ... 031 708 1154
TM 44 BonhrshCres Crssmr ... 031 404 0369
TP 27 GrsmreDve RglnyPrk ... 031 706 3445
TR 16 66 Av Umhlitzna ... 031 403 0747
TS 60 GrasmereAv Msgrve ... 031 401 0400
TS 9 stnsi 3 Pimt ... 031 269 3425
V 20 GlffbunyPlce Eastbry ... 031 500 3785
V 443 Road 706 8 Cycad Cl Shlkcrs
Chtswrth ... 031 400 7561
NAICKER U 74 Entabeni Rd PrdseVly ... 031 708 1736
US 183 FinwoodRd Avca ... 031 708 3317
UT Harmony 3 2Av Mvrn Qnsbrgh ... 031 916 2551
V 143 Arna ParkDve Crtdne ... 031 563 4231
V 9 Axminster St Mvrn Qnsbrgh ... 031 401 1992
V 51 James BoundaryRd Escmbe ... 031 706 3640
V 302 BrayfordAv Snfrd ... 031 464 6037
V5 Chardy Ga Crtd ... 031 500 5552
V 39 ChaaraRd Chirnhls ... 031 505 1689
V 127 Chiltern Dve Pimt ... 031 262 7969
Malvrn Heights ContnRd ... 031 259 1104
Malvrn Heights ContnRd Mvrn ... 031 464 4626
V 43 CriscndaPlce AreaaPrk ... 031 207 5449
V 44 CrottdeneDve Crtdne ... 031 401 7743
V 12 DundinRd Crssmr ... 031 409 3042
V 8A Davel Rd Ashby Pnetwn ... 031 700 9106
V 101 DeerrlSt Crtdone ... 031 403 9694
V 28 ElmswdGa Wdvw ... 031 502 3083
V 121 Fount HavnDve FrstHvn Dbn ... 031 505 1085
V 381 FremantleRd MiVrnn ... 031 402 4404
V 72 GreenvaleAv WstcIf ... 031 403 3459
V 37 Harish Rd Nagna ... 031 462 4676
V 19 HomleighRd Rsvrhls ... 031 262 0456
V 26 Horner Rd Bayvw Dbn ... 031 400 0567
V 41 KasualRd Mrwnt ... 031 462 1727
V 35 LadlepalmCres Pnxw ... 031 505 7557
V 42 LarkspurRd Springfld ... 031 209 1536
V 84 LightHseRd Ocnvw ... 031 466 6625
V 32 MainprkWy ShstrPrk ... 031 505 0918
V 34 MenathRd St MbnrHts ... 031 400 3044
V 25 MorewoodRd Pimt ... 031 269 2013
V 47 PelicanDve Havnsde ... 031 405 1539
V Carrngtn Gardns Ptcann Rd Umblo ... 031 261 6309
V 1 PwrlneSt Wstcif ... 031 404 9057
V 23 PyreneesSt Shlrcrs ... 031 409 7985
V 44 Rgntonkage ... 031 505 3308
V 465 Road 706 Mntfrd ... 031 404 6216
V 700 Road 706 Mntfrd ... 031 404 0171
V 5 Road No 704Dve Montfrd ... 031 401 4766
V 91 Road No 726Rd Montfrd ... 031 404 1785

NAICKER (CONTD)
V 42 SaulterDve MrnnhPrk ... 031 700 5955
V 80 StanrdreCres Brkdle ... 031 505 6696
V 59 ShlkringRd Mrbnk ... 031 468 6495
V 43 StkstlleAv Cstleh ... 031 578 5757
V 3 SuisgenRd Ispngo ... 031 902 4496
V 36 SwartbergSt Shlcrss ... 031 409 7762
V 16 Swift Cres Lotusprk ... 031 902 8856
V 2 TamarynPlce Arenaprit ... 031 404 3249
V 1 Tate Vie The VlieRd Lwrllvo
Amnzmt ... 031 916 3494
V 29 ThorntreeAv Svnnhprk ... 031 706 1477
V 6 TipstonePce Whtstne ... 031 500 6330
NAICKER V 106 TygerAv GreenwdPrk ... 031 563 1714
Cel ... 082 414 8368
NAICKER V 27 Wedgwd Ct Lmgniprk ... 031 564 8277
V 1 MilshCrt 5 Pntwn ... 031 702 5550
V 1 RalphCrt 19 Pntwn ... 031 702 5106
V SCwLke ... 031 579 2133
V 30 Road 704 Chtswrth ... 031 403 9047
V4 4 DunnottarAv Sdnhm ... 031 207 6702
NAICKER VA & SONS Bdrs & Grassing 165 Fulham Rd
Rsrvrhls ... 031 262 2673
NAICKER Vadivalool 230 Road 502
Crftdne ... 031 401 2772
Vadvelu 30 Road 710 Chtswrth ... 031 404 5470
Vedenghee Pengelly PeachvnPlce
Crssmr ... 031 466 6456
VG 50 CamperDve Hvnsde ... 031 402 2747
VI 5 Road 704 Mntfrd ... 031 401 4750
Vilvanathan 138 RingwoodAv Wdvw ... 031 505 2383
VM 15 66th Av Umhlitzna Dbn ... 031 403 1114
VN 10 DeasmorePlce GrveEnd ... 031 502 3026
VN Stand 95 Stckvl ... 031 767 3331
VP 8 Elpsm Downs Ronald Rd Mntor ... 031 469 1860
VP 3a SamsundersRd Glnstn ... 031 902 1175
VP 171 Road 703 Chtswrth ... 031 404 4916
VR 8 PunjabCrcle Mrwnt ... 031 462 1238
VS 79 Clancy Av Mrrnnplk ... 031 207 8773
VT 14 KaprmiRd Mrwnt ... 031 468 6097
VU 14 MontdeneDve Mntfrd ... 031 401 7776
W 8 DanbrookPlce Brkdle ... 031 505 0958
W 66 FairlghtRd Mvrn ... 031 463 1126
W 10 GaidwnPlce Wdvw Dbn ... 031 505 1408
W 40 Herish Rd Nagna ... 031 706 4761
W 182 Avalen Cres Nithcroft ... 031 500 1362
VP 39 3rornvale Plce Rydvle ... 031 507 2897
W 44 CorlanderCise Crssmr ... 031 409 1969
W 71 GrffviePlce Lngcrft ... 031 507 4919
W 61 DhanwarAv Mrbnk ... 031 468 7820
VT 71 DiamondCise Shlrcrss ... 031 469 3052
W 9 GrasslandAv Svnnahprk ... 031 706 8477
W 55 HawkSt Shrwstn Dbn ... 031 403 3776
W 4 HohnCise Mvrn ... 031 464 8154
W 336 IhandaRd PeterRd ... 031 577 1390
W 26 Kenford Rd Kervil ... 031 563 8097
W 51 KharwaRd Khrwstn Khrwstn ... 031 401 4554

NAICKER (CONTD)
Y Khorshid Creek Khorshed Rd Mlvrn ... 031 464 6591
Y 15 Lamson Ave Havnsde ... 031 400 5027
Y 12a LotusDve LotusPrk ... 031 902 9148
Y 19 MrgreigonRd Sdnhm ... 031 208 9994
Y 49 Road No. 727Rd Montfrd ... 031 404 1600
Y 7 Roberts Plce Dwncff ... 031 266 0056
VP 89 Rise HeightRd ArenaPrk Dbn ... 031 404 7363
Y 19 SeefortRd Highhvds Hls ... 031 702 6941
Y 100 ShrrginDve Skrgin ... 031 402 0880
Y 3 SkyvkK Rd Bayvw ... 031 400 1627
Y 240 SkyridgeCrcle Moortn ... 031 404 8692
Y 2 Snowfern Plce Rdfrn ... 031 507 9125
Y 6 Wren St Khrwstn ... 031 401 9909
YA 12 Camper Dr Havnsde Dbn ... 031 400 1410
Yagamsham 9 PommernLne
ElfrqrmHigts ... 031 564 1928
YG 73 AmberdaleRd Birdie ... 031 578 7238
YP Hmz Manzl Crescent St Sdnhm ... 031 207 9565
YP 8 HarwoodRd Birdie ... 031 404 3854
NAICKERS CARTAGE CONTRACTORS
Sand & Stone Suppirs 16 BakerSt
Qnsbrgh ... 031 464 2114
NAICKERS CURRY DEN 759 North CoastRd
GreenwdPrk ... 031 563 7320
NAICKER'S K TRANSPORT 35 GreenvleWd
Qnsbrgh ... 031 401 0384
NAIDARAH SUBBIAH T 173 HannafordDve
Qnsbrgh ... 031 506 1118
NAIDO A 409 BrckfildRd Sdnhm ... 031 207 5449
S 14 Bamboo Lne Pnetwn ... 031 701 9468
NAIDOO 81 Botnc GardnsRd Msgrve ... 031 201 6909
ID DawnsnRd Wdvw ... 031 266 0287
18 Equinox Rd UmshlogaRdge ... 031 566 5359
14 Hansa Pire Nagna ... 031 701 3433
243 High Trce Crssmr ... 031 409 1693
7 Inds TripkI Skrgin ... 031 401 4460
107 KensngtnDve Bayvw ... 031 563 9913
5j LotusDve Lotusprk ... 031 912 1500
2 McDonald Rd Cnglla ... 031 307 6607
11 ModtkiePlce SfdrmPrk ... 031 404 8872
8 PelicanDve AsterRd Mrwnt ... 031 462 9813
Trevl WndrmreRd Windermre ... 031 303 2895
A 2 1 Cres Rockfrd ... 031 572 2169
A 71 Way Rckfrd Dbn ... 031 539 1766
A Lgbro Plce 50 Av Umhlitzna ... 031 401 4164
A Ahrens Rd 14 Wntwrth Dbn ... 031 467 8365
A 23 AldergateAv 31Dtrje ... 031 549 7046
A 54 Alpine Dr Shlrcrs ... 031 409 9543
A 50 AlpinePlce Shlrcrs ... 031 409 6786
A 72 AlwarRd Austrvl ... 031 468 6716
A 18 AmbosstnRd Havnsde ... 031 401 5467
A 25 AnderssnRd Mrnnhpk ... 031 564 0648
A 60 ArbnhmeCres ArenaPrk Dbn ... 031 403 9201
A 19 Asterola Av Woodhrst ... 031 404 1524
A 128 AstraDve Wdvw ... 031 505 0647
A 31 AutumpnAv ShstrPrk ... 031 505 0647

NAIDOO (CONTD)
A 15 AvalwoodRd Skrgin ... 031 403 416
A Autmn Hil 46 Badn PowiPlce Nrthdne
Qnsbrgh ... 031 708 597
A 74 BandsideCise Cnede ... 031 505 4721
A 62 BranlieRd Brrdie ... 031 578 1191
A 1 BeleyveRd worapdCres ... 031 902 3161
A Belmnt Mews Belmont Rd Kenvil ... 031 564 798
A 35 BidariRd Mrwnt ... 031 468 893I
A 23 BrandrigsiSt Shlrcrs ... 031 409 3621
A 34 BlueCres Rsecff ... 031 404 8581
A 24 BluefernPlce Rdfrn ... 031 500 185
A 31 BryvePlce Grveend ... 031 539 2500
NAIDOO A 40 BoltonRd Pimt ... 031 269 3191
A 77 BradcrfI CI Lngcrft ... 031 507 8531
A Silerin Gardns BrckfieldRd Sdnhm ... 031 207 605
A Eden Helghls Brckhilld DbnCntrl ... 031 332 074I
A 2 BridgeviCres Rydvle ... 031 500 533I
A 44 Burbera Rd Mrewnt ... 031 461 2266
A 35 BurgersRd Austrvl ... 031 468 8113
A 1 CanaralMws Rsvrrhls ... 031 262 5621
A 75 CatiehavenDve Cnede ... 031 505 5856
A 56 Cerisse St DbnCntrl Dbn ... 031 309 3585
A 33 CentreRd Bayvw Dbn ... 031 400 4157
A 35 CsstvlePlce Rydvle ... 031 500 7352
A 49 CentrbrkDve ShstrPrk ... 031 505 5677
A 1 Chedi CI SmrstPrk UmhlingaRcks ... 031 572 4322
A 28 Chicory Rd Crssmr Dbn ... 031 409 2524
A 35 CikagrveCres Grve End ... 031 502 5088
A 78 Clancy Av Mrnngsde ... 031 207 7987
A 242 ClaytldAv Clyltd Dbn ... 031 502 6179
A 65 ClaysideCres Cnede ... 031 506 1190
A 37 ClearwtrvDve FrstHvn Dbn ... 031 505 2318
A 6 ClesvrdPlce Escmbe ... 031 463 3017
A 70 ClosemorvCise Stnmre ... 031 539 1701
A 101 Colorado Crcle Bayvw ... 031 400 3008
A 151 Colorado Crde Bayvw ... 031 400 0025
A 53 Colorado Crcle Bayvw ... 031 400 0029
A 3 Colorado Cres Bayvw ... 031 403 9238
A 8 ConferTrce Bayvw ... 031 400 9332
A 2 Cosda Crtdne ... 031 401 1858
A Cameiot CoronatinRd Mvrn ... 031 464 0695
A Fern Gardns Crescent St Sdnhm ... 031 207 1506
A 121 CrestneRd Whtstne ... 031 507 2897
A 156 CrissroDve Crssmr ... 031 409 3126
A 216 DahliaRd Sprngfld ... 031 208 3832
A 38 DahliaRd Sprngfld ... 031 209 1800
A 59 Darmoorsa Cres Moortn ... 031 404 5444
A 86 DarmorsaCres Moortn ... 031 404 4669
A Rudy Park Mews 15 Dawrnea Rd Mvrn
Qnsbrgh ... 031 463 3154
A 25 DawnvestRd
Nwiinds Twn Cntre ... 031 578 6029
A 175 DesaiCres ElfnghmHigts ... 031 564 1524
A 91 DerriSt Mvrn ... 031 400 2231
A 92 DetroitSt Hvnsde ... 031 401 4667
A 173 DrewsvRd Rsvrrhls ... 031 262 4733
A 96 DunnottarAv Sdnhm ... 031 208 8662
A 23 ElvenrsCt CI Lngcrft ... 031 507 2771
A 44 EarlicroftCse Lngcrft ... 031 500 4161
A 362 EarlsfldDve Hwindsdw ... 031 578 2842
A 76 Emerald Av Moortn ... 031 404 5996
A 16 EqualityAv Crtndne ... 031 401 1837
A 357 HighbrayDve Wstcff ... 031 402 0023
A 65 FalrlghtRd Mvrn ... 031 463 2346
A 16 FarreyRd Ldsmth ... 031 400 1170
A 10 FernmPline Pntwn ... 031 505 948I
A 35 FernAv Ngna ... 031 706 1603
A 11 Fincn Trce Rsvrrhls ... 031 262 1210
A 1 FishesideDve Escmbe ... 031 464 6538
A 24 RapscthePlce NwindsV ... 031 578 1246
A 16 PamboynivAv Mrnnplk Dbn ... 031 564 1038
A 248 Fleet St Wstcff ... 031 401 7848
NAIDOO A 24 Fence NghtngleDve
Qnsbrgh ... 031 402 1424
NAIDOO A 268 Camer Cl ... 031 468 5149
A 23 FirstmwDve Rdfn ... 031 505 7576
A Mrngsde Vige Fyte Rd Mrngsde ... 031 303 7606
A 23 FreihPlce VLebckPrs Dbn ... 031 402 5491
A 15 GarnetPlce LotusPrk ... 031 902 8266
A Otwa Court 110 GbgsIkst DbnCntrl
Dbn ... 031 368 7643
A 50 GoldneldGdns Earisfid ... 031 578 2769
A 98 GraftonSt Ocnvw ... 031 466 4417
A 20 GrymreDve RgncyPrk ... 031 706 5462
A 26 Gravity Dve Havnsde ... 031 404 8941
A 1 Gray Pire Nrthdne ... 031 708 2222
A 311 GrayPrkI BrghtnRch ... 031 467 8429
A 494 GraynRd Umblo ... 031 261 7436
A 79 GrovefndDve Stnmre ... 031 539 2463
A 30 HavnsidaDve Havnsde Dbn ... 031 400 5793
A 36 HawkiesRd Khrwstn ... 031 403 1883
A 9 5 HayfldGdns Earisfid ... 031 401 0385
A 58 Herman Drve Wdvw ... 031 404 5547
A 18 High Te Moortn ... 031 404 3518
A 18 HinleyCres Shlkcrss ... 031 409 4248
A 10 HooversRd Shlrcrs ... 031 409 6103
A 15 HopevalePlce Rydvle ... 031 507 2937
A 2 HumbyvDve Eastbry ... 031 500 6082
A 4 ImpkaA Dr Mbnrgts Dbn ... 031 400 7193
A 47 ImperalRd Hvnsde ... 031 400 3689
A 59 JacarandaAv Mbnrghts ... 031 400 2777
A 320 JacksSt Rd Crvd ... 031 564 0877
A 36 JamesAv Ispngo ... 031 902 1877
A 21 Jannu Rd Mrewnt ... 031 462 9813
A 4 KingsfrnSt Skrgin ... 031 465 937I
A 19 KrantzvnPlce Crftdne Chtswrth ... 031 401 445
A 21 LarkspurRd Sprngfld Dbn ... 031 209 4055
A 25 LeslieFr Brrdie Dbn ... 031 578 2400
A 21 LesaliePlce Rydvle ... 031 329 3056
A 97 Letrham Dr Mvrn Dbn ... 031 507 7850
A 51 LckstnePlce Whtstne ... 031 137 1169
A 639r MagsbrgSt Shlrcrs ... 031 409 7780
A MnnklesPI Ksnd Pbn ... 031 562 7669
A 23 Masha Cres Moortn ... 031 404 4676
A 64 Memony Rd Pimt Dbn ... 031 269 6714
A 29 GulmaCres FrstHvn Dbn ... 031 505 7436
A 43 MllkhavenPlce FrstHvn ... 031 505 1159
A 43 Mole Grve Moortn ... 031 404 6253
A 6 Mossfern Lne Rdfrn ... 031 500 2781
A 18 NabhalaCres Hrnagr ... 031 409 4669

# Index

Note: Page numbers in **bold** type refer to figures
Page numbers in *italic* type refer to tables